Your Towns and Cities in the Great War

Swansea
in the Great War

Author Profile

Bernard Lewis is a retired local government officer who, although born in Swansea, now lives in Neath. He completed a Diploma in Local History in 1995 at the University of Wales (Swansea) and has since had three local history books published: *Swansea and the Workhouse: The Poor Law in 19th Century Swansea* which was published by the West Glamorgan Archive Service in 2003; followed by *Swansea Pals: A History of the 14th (Service) Battalion, the Welsh Regiment, in the Great War* (Pen and Sword Books, 2004); and *Foul Deeds and Suspicious Deaths Around Swansea* (Wharncliffe Books, 2009).

Swansea in the Great War represents the results of more than a year of research in local archives and the contemporary press reports, and also includes information received from many relatives of those who served at the front, or lived in the town, during the war.

Bernard is married to Elizabeth and they have one daughter and four grandchildren.

Your Towns and Cities in the Great War

Swansea
in the Great War

Bernard Lewis

Pen & Sword
MILITARY

Dedication

Remembering the people of Swansea who 'did their bit' in the Great War, in the service of a just cause.

First published in Great Britain in 2014 by
PEN & SWORD MILITARY
an imprint of
Pen and Sword Books Ltd
47 Church Street
Barnsley
South Yorkshire S70 2AS

Copyright © Bernard Lewis, 2014

ISBN 978 1 78303 294 5

The right of Bernard Lewis to be identified as the author
of this work has been asserted by him in accordance with the
Copyright, Designs and Patents Act 1988.

A CIP record for this book is available from the British Library.

Printed and bound in England
by CPI Group (UK) Ltd, Croydon, CR0 4YY

Typeset in Times New Roman

Pen & Sword Books Ltd incorporates the imprints of
Pen & Sword Archaeology, Atlas, Aviation, Battleground, Discovery,
Family History, History, Maritime, Military, Naval, Politics, Railways,
Select, Social History, Transport, True Crime, and Claymore Press,
Frontline Books, Leo Cooper, Praetorian Press, Remember When,
Seaforth Publishing and Wharncliffe.
For a complete list of Pen and Sword titles please contact
Pen and Sword Books Limited
47 Church Street, Barnsley, South Yorkshire, S70 2AS, England
E-mail: enquiries@pen-and-sword.co.uk
Website: **www.pen-and-sword.co.uk**

Contents

Acknowledgements

I have to gratefully acknowledge the help and assistance I have received from a great many people in completing this book.

My first thanks must go to Mr Kim Collis and his excellent team at the West Glamorgan Archive Service, Swansea. I have made extensive use of the relevant records held in the archive and have received much in terms of advice and assistance along the way for which I am very grateful. Mrs Marilyn Jones and her colleagues in the Swansea Local Studies team at the Swansea Library have also been most helpful while I was wrestling with the long reels of newspaper microfilm that proved so invaluable to my research. Members of the Great War Forum website at 1914–1918.invisionzone.com have been unceasingly helpful in a variety of ways and I thank them most sincerely. The Long, Long Trail website (Chris Baker) at www.1914–1918.net also proved a very useful resource. A large number of individuals have helped me in various ways and these include Tony Allen, Phillip Battye, Roger Brown, Mark Butler, Geoff Caulton, Christine Clarke, Eunice Conibear and Elisabeth Hill, Tony Cook, Noel and Alan Cox, David Davies, Hugh Harrison-Allen, Susan Hemmings, Simon Jervis, Steve John, Hugh Jones, Simon Jones, Paul Kendall, Simon Peter Lee, Jeffrey Lewis, Sue Light, Robert Lindsay, Gwynne McColl, Pam McKay, Gareth Morgan, Jean Morgan, the Peace Pledge Union, Alan Penhaligan, John Powell, Gwyn Prescott, Leighton Radford, Terry Reeves, Ynis Richardson, Phillip Sillick, Sotonmate (Great War Forum), Jim Strawbridge, Joe Sweeney, Lesley Taylor, Heather Thomas, Sue and Andy Thorndycraft, Val and Ken Waite, John White, Charles Wilson-Watkins.

I am also indebted to my editor, Pamela Covey, who was very diligent in correcting and clarifying my manuscript where required and did so with a very welcome sense of humour.

I would also like to sincerely thank Mr Roni Wilkinson and his team at Pen and Sword Books for commissioning me to write this work. Roni has done sterling work over many years in furthering the publication of books about the Great War and he is an unflappable pleasure to work with. He didn't even bat an eyelid (as far as I could tell via e-mail) when I told him that my word count exceeded the commission requirement by over 100 per cent! I hope he thinks the result was worth the effort.

Finally, I must thank my wife Elizabeth (Lib) for her unconditional support in helping me to complete this project. After my research and writing were unavoidably delayed by family illness and bereavement, she was a source of constant help and encouragement in enabling me to 'catch up' on lost time, as well as acting as honorary sounding-board and proofreader. I am deeply in her debt.

Bernard Lewis
Neath, January 2014

Introduction

This book is a history of some of the significant events that affected Swansea during the Great War of 1914–18. As such, it is a history of how the war affected Swansea and its people at that time rather than a history of the war itself. The reader will not, therefore, find within its pages detailed coverage of the various stages and battles of the Great War as it developed on several fronts. That said, many of the momentous actions that did take place between 1914 and 1918 will be mentioned but only in as much as there was a Swansea man (or woman) linked to the story.

Swansea in the early part of the twentieth century was a bustling town and port that still relied on industry of all types for its continued economic wellbeing but it was for its heavy industry that Swansea was best-known. Indeed, in 1911 the largest employment sector for males over the age of 10 in Swansea was that of iron, steel or tinplate, with about 5,600 being so employed. Other important sectors of the local economy were engineering (3,600) and building and construction (3,300), while certain forms of transport within the town accounted for another 4,400 men or youths. Over 2,000 men were also employed in the docks, a figure that had received a boost in 1909 with the opening of the King's Dock.

Map of Swansea Docks. *(Author's collection)*

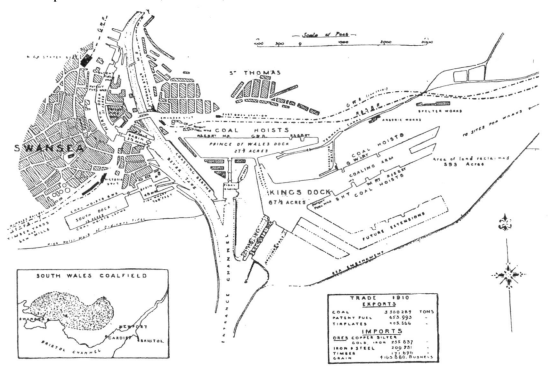

High Street, Swansea. In 1914 it was the main shopping area in the town. *(Author's collection)*

Like many other towns in the latter part of the nineteenth century, Swansea had experienced a tremendous growth in population as industrialization, almost literally, forged ahead. The infrastructure of the town had struggled to keep pace with this expansion and, as things finally slowed down a little, the town councillors and aldermen began to look at the question of town improvements. In the early part of the twentieth century they set out to acquire the tramway system from the private company that ran it for the greater benefit of the town and its people; were building a new reservoir at Cray to remove the problem of water supply; had opened a municipal telephone exchange (which soon had 600 subscribers); and there were plans afoot to expand the borough. Improvements were also made to the layout of Castle Street and there were plans for a large municipal housing estate at Townhill, as well as the hope of a modern civic centre to be erected at either Victoria Park or Northampton Place (near the modern-day Kingsway).

The war certainly set back some of these plans, delaying the Townhill housing estate by several years and putting the new civic centre plans back by as much as twenty. It was natural that, when the war came, the Corporation and its officials would certainly be in the administrative front line, if not actually in danger at the front. Indeed, from the early days of recruiting for a Swansea town battalion, dealing with food shortages, trying to keep unemployment under control, providing for Belgian refugees, trying to run municipal services that had lost numerous men to the armed forces, assisting with fundraising initiatives in support of the war aims and sorting out a host of other issues, it fell to the Corporation to do whatever it could to ensure that every ounce of municipal strength was put into supporting the war effort.

Neither was it simply a case of old men on the Corporation encouraging young men to fight, with no worries of their own. The 1914 Mayor of Swansea, T.T. Corker, not only helped to form the Swansea Battalion; he also saw his son Frank leave with it for the front as a second lieutenant. Corker senior died suddenly in 1916; worn out, many said, by his exertions as mayor in respect of the war effort. His son did not return home from the front, being killed in action a few months after the death of his father. Corporation member William Laugharne Morgan who ran a coal business in the town lost his son Lewis in a flying accident (he having previously lost a leg in combat), while Alderman Tom Merrells had the worry of three sons at the front, one of whom was captured by the Germans.

There were similar worries and concerns in a great many houses in Swansea as loved ones enlisted or were, from 1916 onwards, conscripted into the armed forces to be deployed to an uncertain fate. Even at home, those who worked on the sea faced risks from the unseen presence of German U-boats in the waters of the Bristol Channel and beyond, while men and women who were employed locally in munitions work ran the risk of chemical poisoning or being blown up in accidents. Problems with food supply increased the risk of malnutrition, especially among the less well-off, while the worldwide influenza epidemic in 1918 placed even those who believed they were billeted safely at home under the threat of an unexpected death.

From 1914 onwards, Swansea and its people, in common with every other town and city in Britain, had to face a dangerous and uncertain future as war raged in Europe and beyond. This book tells of how the war affected the town, as well as recounting some of the stories of those who endured hardship and tragedy in the four long and often heartbreaking years that followed.

Wind Street, Swansea. Much commercial activity was centred here, including a number of banks. (Author's collection)

Chapter One

Recruitment and Conscientious Objection

In August 1914 the British army could boast of having almost 250,000 men under arms. Almost half that number, however, was not available for use on the continent of Europe in the short term. They were performing possibly mundane but nevertheless important work in the distant outposts of Britain's huge empire. India, the jewel in the crown of that empire, had no fewer than fifty-one infantry battalions and nine cavalry regiments within its borders. The figures for South Africa were four and two respectively, while smaller contingents patrolled in Egypt, the Sudan, Gibraltar, China, Malta (which for a small island had a surprisingly high figure of five infantry battalions) and several other remote corners of the Empire.[1]

Britain's army was professional in every sense of the word. The men were well-trained by the standards of the day and soldiering was their 'job'. It was what they were paid to do and it was a career path that they had voluntarily chosen to follow, forced enlistment (conscription) being unknown at that time. In their family background there might have been compelling reasons why an army career had seemed attractive, of course. Their family life might have been troubled; employment, and therefore money, might have been in short supply; or perhaps their activities at home had led to unwelcome attention

Lord Kitchener.

from the local constabulary and it had seemed best to simply get away for a while. In any event, every man was a volunteer and none had been coerced into joining the service. Britain had traditionally maintained a relatively small standing army composed entirely of volunteers, with the defence of mainland Britain and the British Empire being largely entrusted to the might of the Royal Navy, which was at that time the largest and most powerful navy in the world and well able to exert its power across the globe in times of crisis.

The British army had seen action in a variety of settings since it fought in the Crimean War of 1853–56. It had been engaged in the Indian Mutiny of 1857 as well as undertaking actions in the Sudan, Afghanistan, South Africa (against both Zulus and Boers) and the Boxer Rebellion in China, to name but a few. With the exception of the Crimean War, however, it had not fought on mainland Europe since the defeat of Napoleon in 1815. Compared to the armies of France and Germany, the British army was actually quite small at around 250,000 regular soldiers. The German army of 1914, for example, stood at around 800,000 regulars.[2]

In August 1914 Lord Kitchener, the hero of Khartoum, was the newly-appointed Secretary of State for War. Unlike many of his contemporaries, he was not in the 'It'll be all over by Christmas' camp and foresaw a long and potentially bloody struggle ahead if France and Belgium were to remain free from permanent German occupation. On that basis, and within days of the outbreak of war, he issued his famous appeal for volunteers. Kitchener asked for 100,000 men aged between 19 and 31 to come forward and expand the ranks of the British army for the present emergency. They would be required to serve for a period of three years or until the end of the war. From the declaration of war on 4 August to 8 August 1914, just over 8,000 men had voluntarily come forward to join the colours. In the week that followed, possibly roused by Kitchener's stirring appeal and by news of the heavy fighting in Belgium, almost 44,000 more arrived at recruiting offices across the country. By the end of December 1914 a staggering 806,000 men had come forward in support of what must have been seen as a just cause.[3] Although this was a very commendable figure, it nevertheless represented only a portion of those who could have come forward for military service had they so desired. The plain fact was that many saw the war as being no real business of theirs. The 'over by Christmas' idea meant that many thought that it probably wasn't worth their while volunteering as the war would, in any case, be over before they were trained and ready for action. Others had families to care for or important jobs to perform. Some had parental responsibilities or elderly parents in need of care.

There was a plethora of reasons why a man should not volunteer and many thought that, at the end of the day and on a purely personal level, what difference would one more man really make? The recruiting figures were being applauded in the press, so

Early recruiting in London. Swansea also experienced a rush.

Swansea women queue for their separation allowances from the military.
(West Glamorgan Archive Service [afterwards WGAS] D/D Z 187/1)

some would have understandably thought that the army could probably manage quite well enough without them and simply sat on their hands as the recruiting parades marched by. Others would not join due to strongly-held conscientious beliefs, while still more simply baulked at putting their own lives at risk for the sake of countries they had never visited and with which they had no affinity. Some probably just feared for their lives. Joining the forces was voluntary and in the Great Britain of 1914 a great many decided not to do so.

Swansea, in common with every town in the country, saw recruitment wax and wane over time. In the earliest days of the war there was a great amount of bustle in the town as army and navy reservists left to join their units, having been recalled to help deal with the crisis. Similarly the Territorial Force, those part-time and so-called 'Saturday soldiers', had reported for duty with their particular units. The mayor and Corporation of Swansea naturally felt that it was their loyal duty to try to co-ordinate matters locally in aid of the war effort and the formation of a civil defence guard for the town was soon under consideration. However, this idea failed to find favour with the War Office. Fighting units that could be deployed for action overseas were the priority, rather than the creation of a corps of potentially half-trained guards to simply look after the local docks and bridges.

The early recruiting arrangements at Swansea, run under the auspices of the military, proved to be seriously defective. Such was the slowness of the procedure that lengthy queues drove some Swansea men to travel to Cardiff where, apparently, matters were dealt with in a much more speedy and efficient manner. The Mayor of Swansea, Thomas Taliesyn Corker, was receptive to the proposal made by both Mr Cory Yeo and Sir Alfred Mond

Thomas Taliesyn Corker,
mayor of Swansea during 1914.
(South Wales Daily Post [afterwards SWDP])

that the town should form its own infantry battalion.

This idea was accepted with some caution by the War Office and the mayor quickly arranged a meeting with the major employers in the town to gauge what degree of support might be anticipated. The idea was endorsed and a patriotic meeting was subsequently held in the Albert Hall, Cradock Street, on 16 September 1914 to explain the idea to the public. The suggestion was greeted with acclaim and a large number of cash donations were promised (an important point, since the War

The Swansea Guildhall of the Great War period. The new Guildhall opened in 1934. *(Author's collection)*

Office initially would not undertake to meet the costs of raising such a battalion). An advertisement for recruits to what would be the Swansea Battalion (later officially named the 14th (Service) Battalion of the Welsh Regiment) was published and recruiting commenced at the Guildhall (now the Dylan Thomas Centre). In the first four days of recruiting for the new battalion, the number signed up stood at a somewhat disappointing 254. However, it should be noted that an estimated 8,000 Swansea men had already been recalled to the colours or had voluntarily joined other units.

Progress in the formation of the battalion (requiring about 1,300 men) remained slow as the months moved on. The press of the day reported that by 18 October 1914 the

A recruiting march in Swansea with the Albert Hall in the background. *(Charles Thomas)*

number recruited stood at 436 but this had edged up to 950 by 24 November. By early December 1914 the battalion, though still a little short in numbers, left Swansea for further training at Rhyl. The departure of the Swansea Battalion from the town did not mean the end of the town's recruiting efforts, of course. Men were still needed for numerous other units as increasing casualties at the front required a constant stream of replacements that were proving somewhat hard to come by. In May 1915 Sergeant Griffiths of the 2nd Welsh Battalion was home on leave having been wounded and was strolling in the Port Tennant area of the town. He was surprised by

> the presence of many young fellows – a good number well known to me and I to them – who were lounging about dressed in their Sunday best...after a while I got into conversation with a young chap and being unable to contain myself any longer, I asked him if he had tried or thought of enlisting. His reply was 'No'; adding 'Besides, what have I got to gain?' [4]

A veritable rash of recruiting meetings, almost a hundred in total, had been held in Swansea and the surrounding district in May 1915, though it was noted that 'the response in many directions had not been what it should be'. One such meeting had been undermined by a group of young men holding a meeting of their own at which they formally resolved not to enlist. A local minister took to the pulpit at another to preach a message of peace that left no room within his flock for recruitment to the army.[5] As the military authorities (with political backing) cast their patriotic net ever wider in the quest for volunteers by increasing the maximum age for volunteers to 40 years, even some of the senior officials of the Swansea Corporation came under pressure to enlist.

The Swansea Watch Committee indicated that its employees who were under the age of 40 might wish to consider whether they were actually serving their country to the best of their ability by remaining in their Corporation posts or whether their efforts should be directed to service in a war-related activity, if not by actually serving at the front itself. Mr Heath, the borough surveyor, stated that while he would be happy to join up, he thought that his particular skills were best deployed in the service of the Corporation and town of Swansea. After all, the town still had to be run,

Comic recruiting postcard.
(Tony Allen, www.worldwar1postcards.com)

"LOR! AND HERE I'VE TRIED FOR THIRTY YEARS, AND CAN'T GET ONE!"

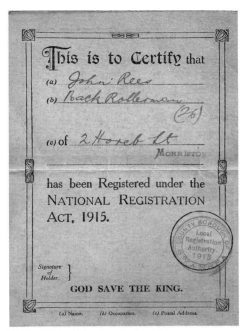

National Registration Act card. *(Gwynne McColl)*

even if there was a war on. He noted that if a rule requiring all the under-40s employed by the Corporation to enlist was brought in, it would leave the borough surveyor's office to be run by its current deputy head plus an office boy, while the town clerk's office would be in the same unfortunate and unworkable situation.[6]

The government knew that the ever-growing demands of the military for more manpower meant that something much more formal simply had to be done to improve the rate of recruitment. This was a matter of some concern as the British army had always consisted of volunteers and many well-placed people, both within and without the government, wondered what the public reaction would be if forced military service was to be introduced by way of conscription. A cautious move forward was made with the passing of the National Registration Act of 1915 which required the names of all persons aged between 18 and 65 and not already serving in the military to be recorded. Details of the person's occupation were also to be provided and this enabled the government to winkle out the number of men of military age who were not already in the forces and perhaps not in a civilian occupation that was deemed essential to the war effort. The initial results of this survey in September 1915 showed that about 3,400,000 men of military age were not in the armed forces and another 1,600,000 were in civilian occupations which currently exempted them from being called up. Among this cohort of 5,000,000 were some 2,000,000 single men.

Another step on the road to conscription was then taken with the appointment of Lord Derby as the government's Director-General of Recruiting. Derby brought forward a scheme in October 1915 under which men aged over 18 and below 41 could, if they were so minded, volunteer for immediate service as was the current practice or they could 'attest' that they would accept being called up at a later date if the exigencies of the war so required. Of the 2,000,000 single men identified by the National Registration Act, only 50 per cent subsequently signed up promptly or attested under the Derby Scheme. The figure was even worse for the married men, with only 40 per cent of the 3,000,000 taking positive action regarding current or future service. Even when the fact that some of the men were naturally performing important roles in civilian jobs was taken into account, the overall results were still extremely depressing, both for the government and the military.[7]

The dwindling number of voluntary recruits finally forced the government's hand

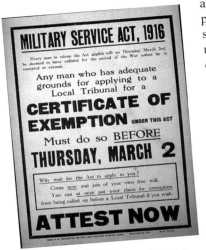

Poster advising those who think they should be exempt from military service to make application.

and in January 1916 the Military Service Act 1916 was passed, ushering in the era of conscription. The act was sweeping in its application, essentially deeming all unmarried men (or widowers with no dependent children) aged over 18 and below 41 to have been enlisted into the army and then transferred to the reserve while they awaited their formal call-up. This automatically placed a large number of unmarried men (unmarried as at 2 November 1915) aged over 18 and below 41 at the disposal of the military, although there were exemptions. These included those with business or domestic arrangements that would suffer considerable disruption in the event of a call-up. Additionally, those who suffered from ill health or had an infirmity that rendered them unfit for military service, as well as those who had a conscientious objection to undertaking combatant service, were also to be excused. There would also be some whose civilian work was of greater value to the country than any military task they might be asked to perform.

Persons who thought that they qualified for exemption under one of the permitted reasons would have to apply to a local military service tribunal for their case to be considered and, if approved, for the necessary certificate of exemption to be issued. Certificates could be granted on an absolute, conditional or temporary basis, depending on the particular circumstances of a case. There were also exceptions where particular men would not be required for military service with the army and these included ministers of religion and men who were already serving in the Royal Navy or Marines.[8]

The Local Government Board duly requested the Swansea Corporation to establish a local military service tribunal for its area, its role being to hear applications from those who sought exemption from service. The local tribunal was to consist of five members of the Corporation, plus a representative each from the Chamber of Commerce and the Labour Association. There would also be a military representative to put forward the views of

The exertion of moral pressure on men with regard to enlisting.

Daddy, what did YOU do in the Great War?

Another example of moral pressure on potential recruits.

the military on applications for exemption. The Swansea tribunal soon found it had plenty of work to keep it busy. In late February 1916 the tribunal met in the afternoon to be confronted with no fewer than sixty-five persons, each of whom wished to present a case for their exemption from military service. Decisions often seem to have been arrived at briskly, with sympathy for the applicant frequently being in short supply.

For example, a clerk in a local foundry applied on the grounds that he supported his widowed mother. It was ascertained that he had two brothers, though they apparently contributed nothing to his mother's upkeep. He accepted that out of the £1 a week he gave his mother she maintained him and he was told that, as his mother would qualify for an allowance from the military in respect of her son's service, he would have to go into the army and his request was therefore refused. Many cases were brought by employers keen to retain the services of an 'indispensable' member of staff. The tribunal's killer question on this type of claim was: 'What would happen if the man went?' Almost invariably the answer was along the lines of 'We'd have to muddle along without him and it would be very inconvenient.' Inconvenience did not rank highly with the tribunal and such requests were invariably refused. When one burly applicant told the tribunal that he kept his mother and sisters on a sum that was less than they would get by way of an allowance from the military were he to enlist, he was told: 'Your mother will be certainly better off when you are in the army. Get in as quickly as you can!'[9]

Another applicant stated that he could not undertake military service as his life was insured for £500 and the policies would be voided were he to join the armed forces with its attendant risks to life and limb. It transpired under questioning, however, that the policies had actually been purchased since the outbreak of the war and this might have been a simple, if ultimately unsuccessful, ploy on his part to avoid enlistment.[10] In another case a mother applied on behalf of her son as he worked as a haulier and also managed a small farm. The application was refused with the comment: 'Wouldn't you like him to go out to the front and see him coming back with the VC?' A former regular soldier had served before the war and then taken part in the early battles before reaching the end of his contracted engagement with the army. Having seen quite enough action at the front, he opted not to extend his service and returned

The Ben Evans store reassures its male workers that their jobs will be safe while they are serving with the military. *(WGAS TC/27/55)*

SPECIAL NOTICE.

ALL Men who are leaving, or have left, to join His Majesty's Forces, will have their situations kept open for them.

The Wives of the Married Men will receive Half Pay during their Husband's absence.

"GOD SAVE THE KING."

BEN. EVANS & CO., LTD.

A postcard making fun of conscientious objectors. *(Tony Allen, www.worldwar1postcards.com)*

home happy in himself that he had 'done his bit'. He had been in France for fifteen months and had taken part in the arduous retreat from Mons. He thought there were many young, single men who were working in munitions factories who could be called on to fill up the ranks. Despite his record of previous service in dangerous areas, his application for exemption was refused and he was told that he would have to return to the army.[11]

A group of men that frequently felt the scorn of the military service tribunal members was that of the conscientious objectors. The Military Service Act had, in fact, granted an exemption for conscientious objectors but it was only from the 'undertaking of combatant service'. This meant that while a conscientious objector could not be asked to fight or carry arms, he could still be required to perform duties that were of benefit to the military such as road-making, carrying supplies or any of the numerous other non-combatant tasks that helped to keep an army in the field. In Britain in the First World War there were around 16,000 conscientious objectors (in the Second World War the figure was 60,000).[12] Conscientious objection had not been an issue in earlier wars as the military had entirely comprised volunteers. It was, therefore, essentially new territory and if the government thought that the commendable exemption clause for conscientious objectors contained in the Military Service Act was the end of the matter, it was in for a big surprise.

In the same way that many men had to attend a military service tribunal to state their case for exemption from service due to possible family, medical or business reasons, so it was that conscientious objectors also had to attend and explain their position. Only about 2 per cent of the cases heard by the tribunals actually related to conscientious objectors, although being accepted as a genuine conscientious objector was not necessarily as straightforward as it might have seemed. Many tribunal members seemed to think that an applicant's conscience had only surfaced once conscription had arrived. Prior to the advent of conscription in 1916, a man who had objections of conscience needed to do nothing regarding military service as the army and navy depended solely on volunteers to fill up their ranks. It was only after the introduction of conscription that a man was formally required to attend a tribunal and state his case for exemption from service on conscientious grounds.

For many conscientious objectors a simple exemption from combatant service (the requirement to fight and handle weapons) was enough. These men were content to don a uniform, observe military discipline and perform duties in support of the army provided it did not mean bearing arms. This could include construction of huts and baths for the soldiers, carrying out road and railway maintenance or sanitation work. Indeed, a non-combatant corps of the army was especially established to accommodate such men. Another group of conscientious objectors was that known as the 'alternativists'. These men refused to work under military control or do any work that would directly assist military operations. They would not wear a military uniform or conform to military discipline. They were, however, prepared to work under civilian direction on tasks that did not directly benefit the military. Many were subsequently assigned to roles in forestry and farming in Britain, though work in schools and hospitals was also undertaken in some cases. The final group of conscientious objectors was the one that caused the government the most difficulty and anguish. These men were known as the 'absolutists'. Most of this group were committed pacifists and found war abhorrent. As such they totally refused to complete any form of work as an alternative to military service; the argument being that if an absolutist performed, for example, forestry work he was then potentially freeing up another forestry worker (who did not have a

Contemporary press coverage of the Swansea Military Service Tribunal hearings.
(Cambrian)

"TO SAVE HIS SKIN."

FINE SPECIMEN OF "C.O." AT SWANSEA.

"REASONS" FOR EVADING MILITARY SERVICE.

There was a conscientious objector of the first water at the Swansea County Police Court on Saturday, when William McLeod (24), labourer, was charged with failing to report himself when called upon for military service.

Capt. Harold Williams, the military representative, said he had received a letter from McLeod after the first calling up notice had been sent him, in which he said he was sorry he could not answer the call, as his religious convictions would not allow him. For twenty months previous to April last he worked at Mond Nickel Works, where he understood he was protected from military service, as he was categorised in B1, and was directly engaged in the process work there. He was, however, called up, but refused to answer the call. He went to the recruiting office and explained that he was quite prepared to undertake any work of national importance, but could not under any consideration join the Army, as it was contrary to

His Understanding of the Bible

to take any part in the destruction of human life.

"Presumably he preferred only to make shells for someone else to do it," observed Capt. Williams). He asked to go to another munition works ("where he was safe," commented the captain).

Further, in a letter McLeod said he had been employed as a warehouseman for the past three weeks.

"He told the firm that he had been sent there from the Labour Exchange, which was deliberately untrue," added the military representative.

Concluding the letter defendant had said: "I am quite prepared to do any other form of work so as to be serving my country in some way" ("or so that he could save his skin!" ended Capt. Williams).

P.C. Roach, Llangyfelach, deposed to arresting McLeod. He agreed with Captain Williams that prisoner would be doing far better work in France than "kicking up the dust" at Clydach. "It's the duty of every young man," added the constable.

Corpl. Rea, of the Recruiting Office, gave evidence as to calling up, etc.

The Chairman said the case was a very bad one, and fined defendant £5 and handed him over to the military.

VALLEY BRICKLAYER HANDED OVER.

At Pontardawe on Friday, Dd. Lewis, bricklayer, Godre'rgraig, was charged with being an absentee under the Military Service Act. Defendant said he was a conscientious objector on religious grounds. He was fined 40s. and handed over to the proper authorities.

conscientious objection) for service at the front.

Press reports of the time give occasionally vivid descriptions of the tribunal proceedings relating to conscientious objectors. A Llansamlet haulier appeared and was asked: 'Since when have you had a conscientious objection?' The reply was 'Always'. The next question was 'Will you attend to the wounded?' and when the answer was negative it was commented: 'You are enjoying the same privileges as other people willing to serve their country, and you say you won't do anything?' Following another negative answer the man was nevertheless told to report to the recruiting office for enlistment, his application for exemption being refused. A tinplate worker at the Baldwin's Works told the tribunal:

> Being a believer in the Lord Jesus Christ I claim permanent exemption on the ground that it is contrary to His teaching, as set forth in St Matthew and Romans, in the matter of killing and also to the swearing of the oath.

The tribunal questioning of that man covered issues such as whether he would allow the Germans to come to Britain and kill him. Would he allow the Germans to kill his mother? Did he actually possess any intelligence? Would he only drop to his knees and pray for protection from God if a blackguard were to strike him? His application was refused. A young worker at the Cwmbwrla Works indicated that he was prepared to make munitions but not to use them, as a matter of conscience. The mayor, sitting as a tribunal member, commented: 'What is the difference if you hit a man down or give the stick to me to hit him down? Your conscience will let another man hit the fellow. It is a rather convenient conscience and not consistent, young man.' The applicant stated that he would rely on God for protection, being his servant. His application was rejected.[13]

Some conscientious objectors refused to play any part in the military process and simply failed to respond to the call-up paperwork or did not attend a tribunal to state their case for exemption. Where a man failed to appear for duty, it was customary for the local policeman to pay him a visit and ascertain what had gone wrong. After all, perhaps the man had been ill, the paperwork had not arrived, or the date on which he was due to report had simply been forgotten. The local 'bobby' at that time usually lived among the community he protected and would probably know the man and his usual friends and haunts personally, making his apprehension much easier. Where no reasonable excuse was presented, however, the man would be duly arrested

"CLAIMED LIBERTY OF CONSCIENCE."

TINPLATER "C.O." HANDED OVER AT SWANSEA.

At Swansea Police Court on Monday, John Rees (33), tinworker, was charged with failing to report himself for military service.

Corpl. Rea gave the usual formal evidence, and defendant, when asked whether he had anything to say, replied, "I reckon it is through the maladministration of the Military Service Act I am here. I applied for absolute exemption on the ground that I was a conscientious objector, and it was refused. The responsibility therefore is not upon me but upon the military authorities. British law stands for liberty of conscience; I am denied liberty of conscience. I still hold to my conscientious objection. I am bound to be a Christian, in spite of all."

He was handed over to the military.

Press coverage regarding an application for exemption from military service.
(Cambrian)

and brought before the local police court for failing to report for military service. In most conscientious objector cases the offender would usually be fined and then literally 'handed over to the military', two soldiers being on hand to take the man away once the verdict was announced.

The Watters family lived at Pilton Green, near Port Eynon on the Gower Peninsula. The family worked two forges and provided blacksmith services at seventeen Gower locations and as such were an important part of the local community. Hubert Victor Watters was almost 32 when he received his call-up papers on 25 September 1916. He had appeared before a local tribunal at an earlier date to seek exemption, possibly on the grounds that his blacksmith work was vital to the Gower farming community. That must have been unsuccessful, as was a direct appeal to the Board of Agriculture and Fisheries that was supported by a petition from the local farmers. As the Board stated: 'The Board have no power to alter or review a decision given by a Tribunal.' A question was even raised in Parliament regarding the case, as it was felt by some that the Gower Rural Military Service Tribunal had acted perversely in refusing to grant Watters exemption. It was claimed that the chairman of the tribunal had a grudge against Watters and had previously threatened to gain his revenge in some way. It was stated that Watters' claim for exemption was based on the fact that he was performing work of national importance, in addition to his objections of conscience. The military representative at the tribunal hearing had bluntly informed Watters that he 'was a traitor and only fit to be on the point of a German bayonet or in a lunatic asylum.'[14]

Hubert Watters subsequently failed to report as directed for military service and was brought before the Swansea police court in October 1916. In mitigation Watters' representative stated that his client was the secretary of the local Oddfellows' Lodge and needed a week's adjournment in order to be able to hand over the books to his successor. Additionally, it was stated that Watters had two forges in operation and attended to all the blacksmithing

Making sure that Welsh-speakers who wish to claim exemption from military service get the message!

ABSENTEE FROM GOWER

HANDED OVER TO MILITARY AT SWANSEA.

Herbert Victor Waters, Pilton, Gower (31), single, was charged with failing to report himself for military service. Defendant admitted the offence.

Captain Harold Williams appeared on behalf of the military authorities, and Mr. Arthur Davies for defendant.

Mr. Davies said that his client was the secretary of an Oddfellows' Lodge, and they had called a meeting to be held on Tuesday next to appoint a new secretary, and he asked that the case should be adjourned until Wednesday next so as to enable defendant to hand over his books.

Captain Williams strongly objected, and his objection was upheld.

Mr. Davies said the case was not one of the ordinary kind. Defendant was an agricultural blacksmith and had two forges in Gower. He attended to all the wants of the farmers in Gower.

Defendant was fined 40s. and handed over to the military.

Hubert Watters applies for exemption from military service. (SWDP) needs of the farmers of Gower. If any mention was made of a conscientious objection at this hearing, the local press of the time did not report it. The representations came to nought and Watters was fined £2 and handed over to the military.[15]

On 14 October 1916 the formal process of getting Watters into the army continued with the completion of his army Record of Service form, though it seems there were difficulties in that respect. The front page of the form containing the man's personal details was only partially completed and remained unsigned. The writing did not appear to be in Watters' hand and it seems probable that the form was prepared by a recruiting clerk and that Watters had then refused to sign it. Perhaps he had planned a campaign of non-co-operation with the military authorities but in any event he was posted to the 60th Training Reserve Battalion as a first step towards eventual deployment to a front-line unit.

In mid-October 1916 Watters was held in detention for five days, awaiting a military court martial to answer a charge of refusing to follow the lawful commands of his superior officer. In the case of a conscientious objector this was often a simple refusal to put on a military uniform. He was tried and found guilty with a punishment of six months' imprisonment with hard labour, although seventy days of this was remitted. He started to serve his time in Wormwood Scrubs but in the event he did not have to complete the full sentence as he was transferred on 14 December 1916 to the Army Reserve, a step that enabled him to willingly undertake 'work of national importance under the direction of the Brace Committee'. The Brace Committee was the body established by the government to oversee the employment of conscientious objectors. Watters signed an undertaking to the effect that he would work with 'diligence and fidelity', would reside where required and would abide by the regulations set by the committee. Any failure on his part would see him sent back to complete his prison sentence.[16]

Hubert Watters was sent to a road-work camp at Ballachulish, Argyleshire, to help construct a road from that place to Kinlochleven. He was employed as a blacksmith and provided with a forge. As the road construction required heavy rock-breaking work, Watters understandably dealt with a regular stream of tools and equipment that required sharpening or repair. Despite the work that he was required to complete, he was also able to attend church services as well as partake in educational classes at the camp which consisted of about nine huts for the men, plus a dining room, reading room and several buildings that were required in connection with the work tasks, including the smithy.

The setting was idyllic (although the climate could be harsh) and the work at the forge was not too demanding, Watters noting that: 'I used to do more work in 2 hours than I do all day now. We try to make the scheme a great financial failure; we succeed, I can assure you.' Indeed, the government agent supervising the road-building work commented: 'The road will take 2 or 3 years if ordinary men were used; 17 years if C[onscientious] O[bjector]s have to do it!' Further work was undertaken at Caolasnacon, near Glencoe in Scotland, as well as at the Wakefield Work Centre which was the former Wakefield Prison. In June 1918 Hubert Watters signed an undertaking that he would meet all the requirements necessary for him to take up 'exceptional employment'. This essentially freed him from military control in order that he could work at a place determined by the Brace Committee (the Committee on Employment of Conscientious Objectors). In the case of Watters, that place was to be his father's farm at Pilton Green. This had the doubly

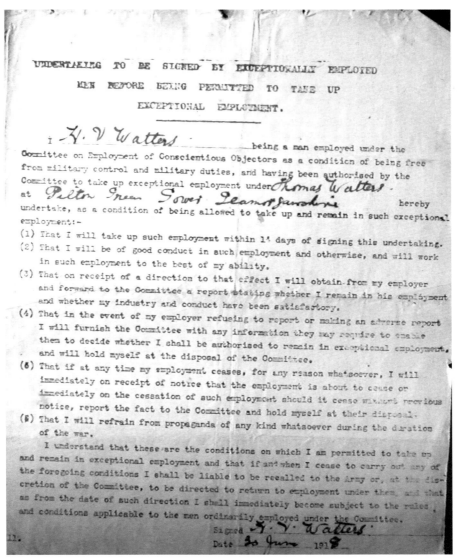

UNDERTAKING TO BE SIGNED BY EXCEPTIONALLY EMPLOYED MEN BEFORE BEING PERMITTED TO TAKE UP EXCEPTIONAL EMPLOYMENT.

I _H. V Watters_ being a man employed under the Committee on Employment of Conscientious Objectors as a condition of being free from military control and military duties, and having been authorised by the Committee to take up exceptional employment under _Thomas Watters_. at _Pilton Green Gower Leamorganshire_ hereby undertake, as a condition of being allowed to take up and remain in such exceptional employment:-

(1) That I will take up such employment within 14 days of signing this undertaking.

(2) That I will be of good conduct in such employment and otherwise, and will work in such employment to the best of my ability.

(3) That on receipt of a direction to that effect I will obtain from my employer and forward to the Committee a report stating whether I remain in his employment and whether my industry and conduct have been satisfactory.

(4) That in the event of my employer refusing to report or making an adverse report I will furnish the Committee with any information they may require to enable them to decide whether I shall be authorised to remain in exceptional employment, and will hold myself at the disposal of the Committee.

(5) That if at any time my employment ceases, for any reason whatsoever, I will immediately on receipt of notice that the employment is about to cease or immediately on the cessation of such employment should it cease without previous notice, report the fact to the Committee and hold myself at their disposal.

(6) That I will refrain from propaganda of any kind whatsoever during the duration of the war.

I understand that these are the conditions on which I am permitted to take up and remain in exceptional employment and that if and when I cease to carry out any of the foregoing conditions I shall be liable to be recalled to the Army or, at the discretion of the Committee, to be directed to return to employment under them, and that as from the date of such direction I shall immediately become subject to the rules and conditions applicable to the men ordinarily employed under the Committee.

Signed _H. V. Watters_.
Date _30 June_ 1918

Hubert Watters accepts 'exceptional employment' so that he can return to his usual place of work while still being subject to military authority should he default in any way.
(Clive Watters)

happy effect of getting Hubert back into his usual employment, which was of great use to the local farming community, as well as making him one less conscientious objector for the military to have to worry about. In May 1919 he was finally released from the control of the committee and was free to live and work where he pleased, although the military still held a notional claim on his possible service until 1920.[17]

Abram Watters was one of Hubert's brothers. Unlike his brother Hubert, Abram, after a dalliance with performing alternative work, adopted an 'absolutist' stance and refused to answer to any military or civil authority in relation to the war. He thought that the woodcutting work he was offered at Weston was liable to undercut the work of the professional woodcutters and, additionally, his work was essentially freeing-up another man for army service. He stated that the conditions at Weston were poor and unsanitary and the work was hard. Hard labour in a prison could not be any worse, in his opinion. By early 1917 he was indeed in a prison for his beliefs, having been initially sentenced to two years, although this was later reduced to six months. This was scant consolation for Abram who told his parents that though he would be eligible for release in July 1917, 'This is not entirely good & means that I shall receive another court martial after the necessary rigmarole is gone through, and then I shall presumably be returned to prison again.' His relationship with his soldier escorts had been surprisingly cordial. On his arrival at Kinmel Camp, near Abergele, he found the guardroom soldiers offering 'the best of friendship', while the military escort that accompanied him to prison 'behaved in the most kindly way that was compatible with their duty'. This kindness was not shared by all that he encountered, however, as he added that: 'It does not take long to teach a man to put his human nature in his pocket. And a soldier can only be efficient when he has overcome his humanity.'

The 'necessary rigmarole' referred to by Abram was the practice of imprisoning conscientious objectors for failing to obey military commands and then, upon their release, repeating the process again by the fresh issue of the order that had previously been disobeyed. In many cases the objector ended up back in prison again, waiting for the next move in what was virtually a game of 'cat and mouse' with the authorities. However, the authorities did not see it as a game. In May 1916 about fifty conscientious objectors were taken from their places of imprisonment (which were Richmond Castle, the Harwich Redoubt and Seaford) and transported to France. Once in France they came under strict military law, now regarded as serving at the front, and were told that were they to disobey an order they would face the risk of death by firing squad. Thirty-five of the fifty still refused to carry out military commands and were court-martialled, found guilty and sentenced to death. Sir Douglas Haig, commander of the British forces on the Western Front, had the common sense to commute the sentence in each case to one of ten years' penal servitude.[18]

Not all were so lucky, if lucky is the correct word for receiving a ten-year sentence. When W.E. Burns, a conscientious objector from Manchester, went on hunger strike in Hull Prison he was force-fed a mix of milk and cocoa by way of a tube that was supposed to be inserted into his stomach via his nose. The doctor administering the mixture managed to pour the liquid into Burns' lungs rather than his stomach and he choked to death. Others, including the Walker brothers from Stroud Green in London, were beaten several times in an effort to get them to see the error of their ways. One objector was stripped naked and dragged through a filthy pond nine times in an effort to break his will. The Peace Pledge Union indicates that during the Great War over seventy conscientious objectors died as a result of the treatment they received in prisons or work camps.[19] Clearly the path to conscientious objection was not an easy one.

Another of the Watters family to come to the attention of the courts was Massena Garnet Watters. He was a member of the Briton Ferry branch of the No Conscription Fellowship and in May 1916 was charged with distributing circulars at Briton Ferry that were likely to prejudice the training and discipline of His Majesty's forces. The first circular was entitled 'Two Years' Hard Labour for Refusing to Disobey the Dictates of Conscience', while another concerned itself with the case of a conscientious objector in the ancient world. Watters and another man had been handing out the leaflets to those attending places of worship on a Sunday. The defence claimed that thousands of the leaflets had actually been distributed throughout the country, while items of a similar nature had also appeared in the public press. The defence arguments did not sway the court, however, and both men were sentenced to one month's hard labour.[20]

Another Swansea conscientious objector was Harold (Hal) Beynon whose widowed mother lived at Watkin Street, Swansea. Hal had been employed at a printing works before the war and after his call-up papers arrived, failed to report for military service and was accordingly brought before the Swansea Court in January 1918. He pleaded guilty and was fined £5 and handed over to the military. A failure to obey orders resulted in a court martial at which he was sentenced to six months in prison with hard labour. Hal served some of his sentence at Wormwood Scrubs and Dartmoor before he apparently accepted work on the Home Office scheme for conscientious objectors and was subsequently moved to Gloucester. In October 1918 Hal Beynon died while at Gloucester as a result of influenza and pneumonia. It is possible that his treatment while in prison, together with the hardship experienced on the work scheme, might have weakened him but it must also be remembered that in late 1918 a worldwide flu pandemic was raging and his death might be solely due to that cause. His death certificate records that he was 25 years of age. Hal's family had certainly not abandoned him due to his beliefs and his brother was present at his death.[21]

John Oliver Watkins worked in the Estate Office of the Swansea Corporation. In later life Watkins became a successful estate agent in Swansea with his own business on Walter Road. It seems likely that Watkins was a Quaker and he took a more unusual stance for a conscientious objector. Though Watkins was not actually named in the press report, a Swansea tribunal hearing held on 14 March 1916 heard representations from the father of a young man who was employed 'in an estate agent's department'. It seems very likely that this was Watkins. His

John Oliver Watkins in the 1930s.
(Author's collection)

father claimed a conscientious objection on the part of his son who was 'a loyal follower of Jesus Christ, who taught us "to love our enemies"'. He then explained that his son had, in fact, already joined the Friends' Ambulance Unit and was prepared to serve at the front by assisting the wounded rather than bearing arms. The Friends' Ambulance Unit had been set up by a group of Quakers on a purely voluntary basis (it was actually open to non-

Friends' Ambulance Unit vehicles. *(WGAS D/D Z 429/6/13)*

Quakers as well). It raised its own funds and did not come under the control of the military or the Society of Friends (the Quaker organization). The unit had been in France since 1914, before conscription was introduced, and its members were all volunteers who were under no obligation to serve with the unit or, in pre-conscription days, in the British military. The Swansea tribunal had cause to seek an adjournment as it was unsure of the precise status of the Friends' Ambulance Unit. In any event, Watkins senior advised the tribunal members that his son would not serve with the Royal Army Medical Corps as that would necessitate his coming under military control, something that his son could not countenance.[22]

The tribunal eventually granted him exemption from combatant service and John Oliver Watkins soon joined the Friends' Ambulance Unit in France. His employer, the Swansea Corporation, was not quite as understanding as the tribunal and declined to pay him the half-pay normally paid to its employees while on military service. This decision was based on the fact that, in their eyes, Watkins was not on military service, having failed to join the fighting forces or the Royal Army Medical Corps.[23]

In France Watkins' unit was attached to a French rather than a British division and was designated by the French as the Section Sanitaire Anglaise 19, a motor ambulance convoy. It consisted of twenty-two ambulances, a mobile workshop and a kitchen. The unit served with several divisions of the French army over time and saw action at the Somme, the Marne, the Aisne and the Meuse as well as other places. It was involved with front-line work in evacuating wounded French infantrymen to hospitals in the rear for medical attention. As such, during its time at the front it suffered damage to several of its ambulances from rifle-fire and artillery shells. The unit also occasionally came under attack from gas shells.

On the night of 10 December 1917 an ambulance was called for by a doctor at a field dressing station close to the front line at Nieuport Ville. Watkins and a comrade made the journey by motor ambulance, under cover of darkness and over a terrain that was littered with the debris of war and a large number of shell-holes. The ambulance was duly loaded with wounded men and began the perilous journey away from the firing-line. The journey proved to be short-lived, however. Peering into the darkness and trying to avoid the barely-visible obstructions in his path, Watkins managed to get his ambulance stuck over an abandoned trench. As he tried unsuccessfully to get the vehicle moving again, a hail of shot and shell fell around both him and the ambulance, also endangering the wounded men. The wounded were quickly disembarked into the scant shelter of the trench, while Watkins and the other ambulance-man began to assemble whatever scrap material they could find close at hand to pack around the ambulance wheels in order that the stranded vehicle could be made mobile again before it was destroyed by enemy fire.

The Germans began firing gas shells which meant that the arduous work had to be undertaken while wearing a gas mask; an essential but very uncomfortable necessity. The mustard gas slowly permeated Watkins' clothing as he worked, resulting in burns to his body and legs. The ambulance was, however, finally got moving again, the wounded re-embarked and the escape achieved. For his actions on the night of 10/11

A damaged Friends' Ambulance Unit ambulance. Working close to the front brought with it inevitable dangers.
(WGAS D/D Z 429/6/13)

Friends' Ambulance Unit personnel. *(WGAS D/D Z 429/6/13)*

December 1917 John Oliver Watkins was later awarded the French Croix de Guerre medal for gallantry. The Swansea Corporation, on hearing this news early in 1918, decided that perhaps it had been a little harsh in refusing to pay Watkins the customary half-pay while he was with the Friends' Ambulance Unit. To remedy the situation (in their opinion), it was finally decided to award him half-pay but only from the beginning of 1918, thus still denying him the half-pay he was arguably due while he was at the front in 1916 and 1917.[24]

On 11 November 1918 the Friends' Ambulance convoy was close to the front line, near to Sedan. Watkins recalled that he was, in the time-honoured manner, peeling potatoes ready for the midday meal when rumours began to circulate about an

French note advising of the Armistice on 11 November 1918. *(WGAS D/D Z 429/6/6)*

armistice, though gunfire could still be heard to the north. A little later a French soldier appeared and affixed a notice to the church door. This was a not uncommon occurrence but Watkins' curiosity was aroused and he decided to investigate. He strolled across to the church to find that the roughly-scrawled notice announced the signing of the Armistice and, effectively, the end of the war. Within a day or so of the announcement a stream of released prisoners of war of various nationalities, most of them dressed in rags, entered the village of Vendresse where the ambulance convoy was now located. Watkins and his comrades did what they could to help, dressing blistered feet and bathing painful sores. What little spare rations could be mustered were served to the hungry throng which numbered in the thousands. In a single afternoon, 23 gallons of cocoa were served before it ran out with many men left thirsty. Many French refugees also tramped into the village and were helped to return to their long-abandoned homes by way of a lift in an ambulance.[25]

With the fighting over and the Friends' Ambulance Unit no longer required at the front, Watkins returned to Swansea to take up his former position in the office of the Borough Estate Agent. Almost a year later he tendered his resignation and embarked on a very successful business career in the town.[26]

The treatment of conscientious objectors became a matter of grave concern to the government. Clearly it was thought that those who had a genuine objection of

Certificate presented to John Oliver Watkins in recognition of his services during the war.
(WGAS D/D Z 429/6/10)

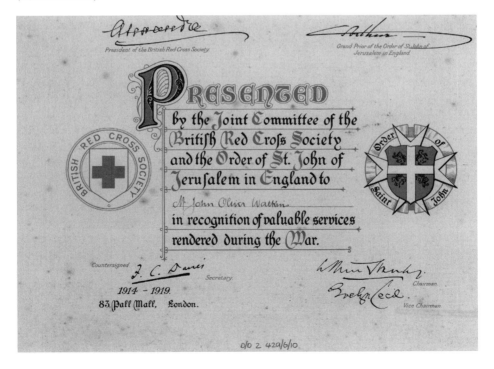

conscience to bearing arms should be exempted from military service. The difficulty arose in determining just who was sincerely genuine in their beliefs and who was using arguments of conscience solely to avoid being enlisted. It should have been possible, in many cases, for the word of a local clergyman to act as confirmation of a man's true beliefs and religious practices, although it seems that very often this was not sought or even accepted as military service tribunals tried to cope with a heavy workload. Many cases involved issues of family or work rather than conscience but all seemed to have been dealt with in a brisk, generally unsympathetic and often unfair manner.

When it became clear that many conscientious objectors would still not bend to military rule, even after being forcibly enlisted, harsher treatment was meted out to them up and down the country with the result that the government became very concerned that the possible death in custody of one or more of them would be laid to its account. Many conscientious objectors actually suffered harsh and inhumane treatment before matters were reined in by a shaken government, with the offer

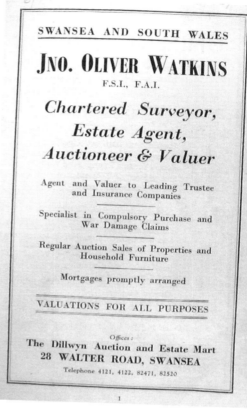

Post-war advertisement for the firm of Jno. Oliver Watkins. *(Author's collection)*

of alternative schemes of work being made in place of military service in appropriate circumstances. Until that time, many conscientious objectors had to stick to their beliefs in the face of cruel treatments and public disapproval. It was not in any way an easy option to pursue.

There were others who did not voluntarily join up or claim a conscientious or other objection to military service. For example, when a police constable saw Thomas Lee at Ravenhill, Swansea, Lee, to use the modern phrase, 'legged it' up the road with the constable, his suspicions aroused, in pursuit. He was soon apprehended and brought before the courts where he admitted being an absentee under the Military Service Act. He was fined £5 and handed over to the military.[27]

Some men took even more desperate measures to avoid military service, sometimes with the aid of others. William Ernest Jones, a hairdresser at Swansea, was found guilty of supplying men with a drug that was intended to render them temporarily unfit for military service. He had approached Henry Brown, via an intermediary named Hudson, knowing that Brown was due to attend a medical board to determine his fitness for service in the army. Jones had asserted that for a total of £8 he could supply a pill that would affect Brown's health in such a way that an army doctor would have to fail him. He claimed to have done this in his own case with no lasting effects on his health. He also claimed to have sold pills to men who were waiting outside the Mond Buildings at Swansea before attending a medical board. He had sold a dozen or so tablets on the spot at 10 shillings each. What Jones didn't know was that when he had spoken to Hudson, that public-spirited individual had 'played along' but promptly taken his information to the police. When Jones subsequently met with Brown, he did so unaware that Superintendent Hayse and Detective Sergeant Gubb were listening from the next room. On proffering the pill to Brown, a surprised Jones was duly 'nicked' and received a six-month prison sentence. The pill had contained a huge dose of nitro-glycerine as well as potassium nitrate and this concoction was capable of temporarily affecting the heart in an adverse manner, thus enabling a man to fail an army medical.[28]

James Meek and George Gardiner also got on the wrong side of the law in attempting to keep Mr Waller, a boot-shop manager, out of the warm embrace of the army. Waller had managed to avoid being enlisted in the past but due to a change in his call-up categorization by the military, he now found himself anxiously awaiting his enlistment papers. Gardiner had previously worked in the local recruiting office and he knew Meek, who worked at the Docks Labour Exchange. The two men conspired, for a payment of £3, to issue Waller with a forged form that would state that he held a false position and that untruth would help to earn him exemption from military service. Mistakes on the form had been explained to Waller as simple clerical errors but when, much to his surprise, he still received his call-up papers, his suspicions grew and he took the form to the authorities. It was pronounced a forgery and Meek and Gardiner soon felt the weight of the law upon them. At trial the pair were each sentenced to twelve months in prison.[29]

There does not seem to have been any great movement of the masses in Swansea against conscription into the armed forces. While individuals may well have stated their particular case before a tribunal in order to gain exemption from military service, the mass of those affected by a call-up seem to have accepted the issue with resignation, if not enthusiasm. When conscription had been on the horizon there were a small number of meetings, held in Swansea in December 1915 and January 1916 and organized by the Independent Labour Party, to argue the case against it but little seems to have resulted in terms of any organized mass protest.

Indeed, despite the individual attempts made to avoid military service, the local press of 1918 commented that about 15,000 Swansea men had actually served in the Great War, most of them apparently in the navy, though how precise those figures are is open to debate given the inadequacy of the recording systems of the time. What is known for certain is that almost 3,000 men with a strong link to Swansea were killed during the war, most (but not all) of their names being inscribed on the plaques at the cenotaph on the Swansea foreshore. That represents a fatal casualty rate of almost 20 per cent of those thought to have served, not including those who were wounded but survived. All in all the figures represent a colossal amount of loss and suffering in Swansea and its surrounds which remain unprecedented in scale. While many went forward willingly to serve king and country, it is unsurprising that others sought to avoid running the risks of an early death or serious injury.

Notes
1. Charles Messenger, *Call to Arms: The British Army 1914–18*, pp.20–21.
2. http://germanhistorydocs.ghi-dc.org
3. Messenger, op. cit., p.96.
4. *Cambrian*, 7 May 1915.
5. *Cambrian*, 21 May 1915.
6. *Cambrian*, 18 June 1915.
7. Messenger, op. cit., pp.130–32.
8. Military Service Act, 5 & 6 Geo. 5, c. 104.
9. *Cambrian*, 3 March 1916.
10. *Cambrian*, 31 March 1916.
11. *Cambrian*, 13 October 1916.
12. Peace Pledge Union, 'Refusing to Kill', p.4.
13. *Cambrian*, 17 March 1916.
14. *South Wales Weekly Post*, 28 October 1916.
15. *Cambrian*, 20 October 1916.
16. Watters' family archives.
17. Ibid.
18. Peace Pledge Union, op. cit., p.50.
19. Peace Pledge Union, op. cit., pp.56–7.
20. *Cambrian*, 19 May 1916.
21. Information provided by Tony Cook.
22. Peace Pledge Union, op. cit., pp.43–5; *Cambrian*, 17 March 1916.
23. West Glamorgan Archive Service (afterwards WGAS), TC/3/38.
24. WGAS, TC/3/38.
25. WGAS D/D Z 429/6/1.
26. WGAS, TC/3/39.
27. WGAS, P/S S/149.
28. *Cambrian*, May/June 1918, edition date missing.
29. *Cambrian*, 23 July 1918.

Chapter Two

Strangers in our Midst

The Swansea of 1914 was, of course, an important shipping centre and it had been the Swansea Corporation that had policed the docks from 1886 until 1891, after which the responsibility was accepted by the Harbour Trust. It was possible for the Harbour Trust to nominate special constables to ensure security at the docks, subject to the approval of the local justices. These constables had the power to board ships to stop or prevent a felony from taking place. They could also act to stop or prevent prostitution, although it should be noted that as vessels were essentially regarded as being private dwellings, there was no power to prevent a woman from boarding a ship unless it was suspected that a felony would result. The special constables could also enquire of any person what their business was in the docks area but upon receipt of a credible answer, no further action was possible. Control of the docks was actually made more difficult by it being essentially an open area, accessible from a number of official or unofficial entrances and policed only by a force that was actually inadequate in number. Efforts were made to control the various comings and goings but with so many sailors and others having a genuine reason to visit the docks area it was always an uphill task for the Harbour Trust to exercise effective control.[1]

This lack of control posed possible problems at the outbreak of war since visiting sailors might leave the docks area intent on gaining military and economic information that might be of benefit to an enemy. Additionally, anyone who lived in or frequented the town and whose sympathies lay, for whatever reason, with the enemy had ample opportunity to enter the largely unsecure docks area for nefarious activities. With the Swansea port being of such importance and with a growing naval presence in the dock area, it was eventually declared a 'controlled' port and restrictions on entry and exit were soon introduced.

Indeed, it was not only those transient seafaring or other visitors to the docks that exercised the minds of the authorities at Swansea. With the country in a state of war, it was unsurprising that those foreigners ('aliens') already present in Britain should also come under a degree of suspicion. After all, even if the long-serving German waiter in the local tea room or restaurant did seem to be a decent sort of chap, who could actually tell where his loyalty really lay? Similarly, if a shop-owner's name seemed to be of foreign origin, how could one be sure where his true allegiance might rest? After the Irish and Jewish contingents it was the 35,000 people of German origin that made up the largest alien group in 1914 Britain and it was natural that that group came under detailed scrutiny as soon as war was declared.[2]

At Swansea, on the outbreak of war, the German vice-consul had made a hasty exit back to Germany, while a number of German sailors were arrested while in the port with their vessels.[3] Other Germans present in the town also attracted the attention of the authorities and were promptly interned. The post of Public Analyst for the town was held by Clarence Seyler, a name that drew immediate suspicion; so much so that the Health Committee to which he made his reports was asked to enquire into the precise nature of his citizenship. In the event that he proved to be of German origin he was to be dismissed and replaced by someone who was British.[4] Happily for Seyler, the enquiries cleared him of any Germanic taint.

There was a certain amount of ill feeling present in the town against those of dubious nationality which resulted in some disturbances and damage to property that was suspected of being owned by Germans. It proved necessary to deal with certain claims for damages, made under a Parliamentary Act of 1886, amounting to almost £175, the sums to be paid from public funds by the town Corporation and including the cases of Messrs Kullar and Gustavus whose names were foreign enough to attract the unwanted and damaging attention of elements of the Swansea populace. It was noted that although Kullar was indeed of German origin he had, in fact, been a naturalized British subject for some time. Not that an aggressive Swansea crowd was aware of that legal nicety, of course, when they smashed his windows. Not all the animosity was aimed at foreigners: Mr Price, the High Street grocer, had his windows broken due to what was seen as his profiteering in foodstuffs.

J. Lyons and Co. Ltd deny that Germans are employed in the business. *(Cambrian)*

He also duly claimed compensation for the damage sustained.[5]

A number of German and Austrian men of military age who had not gained naturalization, many of whom had spent many years in Swansea, suddenly found themselves under arrest and facing internment. An unexpected side-effect of this was, in some cases, that their imprisonment rendered their families destitute as the principal wage-earner was no longer able to ply his trade. A number of these men had actually married British women and when the wives' plight (and occasionally that of the accompanying children) was brought to the attention of the Swansea Corporation, efforts were commendably made to assist them.

This proved to be less than straightforward, however. The Destitute Aliens Committee was a body formed by the Home Office in 1914 to deal with issues affecting aliens in Britain at a time of war. When approached by the Swansea Corporation

The makers of Bovril feel the need to deny any alien influence in the firm.
(Cambrian)

for help it was unable to offer any assistance, apparently as British dependants of aliens were clearly not themselves aliens and were thus outside the compass of the Committee's interests. It was suggested instead that locally-based charities in Swansea might usefully be contacted, beyond which the harsh apparatus of the still extant Victorian Poor Law and the workhouse were available where all other means of help had been exhausted. The governments of Germany and Austria had actually lodged funds with the American ambassador in London to deal with hardship among its nationals but again, it seems that such help could only be advanced to the citizens of those countries and not to their dependants whose nationality differed from that of their husband or wife, father or mother.[6]

Some cases of destitution concerning the dependants of aliens certainly came before the Swansea Guardians of the Poor, the body charged with the administration of the Poor Law and admissions to the workhouse at Mount Pleasant. Long-serving guardian and prominent Swansea citizen J.T.D. Llewelyn considered it unthinkable to simply 'leave the women to starve', though it was thought important that there was a uniformity in treatment across the country. The possibility of returning claimants to their countries of origin was broached, although this would not work where the husband or wife was, in fact, a British citizen who had simply happened to marry a now unwelcome foreigner. Other guardians were anxious that any local monies or practical support advanced to aliens or their dependants who were in need of assistance should, eventually, be repaid to the Swansea Board of Guardians so that the local ratepayer should not suffer financially. The issue was fudged somewhat as it was essentially regarded as being a national rather than a local problem and as such needed a consistent response on a countrywide basis.[7]

J.T.D. Llewelyn.
(Author's collection)

The Destitute Aliens Committee was active in the autumn of 1914 in advocating the transfer of the alien internees who were being held in numerous towns (including Swansea) to the former Cunningham's Holiday Camp at Douglas on the Isle of Man. This suggestion was accepted by the Home Office and the paraphernalia of a prison camp soon superseded that of a holiday resort on the island with the usual mix of barbed wire, electric perimeter lighting and armed guards. The first batch of 200 internees arrived on 22 September 1914 and within a month the numbers had swollen to over 2,000. Another camp at Knockaloe accommodating over 20,000 internees was set up soon afterwards.[8]

Carl Oscar Roth had been born in Dresden but had lived in Swansea since he was a young boy. By 1911 Roth was living at Dresden House, 32 Carnglas Road, Sketty, Swansea, the house name being a clear harking back to his origins that he would later have cause to regret. Living with him there at that time were his wife Eva and their four children. His occupation was that of a sausage-skin dealer and in that respect he occupied business premises in Dyfatty Street which was, of course, very convenient for the local slaughterhouse.[9]

Internees at Knockaloe Camp on the Isle of Man. *(Andrew Snelling, via Europeana1914–1918.eu)*

As a man of German origins, of military age and not naturalized, Roth was soon rounded up as a potentially dangerous enemy alien and despatched to the Isle of Man where he was accommodated at the newer and much larger Knockaloe Camp, close to the town of Peel. He was listed in some records as internee number 11862. Though his date of arrival at the camp is not clear, it does seem that he was only released as late as 26 August 1919, almost ten months after the Armistice. The Armistice was, in effect, a temporary cease-fire put in place so that diplomatic negotiations could take place regarding the terms of Germany and her allies' surrender. As such, a prudent approach was taken to the demobilization of soldiers and the release of enemy prisoners and internees, just in case hostilities should restart in the absence of a signed treaty.

The Isle of Man internees were initially sent to the camp at Douglas, where they were placed in tents that could accommodate four men. They were provided with straw mattresses and army blankets while meals, of which there were three a day, were taken in one of the larger former holiday camp buildings. At a later date huts replaced the tents. However, all did not go well at Douglas, the smaller of the two camps. In November 1914 some exceptionally wet weather led to discontent about the conditions within the tents, while the quality of the food was another area of contention. On 20 November 1914 it seems that some of the internees had decided to escape and saw the kitchen adjacent to the dining hall as a weak point in the camp defences. At a given signal, a number of prisoners approached the two guards who were on duty in the dining room in an aggressive manner and this action necessitated the summoning of additional guards from nearby.

The guards, many of whom were old soldiers, were confronted by a hostile crowd of enemy aliens throwing cups, saucers and chairs. A warning volley seemed to have no effect, so the next volley crashed into the threatening throng, killing four and wounding another dozen, some seriously. Another internee was found to have fallen through a skylight to his death in an attempt to escape. The guards were eventually found to have acted reasonably in light of the situation that confronted them. It seems unlikely that Roth was involved in this sad affair as

SWANSEA AND THE ALIENS' PERIL

At a meeting of the Executive Committee of the Swansea Conservative and Unionist Association, in Swansea on Tuesday evening, Ald. J. Hillard presided over a crowded attendance. The following resolution was passed unanimously:—" That this meeting urges upon the Government the necessity of immediately interning all enemy aliens in this country, cancelling the naturalisation of all enemy aliens and expelling all naturalised aliens of enemy origin from any office under the Crown."

Local concern about the problem posed by aliens. *(Cambrian)*

he seems to have been held at the larger Knockaloe camp. That said, it must have clearly reminded Roth and his fellow internees of the risks associated with aggressive behaviour against the camp guards.[10]

The fear of enemy spies being present or arriving in Britain was a major concern in the nervous days of autumn 1914. Due to this a measure designed to help control the activity of aliens was introduced by the government in the form of the Alien Registration Act of 1914. This required aliens resident in an area to register at the local police station and provide details of their name, address, marital status and employment. This gave the police a small measure of control over their activities and provided the government with important information on the numbers of aliens actually living in the country. It wasn't just the 'usual suspects' in the form of Germans and Austrians that had to be dealt with, of course. Numerous seamen of myriad allied or neutral nationalities arrived in British ports on a daily basis, fetching and carrying the food and raw or finished materials that helped to power the British economy and feed its population. Many lodged in the town of Swansea while their cargo was unloaded or while awaiting their next berth on a ship. Additionally, a huge number of Belgian refugees had entered Britain in response to the German invasion of their country and a number of these had made their way to Swansea.

SWANSEA DETECTIVE AND THE ALIENS.

After finding that two Greeks and one Italian had failed to notify their change of address, Detective T. O'Brien was assaulted by the two Greeks and experienced a rough time. The defendants were fined £5 5s. each for the first offence, whilst the two Greeks were fined £20 each or three months for the assault. The proprietor of the eating house where defendants were found, Andres Pavlates, was charged with aiding and abetting, but the charge was adjourned.

Administering and enforcing the registration of aliens legislation was no small matter. In 1917 no fewer than 35,526 aliens were registered at Swansea during the year, bringing the total registered since the outbreak of war up to 68,445. Many of these were, of course, simply visiting seamen who made regular stops at Swansea to load or offload cargo and as such were entirely innocent of any

Troublesome aliens at Swansea.
(Cambrian)

nefarious intent. It was noted that the majority of those registered were typically so recorded on at least three occasions during 1917, indicating the repeat nature of much of the trade at the docks.[11]

Registering aliens who stayed in hotels and lodging-houses was a requirement of the legislation. Prosecutions in such cases where the regulations had been breached might not be without humour. Mr Leakey, a landlord, was brought before the court in Swansea in June 1916 to answer a charge of failing to report and register the presence of an alien lodger by the name of Henry Mawby. As it transpired, Mr Mawby was actually a native of North Wales and his strange-sounding accent was merely that of an innocent North Walian. The charge was dismissed although costs were awarded against Mr Leakey, presumably for not fully explaining the position before the matter reached the court.[12] Not so lucky was Fred Deakin who failed to report an American and a Swede who were staying at his premises. Deakin was fined 10 shillings in each case. Two Norwegians were fined £10 each for being ashore without permission, the prosecuting officer referring to the fact that information that was of use to the enemy was being leaked by neutrals and as such the defendants were rightly viewed with suspicion.[13] George Hans Hansen (Hans being a name guaranteed to set a wartime Swansea policeman's pulse racing) had failed to report that he had switched his lodgings from Port Talbot to Swansea and, additionally, had been found 'prowling around the market at four in the morning'. He was fined £10 with an alternative of fifty-one days in prison.[14]

Visiting seamen were required not to remain ashore in Swansea, without special permission, after 9 pm on any evening. With sailors being sailors, this was a requirement that was often breached. Jens Anderson, a Swedish sailor, was fined £2 plus an interpreter's fee when he was in violation of the requirement. He had what might have seemed to some to be a good defence: when Special Constable Miron had found him, the defendant had been lying unconscious at the top of the Strand and bleeding from the head. Whether this injury had arisen from a fall or an assault was not stated but it had proved necessary to convey Anderson to the hospital, an ambulance trip for which he was charged a further £1.[15]

A case of a potentially more serious nature occurred in July 1917. Charles Howell was apprehended aboard the British schooner *Duchess* which was then berthed at the North Dock, Swansea. Howell, it turned out, had been travelling for the previous two years as a British subject, while his name was really Paul Loll. He had been born in Poland to a German father and a Danish mother. When cautioned by the arresting officer he had responded:

I am glad it has come to this. I have not been able to sleep for two years, since I came here...I am sorry I did not give myself up; it would have been better for me. I thought I would pass as a Britisher.

Enquiries showed that Loll had travelled frequently between Britain and France while actually being a German and therefore an enemy alien. His belongings contained a French police pass and a military pass issued at Swansea. However, it seems that despite the suspicions raised by the actions of Loll, there was not enough evidence to conclude and prove that he had been acting as an enemy spy when using his false identity. Instead, the charges brought against him related to his residing in the port of Swansea, an area that was prohibited to aliens except where explicit permission had been granted, as well as landing in the port without the requisite authority while being an alien. He was sentenced to six months' imprisonment with the chief constable then being authorized to intern him on release. Loll was fortunate that allegations of spying had not been pursued and proven: convicted enemy spies of the Great War era were routinely shot by firing squad at the Tower of London.[16]

With war having been declared on 4 August 1914, it took less than a week for the usually snail-paced British Parliament to draft and approve a measure that would give the government and its various agencies extensive powers to meet the new emergency. The Defence of the Realm Act 1914 (popularly known as DORA), which became law on 8 August 1914, was a hasty affair running to little more than a paragraph. As events unfolded it soon became obvious that something with a little more precision was required and the first revamp (but not the last) arrived on 18 August, before the later passing of the Defence of the Realm Consolidation Act 1914, which came into force in November 1914 and brought all the experience gained so far together into one Act. Other amendments were made as the war progressed.

The Act of November 1914 gave the government unprecedented power over certain activities of both individuals and corporate bodies. Britain was, after all, under the potential threat of invasion for the first time since the days of Napoleon Bonaparte. The Act therefore sought to prevent persons communicating with or obtaining information for the enemy. It was designed to safeguard the armed forces, the principal means of communication and the railways, ports and harbours on which trade and the movement of military supplies depended. In some circumstances privately-owned shipping could be required to defer to any orders deemed necessary by the Admiralty, while factories or workshops might be brought under the control of the Admiralty or Army Council and subsequently moved away from routine work towards

THE VOICE OE THE GROCER.

'Tis the voice of the grocer, I heard
   him complain—
I am tired of working with might
   and main,
What with forms and coupons and
   counterfoil,
My temper is shattered, my blood it
   does boil.
When my bit I have finished of 30
   a week,
The rest of the time the figures I
   seek,
My stocks to the ounce on form I
   must tell,
So I am wishing controller and such
   were—ah, well !
When I come to the end of a very
   hard day,
I climb to my room, too weary to
   pray.
I am thinking of D.O.R.A., whose
   rules I should keep ;
But the orders quick changing
   quite murder my sleep.
And when I leave here for a world
   yet unknown,
My papers for trading will never
   be shown.
If they ask me to grocer, I shall say
   to them, " No, Sir,"
For once is enough to be bothered
   like this.

A Swansea grocer bemoans the red tape he feels has been thrust upon him due to the war and includes a dig at DORA (the Defence of the Realm Act). *(Mumbles Press)*

work required by the military. Any existing works' output of 'arms, ammunition, warlike stores and equipment' was also to be placed at the disposal of the armed forces. In addition, the spread of false reports or reports inclined to cause disaffection among the armed forces was deemed an offence.

DEFENCE OF THE REALM ACT.

—

Surveyor Reports a Mumbles Hotel-keeper.

COUNCILLOR'S PROTEST.

At last week's meeting of the Oystermouth Council the Surveyor (Mr W. P. Pupdicombe) reported that the landlady of a local hotel had, in contravention of the Defence of the Realm Act, neglected to keep a register of meals. He stated that he first called at the hotel in question on the 12th July, when he found there was no register there at all. The landlady was on that occasion absent, but he saw her the next day and drew her attention to the requirements of the law in this connection. On August 8th and 28th he again visited the hotel for the purpose of inspecting the register. On both occasions he found it in an incomplete state, no proper record of meals having been kept.

Replying to one of the members, Mr Puddicombe said he had called

Enforcement of the Defence of the Realm Act caused some confusion between the various local bodies.
(Mumbles Press)

The Act could certainly not be regarded as a 'toothless dog' by any who had the misfortune to cross its requirements. Minor offences could be dealt with in the local magistrates courts where a convicted person could receive a penalty of up to six months' imprisonment (with or without hard labour) or, alternatively, a fine of £100, with the worst of the minor offenders possibly suffering both penalties. However, a much harder line was drawn for those who intended to assist the enemy. In these more serious cases a civilian offender could be treated as though he was on active service and thus subject to military law and, as such, could be tried by court martial rather than in a civilian court. In the event of a verdict of guilty, the penalty was death. This legislation was used to deadly effect against German spies as well as the leaders of the Irish Easter 1916 uprising (although not in the case of Roger Casement, who was tried and executed for high treason).[17]

As the war progressed, so the restrictions under DORA grew. It became necessary for owners of homing pigeons to obtain a permit to keep them due to the fear of the birds being used to pass messages to the enemy. However, the granting of a permit did not prevent some nervous civilians taking pot shots at a passing pigeon on the off chance that it might be an illicit message-carrier.[18] Further restrictions included the limited lighting of shops during certain hours, alongside regulated shop opening/closing times. One permanent change to the British social landscape came about with the adoption of British Summer Time, introduced in May 1916.[19]

Under the Defence of the Realm regulations it became necessary for motor vehicles entering restricted parts of Swansea (such as the docks area) to dim their lights and it was agreed by the Corporation that suitable signs should be affixed to lampposts to warn drivers of this new and novel requirement.[20] The question of dimming externally visible lights in both domestic and business premises arose at a Corporation meeting in September 1916. Mr H.F. Hood, Secretary of the Swansea Grocers' Association, reported confusion among his members over exactly what was required. It was noted that 40,000 explanatory leaflets had been distributed within the town and, despite the chief constable declaring that these were as clear as possible, one member of the association actually thought them to be as clear as mud. Despite these issues, it was still felt that the law should naturally be obeyed. The suggestion that those who failed to dim lights adequately be fined £25, as was apparently the practice in Cardiff, found no support in Swansea.[21]

This regulation had a serious intent. Principally there was a need to dim or even extinguish lights in certain parts of the country in order to prevent enemy aircraft, often in the form of Zeppelin airships, from using such lights to assist their location of a target.

While a Great War Zeppelin did not carry the same bomb-load or have the same accuracy in bombing as a Second World War aeroplane, it nevertheless presented a real threat to towns and cities in Britain. During the period 1915–18 a total of fifty-one Zeppelin raids were made on Britain, resulting in the dropping of 5,806 bombs which killed 557 and injured 1,358 people. A similar number of German raids using fixed-wing aircraft rather than Zeppelins dropped almost 3,000 bombs and killed 857 people.[22] One advantage of the Zeppelin over a fixed-wing aircraft was its ability to quickly ascend above the normal operating height of the aircraft, rendering it immune from attack before making its escape. From a German viewpoint, the raids provided much more than fatalities on the ground and damage to buildings. In raids on London and other important centres of wartime production it was the disruption caused by the raids, often resulting in the loss of production of war material in darkened workshops and factories, which pleased the enemy, not to mention the effect on British morale. In the event, Swansea did not

Zeppelin raids on Britain brought the war to the home front.

see any airborne raiders until 1940 in a later war, when the outcome was devastating for the town.

However, notwithstanding the attempts by the Corporation and police to clarify things, it seems that little immediate or practical light was shed on the subject for the benefit of the town's shopkeepers. In October 1916 twenty-three persons, mostly businessmen, were summonsed and fined from 15 shillings to £2 for failure to adequately obscure their lights.[23] It was not only shop and car lights that were of concern. John Beynon and a couple of his mates transgressed the DORA lighting regulations by setting fires on a hillside; an act that was presumably seen to be akin to possibly signalling to an enemy and certainly drawing unwelcome attention to the town and its shipping, should any enemy U-boats be lurking offshore. Though it seems that the explanations given at court removed any suspicion of collusion with the enemy, Beynon was nevertheless found guilty of what was essentially merely a silly action on his part. He was only required to pay costs of 4 shillings, presumably due to wasting court time.[24]

Another caught out by DORA was David Webborn. His offence had been a failure to post a list of his employees; a useful practice in assisting the authorities in trying to identify possible aliens.[25] A gentleman who also found himself before the courts at Swansea charged with an offence under the DORA regulations was Arthur H. Studd, a man of 'private resources', whose brother was a brigadier general serving at the front while seven of his nephews were also with the colours. Some days earlier Mr Studd had addressed a patriotic Navy League meeting at Swansea attended by the chief constable, among other eminent guests. Mr Studd had been brought before the court due to having been caught sketching in the castle grounds at Oystermouth. When taken in for questioning, several drawings of possible interest to an enemy had been discovered in his

THE HUNS.

GERMAN SAVAGERY AT BELGIAN TOWN.

MURDER AND TORTURE: HARROWING STORIES.

Details of atrocities by German soldiers were given by Mlle. Auslin to a "Standard" representative, at 8, Clanricarde-gardens, Bayswater, where accommodation has been provided for a number of well-known refugee Belgian families.

"Before Aerschot was occupied by the enemy," she said, "it was bombarded by a Zeppelin airship, the streets being torn by the explosion of the bombs. Many private houses and public buildings were damaged, and several of the townspeople injured. When the Germans marched in and occupied the town horrible atrocities were inflicted on the populace. I saw a whole family taken from their house because a man resisted the violation of his wife, and shot in the street, among them being two little children who were hiding their faces in terror in the skirts of their mother's dress.

Boys' Eyes Gouged Out.

"On one of the houses in the town." Mlle. Auslin stated, "two English flags were flying. The house had been deserted, but the flags seemed to excite the German soldiers tremendously. They shot at them with

Stories of German atrocities were often subject to exaggeration, though sadly many were true.
(Cambrian)

belongings, including two of the Mumbles fort. Mr Studd, who was staying at the Hotel Metropole in Swansea, was unaware that he needed a permit to sketch in Swansea (which was a prohibited area) and explained that he was an acclaimed artist and had exhibited in Paris, among other places. The court, having listened to Studd's explanations and heard from a Swansea naval officer that the drawings were of no military value, eventually released him with the charges being dismissed. They were at pains to commend the police for their diligence, noting that they had done the duty expected of them and that others who drew their attention in future might not be as innocent as Mr Studd.[26]

Contemporary records show that local authorities took the DORA regulations seriously: in Swansea in 1917 there were 172 cases where proceedings were taken for breaches of DORA, resulting in 126 convictions. Nineteen of those convicted were imprisoned for varying periods, though none was longer than six months and the majority were sentences of between two to three months. Fines were issued in 107 cases; some of those imprisoned also being fined. In the case of the restriction and registration of aliens, 1917 saw proceedings instigated in 442 cases resulting in 419 convictions. Of those convicted, only three were sent to prison, the majority receiving a fine.[27]

Another group of people that became an issue for Swansea officials and the people of the town was that of the Belgian refugees. The German plan to attack France (the Schlieffen Plan) had been drawn up and fine-tuned over many years and a key component of it was the need for the German army to pass through Belgium, hopefully by agreement but by force if necessary, on its way to attacking France. When matters on the diplomatic front reached crisis point, Belgium duly refused a German demand made on 2 August 1914 for free passage through the country for its armed forces in order for them to reach the French border. With Germany ignoring a British ultimatum not to enter Belgium, Britain entered the war on the side of her hard-pressed Belgian ally on 4 August 1914. A day later German soldiers attacked the fortress town of Liege in Belgium and were initially repulsed by its defenders. By 16 August, however, the town and its numerous forts were in German hands.

As German troops swarmed across Belgium, a terrified host of civilians attempted to keep one step ahead of the advancing enemy. With many enraged Belgian civilians taking pot shots at the Germans (as allowed by the Hague Convention), the invaders resorted to reprisals and harsh actions. At Dinant over 600 men, women and children were shot in retaliation for what the Germans claimed to be Belgian snipers targeting their men. This cruel action, just one of many, naturally served to increase the fears of the civilian population. Many more began to flee their homes for safety and, as the German advance continued down the coast and plains of Belgium, some sought refuge overseas.

The first Belgian refugees arrived in Swansea on 1 September 1914 and were temporarily housed at Ffynone House, the home of Sir Alfred Mond. It was reported that others would soon follow and indeed they duly did.[28] With the prospect of more arrivals in Swansea, the Corporation took a precautionary step on 16 September 1914 and set up a sub-committee, chaired by the mayor and furnished with plenary powers to deal with any emergency relating to refugees. This proved to be a wise move as refugees continued to regularly arrive in fairly small groups, although in October 1914 a larger party of forty-nine exhausted fugitives turned up unannounced at High Street train station, having come from Ostend via Folkestone to Swansea. They had

> travelled for nearly two days. It was a curious and motley crowd, and a pitiful sight, these poor families, the majority of whom were women and children. Some of the latter were from five weeks upwards, whilst there was one old woman of nearly 80 years of age.[29]

As it was the middle of the night and communications had obviously been muddled, there was no official welcoming party to meet them. With the mayor away on business, Alderman David Davies was quickly roused from his bed to deal with matters. The staff of the Great Western Railway Company helped where they could and the Hotel Metropole opened its doors for free refreshments and, a little later, beds for the night.[30]

By the end of October 1914 there were just over 100 Belgian refugees in Swansea; a figure that rose to 293 by late January 1915. At that time there were 89 men, 59 females and 145 children. The men included 28 fishermen, 16 speltermen, 4 carpenters, 4 engineers, 4 vegetable-preservers, 2 colliery agents and a number of men with other occupations, including 2 judges.[31] About eighty of the refugees were accommodated at Maesteg House, St Thomas, the former home of the Grenfell family. The house had been uninhabited for some time and required repairs and ongoing maintenance so that it could be fully utilized. In the first two years of its use for refugee purposes, a sum exceeding £500 was spent to that end. Other properties were also utilized, such as Brynsifi House at Mount Pleasant, the Poplars at Morriston, a number of properties on De-la-Beche Street and the old YMCA buildings (the new YMCA had opened in 1913).[32]

Fund-raising in Swansea in aid of the Belgian refugees was required in order to provide the

Large Grill Room at Popular Prices. Private Rooms for Dinner Parties.   Ball Room, &c. Electric Light throughout.   · Electric Lift. Motor Bus meets all important Trains.

Illustrated Tariff on Application to—   E. T. TUCK, *Manager.*

Interior of the Hotel Metropole, Swansea. It was often the first stop-off for Belgian refugees arriving in the town. *(Author's collection)*

money necessary for their upkeep, although as time went on it was presumed (and hoped) that at least some of the men would find local employment and be able to largely provide for themselves and their families. The Swansea Art Society held a special exhibition at the Royal Institution of South Wales (the modern-day Swansea Museum) in February 1915. This consisted of fifty-seven paintings, completed by its members, which were to be sold to the public and the proceeds to be devoted to the support of the refugees.[33]

In the main the Belgian men did, indeed, prove industrious. When Sir Ernest Hatch, the chairman of a government commission examining the question of employment for Belgian refugees, visited Swansea he found that little needed to be done at government level. Many of the Belgians in Swansea had already found employment in the fishing, metal-processing and carpentry sectors, while others had been placed on public work schemes with the active support of the Swansea Corporation. Some found work in the marble trade, some as cabinet-makers, shrimpers, masons or miners as well as in several other lines of business. Of the Belgian women, many understandably had family duties to perform in looking after children or aged relatives. Of those who were able to work, eight worked as domestic servants, three as dressmakers, one in a shop and one, somewhat surprisingly for the time, as a fisherwoman. About eleven Belgian women or girls had, however, failed to find suitable employment by the beginning of March 1915.[34]

Hatch also noted that the Corporation had willingly extended help in other practical ways. He noted that free education was provided for the Belgian children; no rates were payable; free travel was allowed on the Swansea trams; free medical advice and periodic sanitary inspection was provided; a Belgian nun had been asked to give the children appropriate religious instruction after school hours; and a number of Swansea ladies acted as visitors to ensure that all was properly conducted at the homes allocated to the refugees.[35] Medical examinations were provided when a need was identified and these occasionally indicated a possible clash of cultures. When Matilde Dupree and her father were examined as both were thought to be suffering from tuberculosis, the physician instead reported them both fit but 'grossly over-clothed' and the risk of spreading disease was made worse by the Belgians' habit of 'spitting anywhere'. He had drawn up a notice addressing that issue, which he wished to have translated into Flemish for the enlightenment of the refugees.[36]

Sir Ernest Hatch emphasized that the Belgians were expected to be prepared to work in return for any assistance that was rendered to them. He was satisfied that the vast majority was so inclined, as was the case at Swansea. However, in cases of what he termed 'black sheep' among the refugees, he urged the Corporation and the people of Swansea to exercise restraint wherever possible. He added that in cases where a man proved to be incorrigible and totally unwilling to earn his keep when given the chance, he should then be returned to the authorities in London at the earliest opportunity.[37]

Still, having found employment did not mean an end to problems regarding refugees for the hard-pressed Swansea officials. A number of Belgian fishermen resumed their

**Press coverage of
Belgian arrivals.**
(Cambrian)

trade while using Swansea as a base and temporary home; a very welcome development with much of the Swansea trawler fleet having been requisitioned by the navy. They were largely, at least at first, housed and looked after under the aegis of the Swansea Belgian Refugee Committee. The question naturally arose that as soon as the men were back in gainful employment, how much of the burden of their upkeep and that of their family could they be expected to meet from their earnings? This proved problematic for the Swansea official charged with discussing this question with the fishermen, who proved to be somewhat more elusive to catch than the valuable fish they brought back to Swansea. When they were finally netted they proved, as the official put it: 'Very ready to promise, but very loth [sic] to part with their money.'[38]

PATTI VISITS THE WOUNDED.

BEDSIDE CHAT AT SWANSEA HOSPITAL.

MORE REFUGEES COMING TO THE TOWN.

The houses in De-la-Beche-street, Swansea, on the side of the Albert Hall, have been purchased by the local education committee, and the new municipal secondary school for girls will be commenced on the site next March. In the meantime, however, Nos. 14 and 16, will be ready for the reception of the Belgian refugees in a few days. No. 17 is in the occupation of Mr. Eden and his committee, who are dealing with the unemployment problem so successfully. Brynsifi, Mount Pleasant, is being fitted out

Madame Patti visits Belgian refugees and has the advantage of being fluent in French. They were not the only Belgians in Swansea as Belgian soldiers came to the hospital for treatment. (Cambrian)

While at Swansea, the Belgian refugees ran the full gamut of human emotions. One Belgian couple realized that they were falling in love and decided to get married. The bridegroom had a problem, however, as under Belgian law he required the consent of his parents. This was a little difficult to obtain as a matter of course since his parents were in Ostend, which was under the heel of the German invader. Belgian officials in Britain bent and twisted various rules and, foregoing a Roman Catholic ceremony, it proved possible for the couple to wed at St Thomas Church.[39] Louis Deroubaix had escaped from Mons during the German onslaught on that town. Ending up in Swansea, he had become ill and passed away at the age of 39, leaving two orphaned children. He had died in Swansea Workhouse (possibly only while being treated in its infirmary rather than there as an inmate) and the expense of his funeral was met by the Swansea Belgian Refugee Committee.[40]

Octavia De Cleyn seems to have arrived in Swansea as a refugee together with her husband and two children. In early 1916 Madame De Cleyn had become ill with a heart problem and, despite receiving medical attention, she subsequently died. Her husband, on his return to Swansea from sea, was faced with a dilemma regarding what to do with the children. He needed the freedom to return to the sea to make a living but that was impossible unless the children could be cared for during his absences. He arrived at a solution by lodging the two girls, Maria and Rosa, with Louisa Adcock, a widow who lived in Bond Street, Swansea and regularly took in lodgers to supplement the wages she received as a school caretaker.

A deal was struck whereby, in return for 10 shillings a week, the two girls would be cared for as well as being given the opportunity to attend a Roman Catholic church. Mr De Cleyn continued to ply his trade at sea, sending postcards to the house at Swansea from places such as San Sebastian, Rouen and the somewhat less exotic Tyneside and Liverpool docks. To the delight of his daughters (and Mrs Adcock's children) he also had a friend who worked in the Cadbury's chocolate factory and carefully-wrapped parcels of extremely scarce chocolate were regularly sent to the house. Tensions could be present in the household, however. When Mr De Cleyn was staying at the house while away from sea he could be mildly violent towards the children, something that Mrs Adcock disapproved of. He was also known to threaten the girls that if they did not behave in his absence, their late mother would return and pinch their toes when they were asleep; another practice that earned his landlady's disapproval.

Over the war years Mr De Cleyn's visits to the house resulted in his affection for the widowed Mrs Adcock growing. He twice asked her to marry him but was politely refused on each occasion. A request that she move to Belgium and become his housekeeper was also rebuffed. He later married someone else and moved to France, though the two families kept in friendly contact over many years. Of the two Belgian girls who had lodged with Mrs Adcock, in later life one became a nun while the other told her own children that she had had a fantastic time in Swansea where Mrs Adcock had been like a second mother to her and her sister.[41]

Finding work in Swansea as a refugee was not necessarily a total blessing as much of the available work was of the heavy industry type and brought with it numerous risks. The 38-year-old Louis Van Hess had gained employment as a furnace-man at the Upper Bank Spelter Works. He had been working on the night shift and, for some unknown reason, left his place of work and proceeded to an area where he had no cause to be. He was later found by a charge hand, lying at the bottom of a 10-foot-deep manhole. The pit had not been protected by the customary barrier and with the lighting being poor in that part of the premises it seems that the Belgian had fallen to his death. This was judged by the coroner to be simply an accident and the condolences of the business were extended to the widow and family of the deceased.[42]

Although Swansea, in common with many other towns and cities, extended a warm hand of welcome to the Belgian refugees, the fact remained that they were regarded as 'aliens' and as such had legal restrictions imposed on their activities. Indeed, by the end of January 1915 it had been decided in London that no more Belgian refugees would be sent to places like Swansea (a controlled port), as having aliens in sensitive areas was not considered advisable.[43]

Several Belgian refugees actually had encounters with the British legal system during their time in the town. Pierre Roland was a Belgian refugee who was found in the docks area without the permission of the Swansea Alien Registration Officer and also without proper documentation. The Swansea dock area was a controlled and defended port and as such prohibited to those without the requisite authority; Roland was duly fined £5 and advised that the penalty could have been as much as £100.[44] Jean Bergs changed his address without notifying the Alien Registration Officer and laughed when challenged about his oversight. It was also noted with concern that he carried a small stone hammer about his person and had previously been charged with larceny. He was imprisoned for three months with a recommendation that he should be deported, presumably back to the unoccupied part of Belgium, upon his release.[45]

The refugee Belgians were not forgotten by their compatriots. In April 1916 the Right Reverend Bishop of Wacchter visited Swansea in order to bring pastoral relief to his countrymen and to thank the people of Swansea for their continuing kindness to the strangers in their midst. The bishop understood the suffering that his country was undergoing and the reasons why so many had felt the need to flee. He had been with the Belgian King Albert in the trenches, encouraging the troops, as well as in Malines celebrating a requiem mass with the sound of the German guns booming in the background while the nearby town of Louvain burned. At Swansea the bishop celebrated low mass at St David's Church, the congregation swelled by the presence of about 150 refugees. In the absence of the mayor (Alderman Thomas Merrells), the bishop was formally greeted by Alderman David Davies, who was also chairman of the Swansea Belgian Refugee Committee, on behalf of the Corporation.[46]

The end of the war in November 1918 started the slow process of Belgian refugees being able to return to their own country. Things were not too straightforward at first as there was a question over who was to pay the cost of their return transport, plus the limited availability of suitable shipping, with passenger transport still recovering from the dislocation caused by the war. While Swansea had proved a welcoming sanctuary for the refugees, as the weeks passed after the signing of the Armistice local officials began to get a little anxious that their guests should return to their true homes somewhat sooner rather than later. An enquiry from Swansea to the Local Government Board elicited the blunt reply that: 'There is not the slightest chance of getting rid of any Belgians next week, as the ship we were relying on has had an accident in Antwerp harbour, and is laid up in dry dock.' Some Belgians chose to return home at their own expense, so keen were they to resume their pre-war lives, while at least one man purchased a small boat in which he planned to sail home once the necessary paperwork had been completed.[47] However, it seemed the journey home might not be all plain sailing. A Belgian wrote to the Belgian Refugee Committee at Swansea, asking it to warn his countrymen:

> It took me two and a half days to get a passport from the Belgian Consul. There are thousands here paying for their journey. The best thing people at Swansea can do is to stop where they are, as conditions in Belgium are simply awful.[48]

It was a further two months before the majority of the Swansea refugees finally left the town, almost 400 of them gathering at High Street train station to begin the long journey home. They were mostly women and children but included a small contingent of men, everyone carrying a package or two of varying shapes and sizes. A good amount of broken English was in evidence, having been picked up in conversation while at work in Swansea or in chats with neighbours and helpers. There were understandably mixed emotions as handshakes were exchanged and farewells made between people who had become friends in adversity. As one Belgian lady remarked: 'I like the Swansea people.' However, it was only natural that a return to their country

King Albert I of the Belgians. He fought alongside his soldiers while his wife served as a nurse at the front.

of birth at the earliest opportunity was the preferred option for almost all the refugees, as well as the Swansea officials.[49]

Notes
1. WGAS, TC/51/8384.
2. Ian Beckett, *Home Front 1914–1918*, p.149.
3. Bernard Lewis, *Swansea Pals*, p.18.
4. WGAS, TC/3/35.
5. WGAS, TC/27/41.
6. WGAS, TC/27/21.
7. *Cambrian*, 2 October 1914.
8. Cesarani and Kushner (eds), *The Internment of Aliens in Twentieth-Century Britain*.
9. Information provided by Ynis Richardson.
10. *Cambrian*, 27 November 1914.
11. WGAS, TC/3/37, Chief Constable's Report.
12. *Cambrian*, 23 June 1916.
13. *Cambrian*, 26 October 1917.
14. Ibid.
15. *Cambrian*, 16 March 1917.
16. *Cambrian*, 20 July 1917.
17. Defence of the Realm Act (later amended), 4 & 5, Geo. 5, c. 29.
18. Beckett, op. cit., p.150.
19. Ibid., op. cit., p.128.
20. WGAS, TC/3/35.
21. *Cambrian*, 29 September 1916.
22. Peter Hart and Nigel Steel, *Tumult in the Clouds*, p.284.
23. *Cambrian*, 20 October 1916.
24. WGAS, P/S G/6/1.
25. Ibid.
26. *Mumbles Press*, 7 June 1917.
27. WGAS, TC/3/37, Chief Constable's Report.
28. *Cambrian*, 4 September 1914.
29. *Cambrian*, 23 October 1914.
30. Ibid.
31. WGAS, TC/27/11.
32. Imperial War Museum, IWM/BEL/6/231/3.
33. *Cambrian*, 26 February 1915.
34. *Cambrian*, 5 March 1915.
35. *Cambrian*, 12 March 1915.
36. WGAS, TC/27/11.
37. *Cambrian*, 12 March 1915.
38. WGAS, TC/27/11.
39. *Cambrian*, 29 October 1915.
40. *Cambrian*, 19 November 1915.
41. Information provided by Roger Brown.
42. *Cambrian*, 16 November 1917.
43. WGAS, TC/27/11.
44. *Cambrian*, 17 December 1915.
45. *Cambrian*, 24 December 1915.
46. *Cambrian*, 21 April 1916.
47. *Cambrian*, 10 January 1919.
48. *Cambrian*, 17 January 1919.
49. *Cambrian*, 21 March 1919.

Chapter Three

Medical Services at Swansea

With Britain at war with Germany it was obvious that in the very near future there would be a need to provide for the care of the wounded once they were back in Britain. The army would have its own facilities in the field of course, but once a man was evacuated back to Britain for further treatment, there arose the question of how he was to be cared for until his full or partial recovery or, in some sad cases, death. In 1914 there was no National Health Service and hospitals were typically funded by subscription, by charity or were simply the medical wing of the local workhouse. In Swansea one of the first bodies to prepare for wartime eventualities was the local division of the Red Cross Society. Its committee met on 6 August 1914, only two days after the declaration of hostilities, and decided to set up an auxiliary hospital in the town. To that end an appeal was made via the local press for donations of cutlery, crockery, linen and other domestic items so that a sixty-bed unit could be established and fitted out. An empty shop in the Uplands area was to be used for the receipt of donated items and an instructional ward was set up to assist with training matters.

A search for suitable premises for use as a hospital then ensued with the Sketty Church Hall and the Llewelyn Hall at the new YMCA being selected, as well as the property known as Heddfan which was the home of Mrs Edith Cleeves who was also an

The Swansea YMCA fitted out for hospital use. *(Simon Jervis)*

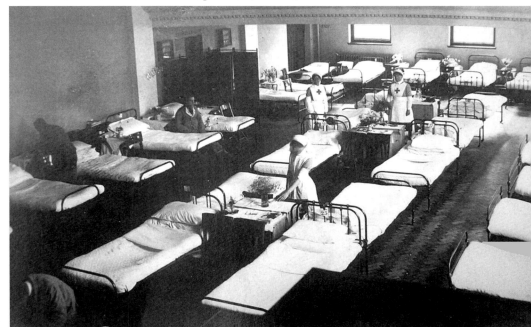

official in the local Red Cross division. St Helen's School was also under consideration at the time when an urgent War Office telegram arrived in Swansea requesting the immediate opening of a hospital for the receipt of wounded servicemen. On 4 November 1914 a hospital was duly opened at the Church Hall in Sketty. The first convoy of wounded men was met at High Street Station by several local Red Cross officials as well as 18 nurses and 12 stretcher-bearers, while 4 cooks, 4 laundry maids and 2 boy-scout orderlies were also standing by. The twelve men who arrived at Swansea had all been wounded at the battle of the Aisne. They received a rapturous welcome on their arrival at Sketty, resulting in several of them being visibly moved to tears. The YMCA at Swansea received its first patients on 3 December 1914, with Heddfan following suit on 4 May 1915.

The YMCA unit started with only 20 beds but was gradually extended until it reached 140 beds by the time it closed in 1919. It is likely that the more serious cases were dealt with at this hospital and many amputations were performed there. The only death

recorded in a Swansea Red Cross hospital took place in the YMCA hospital during 1916. By April 1916 a total of 121 patients had been treated but the heavy casualties resulting from the 1916 offensive in France saw another 187 patients admitted between May and October 1916. The patients were cared for by 4 officers, 19 nurses, 7 cooks and 3 linen-keepers. The unit became so busy that in 1917 the routine YMCA staff and their customers were required to temporarily decamp to the adjacent St Andrew's Church in order to carry out their activities, while the YMCA was devoted solely to medical purposes.[1]

It was still hoped that a suitable building could be identified for use as a larger hospital at Swansea and Miss Dulcie Vivian duly offered up her property known as Parc Wern at Sketty, while Mr Cory Yeo proposed the use of Danycoed at West Cross. The Swansea division of the Red Cross duly took over Parc Wern, while the administratively-separate Red Cross detachment at Mumbles dealt with Danycoed. The Parc Wern house had actually been standing empty for several years but Miss Vivian generously

Nurses and patients from the YMCA. The patients are dressed in the 'hospital blue' uniform adopted by the military. *(Simon Jervis)*

undertook to meet the cost of converting it for military hospital use to accommodate 100 beds. Miss Vivian also had electricity installed, modernized the sanitary arrangements and converted the stables into a recreation room for the wounded, while the War Office provided the hospital equipment. Once Parc Wern was open it proved possible to close the small hospitals at Heddfan and Sketty Church Hall. The property at Danycoed had been the home of Cory Yeo, Managing Director of the Graigola-Merthyr company, but he had relocated to Reading and so was able to offer his former home for use as a hospital. He met the cost of all the adaptations necessary to convert the house for medical use. Forty-two beds were provided and the sanitary fittings were said to be of the most modern designs.[2]

Miss Dulcie Vivian.
(Cymru1914.org)

As the war raged on there was no cessation in the demand for additional medical facilities for treating the wounded. Parc Wern was deemed unsuitable for expansion as it could not be achieved at a reasonable cost, so attention was turned to the new infants' school at Brynmill and that opened as a hospital on 28 June 1917. As matters developed further, Parc Wern became a convalescent home for the exclusive use of officers, the non-commissioned patients being shipped out to the other local hospitals. It could accommodate sixty officers and the first batch arrived in October 1917. The need for extra beds in Swansea did not abate, however, and in 1918 several other buildings were examined for possible hospital use and the possibility of requiring the

Nursing staff at Parc Wern. *(WGAS D/D Z 787/1/d)*

staff at Parc Wern to 'sleep out' so as to free up additional bed space was also considered. Mirador House, the home of Mr and Mrs T.P. Cook was adapted for hospital use and eventually opened on 5 November 1918, although around that time demand understandably slackened as the Armistice was signed, much to the relief of the hard-pressed local Red Cross officials.

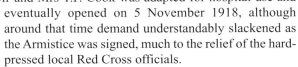

A nurse who served at both Parc Wern and the YMCA hospitals was Miss Hilda Conibear. Miss Conibear had been a schoolteacher before the war but in July 1916 she volunteered for unpaid work with the Red Cross at Swansea. By 1919 she had completed 3,000 hours of unpaid nursing work and was granted the British Red Cross Society War Medal, an award that was instituted in 1920 for Red Cross members (and others) who had worked more than 1,000 hours. Miss Conibear kept a scrapbook in which her hospital patients were free to record their thoughts and thanks. Private W. Lewis (17305) was wounded while serving with the town's own Swansea Battalion, the 14th Welsh. Lewis wrote in the book:

> When war is proclaimed + danger is nigh
> God and the Soldier is every ones cry.
> But when war is over and all things are righted
> God is forgotten + the Soldier is slighted [3]

A group of patients and nursing staff at Parc Wern. *(WGAS D/D Z 787/1/b)*

15,8/16

17/9/16

L/c J. H L Milton
11th (S) Batt. E. L. Regt.
Wounded on the 1st of July in the big Push
Our objective being 'Serre & Beaumont Hamell
But sad to say there are not many left to
tell the tale
For grenade + rifle Shot + shell was like
a Hurrycane Gale.
(With kind regards + Best wishes) Conibear
Parc Wern Hospital Swansea

**Lance Corporal J.H.L. Milton records in verse his
experience of the first day on the Somme (1 July 1916).**
(Eunice Conibear and Elisabeth Hill)

Lance Corporal J.H.L. Milton had been wounded on
the catastrophic first day of the Somme campaign (1
July 1916) while serving with the 11th East Lancashire
Battalion. He wrote:

> Wounded on the 1st of July in the big push. Our
> objective being 'Serre and Beaumont Hamel'.

> But sad to say there are not many left to tell the tale
> For grenade + rifle shot + shell was like
> A hurrycane [sic] gale.

Parc Wern. *(Eunice Conibear and Elisabeth Hill)*

Lance Corporal Milton was a very lucky man. His battalion, the famous 'Accrington
Pals', had advanced across no-man's-land into heavy rifle and machine-gun fire and,
out of the 720 men who took part in the attack, 584 were killed, wounded or missing at
the end of the day. Despite this, one company of men managed to fight its way through
the German barbed wire, across their trenches and into the village of Serre, so reaching
their objective after a Herculean effort. Sadly, they were never seen again.[4]

Another aspect of the work of the Red Cross at Swansea was the provision of trained
men to provide an ambulance service for the transporting of patients from the train
station at Swansea to the appropriate hospital. This detachment consisted of a
commandant and deputy (who also acted as drill instructor), a quartermaster, a medical
officer and a pharmacist. There were also four section leaders, each supervising twelve
men. The men were trained as stretcher-bearers, male nurses, clerks, mechanics, drivers

Mary Vaux. Mary is known to have served with Detachment 132 of the Red Cross at Swansea, probably at Parc Wern and the YMCA.
(Simon Jervis)

and carpenters. To ensure efficiency the unit travelled to Cardiff in May 1915 to observe the detraining of the wounded there and the information garnered was used to establish a scheme of action for use at Swansea. From formation until the end of the war the detachment carried well over 3,000 cases. On two occasions the men were called out to assist in the offloading of survivors from ships torpedoed in the seas around Swansea, although in one case their services were not actually called upon as the survivors were taken elsewhere.

The unit was involved in assisting survivors of the hospital ship *Rewa* after it was torpedoed in the Bristol Channel in January 1918 by the German submarine *U-55* captained by Wilhelm Werner. The *Rewa* was a pre-war steamer that had seen service as a troopship before being converted to a hospital ship. In January 1918 she was bringing wounded men back from Greece when she was attacked and sunk without warning, despite being clearly marked as a hospital ship. After the war Captain Werner was accused of the war crime of sinking ships, including the *Rewa*, without warning. Indeed, on two occasions he had lined up the survivors of the ship he had sunk on the deck of his submarine before submerging and leaving them to drown. He was not brought to justice, however; opting to flee Germany to work on a coffee plantation in Brazil after the end of the war. In the run-up to the Second World War, having returned to Germany, he served as a Nazi Party deputy in the German parliament and during the war served in the notorious SS, choices which perhaps give us the true measure of a ruthless man.

News of the sinking of the *Rewa* reached the Red Cross at Swansea at 7.10 am on 5 January 1918, advising the unit to expect about 100 survivors including about 30 cot cases. A detachment of about thirty Red Cross men reported for duty at the South Dock by 8.45 am, together with four Red Cross ambulances, the police ambulance and an assortment of taxis, private cars and a bus. In all about 540 survivors were landed at Swansea (fatalities in the sinking had surprisingly amounted to only three men), and those in need of medical care were removed to the local hospitals while others were taken to the Sailors' Home, the Exchange Restaurant and the Hotel Metropole where they were fed and clothed. Some 300 pairs of socks plus shirts and vests were provided from the Swansea Red Cross clothing depot. The next day all survivors were taken away from Swansea on hospital trains.[5]

The Swansea General and Eye Hospital had been opened in 1869, having been funded by subscriptions. At the start of the war actions were taken by the hospital committee to reduce the in-patient population as a preliminary step to making the hospital available for military use. With the exception of the north wing, the hospital was to be essentially

closed to the general public in light of
the growing military requirements.
Clinics were to cease and only ten
beds were to be used for convalescent
purposes. Though the military had
requested ninety beds at first, it only
proved possible to make sixty-six
available.

Somewhat surprisingly, some of
the first wartime patients at Swansea
proved to be German rather than
British soldiers. These casualties were
accepted in early September 1914 and
October saw the arrival of over
seventy wounded Belgian soldiers
who had been transferred from the
military hospital at Cardiff. As the

Swansea General and Eye Hospital. *(Author's collection)*

number of patients increased, so the pressure on the hospital's medical staff grew; a
problem that was exacerbated by the calling-up for military service in the medical corps
of a number of the hospital's doctors as well as the matron. The setting-aside of beds for
military purposes obviously had an effect on the treatment of the civilian populace and
the hospital committee was concerned that beds were actually being left unused due to
the anticipated number of military patients sometimes not materializing. The matter was
eased by the military agreeing that beds should be used for civilian purposes when not
immediately required for the treating of wounded servicemen.[6]

By April 1915 matters had advanced so that the capacity of the hospital had to be
increased. It was proposed that those wards that were suitable should be divided down
the centre by a partition to enable the addition of extra beds, while a 'shed' would be
erected on the flat roof of the hospital to accommodate about twenty further beds. The
hospital committee seemed concerned that the hospital would simply be used, to the
detriment of the local populace, as a 'convalescent home' for soldiers who had initially
been treated elsewhere. The military use of beds did indeed lead to problems. In 1916 an
outbreak of septicaemia following childbirth occurred in Swansea and while this would
normally have been dealt with at the hospital, it proved impossible to do so due to a
shortage of beds. Similar problems arose in connection with an increase in the number
of cases of venereal disease in the town, which was not helped by the large number of
servicemen that were stationed at or passed through the town, becoming briefly
acquainted with Swansea ladies of 'a certain class'. To combat that issue it was agreed
that venereal cases involving civilians or members of the armed forces would be dealt
with at the hospital, while cases involving seafaring men or women of loose morals would
have to resort to the less salubrious setting of the Tawe Lodge (the former workhouse)
infirmary. A new hospital building was finally erected to deal with the increased demands,
with funding assistance from the Ministry of Pensions and others, although somewhat
ironically, it did not open until April 1919, five months after the end of the war.[7]

Miss Emily Talbot of Margam allowed her family home at Penrice Castle, on the Gower Peninsula, to be converted into a convalescent home for sick or wounded Australian and Canadian officers. It was planned that this would operate until 30 June 1916, with the possibility of an extension beyond that time. It actually opened in late 1915, the conversion and ongoing running costs being generously funded by Miss Talbot. The proposed staffing was to consist of a butler and a footman with five other men, to include a motor driver and a man to attend to the setting of fires, lamps and so on. The female staff would consist of a housekeeper, cook, kitchen-maid, scullery-maid and three housemaids. If the male staffing level appeared generous, it was pointed out that some of the officers sent to Penrice would possibly be '...so maimed as to be unable to get about themselves without assistance, and some may have to be carried up and down stairs, and the two men...referred to in the list would be allotted this work.'

It was also envisaged that a local doctor would be required to call in once or twice a week to attend to any medical needs and that he would be supported by a resident matron. The number of officers accommodated at any one time would be fifteen. It would be necessary for the existing drawing-room furniture to be removed and replaced with items more fitting for use by military men; such items could apparently be hired from Harrods or some other London firm. Inventories of plate and other utensils would need to be made and separate accounts would have to be kept for the hospital and the Penrice Estate.

The first officers arrived on 20 November 1915 and were assured that:

Miss Talbot desires to make it clear that her house will be entirely given over to the use of the officers and will be conducted, as far as possible, on the lines of an officers Mess or Club with all the advantages of an English Country Estate added. There will be shooting, motoring, and fishing for all the officers who are able to take part in these pursuits.

The home was intended for convalescence and, as such, medical care was largely limited to providing medicine and massages for those officers in need of such services. It was

A modern view of Penrice Castle. *(Robert Edwards)*

Miss Talbot.
(Cymru1914.org)

also a refuge for those whose nerves had been badly affected by service at the front. On that basis, the more seriously wounded officers would not be suitable for a placement at Penrice Castle. It was, after all, still essentially a family home and the agent of Miss Talbot stressed to the military authorities that it would be 'very unfortunate if a fatal ending took place in the house'.[8] There were problems, however. Early in 1916 Lieutenant R.W. Bell,[9] a Canadian officer with the 28th Infantry Battalion, suffered a setback in his recovery. His heart was enlarged and, as things began to look bleak, he was removed for treatment to a private nursing home in Swansea at Miss Talbot's expense. Shortly afterwards he died while still in the care of the nursing home, his mother arriving just after his last moments. The house at Penrice had, however, been spared the distress of a 'fatal ending' within its walls. Lieutenant Beck arrived at Penrice in a very 'nervy' condition and was sent packing back to the military the very next day as the Penrice agent had noted that he had a touch of 'the shakes', apparently brought on by an excess intake of alcohol. His secret stash of alcohol was also discovered, confirming the suspicions.

Towards the end of June 1916 a decision was required as to whether Penrice Castle would continue to receive convalescent officers from the Australian and Canadian forces. While the Penrice Estate agent was happy for the work to continue, it seems that Miss Talbot was in declining health (she died in 1918, aged 78) and had handed matters relating to the use of Penrice as a hospital over to her appointed trustees. The trustees took their responsibilities very seriously indeed and, looking at the ongoing expense of running the house for the benefit of the armed forces with no financial benefit to the Estate, they took the difficult decision to return the house to its former function. The arrangement with the military therefore ended on 30 June 1916.[10]

Another military hospital was established at Horton, again on the Gower Peninsula. This was not reserved solely for the use of officers as had been the case at Penrice Castle. It could accommodate about twenty patients at one time and was inspected by an army officer in 1916 and adjudged to be very good. The patients were seen to be making progress and the

Horton Red Cross hospital magazine article.
(Gower Church Magazine)

GIFTS—RED CROSS HOSPITAL, HORTON.

We have pleasure in publishing the following Report sent in by Miss K. Simons [Ed.]

GIFTS RECEIVED.—Vegetables : Miss Talbot, Mrs Campbell Ford, Penmaen, Capt. Bostock, Mrs Mashiter, Mrs Veale Roberts, Rev R W Lockyer and Rev. H. W. Heaviside. Fruit : Mrs Veale Roberts, Miss Talbot, Mrs Mashiter, Mrs Nicholas Tinned Fruit : Mrs. Lockerbie, Parkmill Ham Mr Little Jones, Cigarettes : Sir A. Mond, Mr David Jenkins, Penclawdd. Daily Papers : Mr Cooper. Illustrated papers : Mrs. Mashiter Rhubarb Mr. Bevan, The Gables. Rabbits and Cakes : Lady Lyons. Jug covers ; Mrs. Pitman.

At present there are twelve patients at the Hospital, all of them getting on well and much appreciating the treatment they are receiving. Letters are constantly being received by the Matron and Staff from patients who have left ; all of them agreeing in the statement that they had a " very good time " at the Hospital, and were sorry to leave. The Visitors at Horton, as well as the inhabitants of Gower, do all in their power to help our soldiers to enjoy their convalescence. Mr. and Mrs. Martin kindly brought a party to the Hospital on August 12 (a wet evening), and gave a most enjoyable concert, and have promised to repeat the entertainment. Mr. and Mrs. Perrott-Bush invited the Matron, Staff, and Soldiers to Llanmadoc Rectory, on August 15 to a Whist Drive and Musical evening. Tea was served in the garden After tea a shooting competition was arranged, then the Whist Drive and after that the evening ended with a most enjoyable musical programme, towards which Messrs. George and Philip Tanner largely contributed. The party left the village of Llanmadoc giving three hearty cheers for their host and hostess hospital was run with good discipline and order. The patients were the subject of a great amount of sympathetic attention from the local populace with regular gifts of fruit, vegetables, ham, newspapers and the all-important cigarettes. The entertainment occasionally provided included whist drives, musical programmes and a trip into the surrounding area by motor car for a limited number of men. There was sometimes a downside to the 'adoption' of the men by the local community. Private Osmund, who had previously been a patient at the hospital, had recovered well enough to be sent back to France where he was subsequently killed in action, saddening many on the Gower Peninsula who had known him while he was a patient.[11]

Entrance to the Swansea Workhouse. *(Author)*

Tawe Lodge, formerly the Swansea Workhouse, was also considered for use in connection with treating the wounded. The original use of the workhouse as an unwelcoming abode for the supposedly workshy poor had largely been superseded over the years by its subsequent use largely as a refuge for the elderly, the sick and orphans. As such, the Swansea Board of Guardians was wary of having to relocate aged and other people who regarded the institution as their home. However, the needs of those who had been injured in the service of their country were also to the forefront of the guardians' deliberations and it was decided to invite a government inspector to review the accommodation and assess its suitability.[12] The outcome of that remains unclear.

As well as the local hospitals that were set up as a result of the Red Cross, St John's Ambulance or voluntary efforts, there were also larger hospitals that were established and run by the military. These were usually based on existing hospitals and were intended to be staffed by members of the Territorial Force Nursing Service (TFNS) which was essentially a body of medically-trained personnel who had volunteered for peacetime service (much like the Territorial Force) with the proviso that they could, of course, be called upon in time of war. The hospitals were, in peacetime, 'normal' hospitals for the use of the general population. However, when war was declared, the hospitals and their TFNS contingents were mobilized and made ready to

A member of the Territorial Force Nursing Service.
(Geoff Caulton, photodetective.co.uk)

accept any casualties that were sent back from the front. In South Wales the 3rd Western General Hospital was based at Cardiff, where it was spread over several locations, and it also had units at Newport and Neath (Penrhiwtyn).

At Swansea Miss Harriette Marion Sandbrook had been employed as a nurse at the Swansea General and Eye Hospital prior to the war. It seems that she had volunteered for service with the TFNS in January 1914 and was then mobilized in September 1914 following the outbreak of war. She was assigned to the 3rd Western General Hospital at Cardiff. Casualties were typically brought to the nearest railway station where they would be met by members of the nursing staff before proceeding to the hospital by ambulance, private vehicle, commercial delivery van or whatever mode of transport happened to be at hand. Wheelchair cases could occasionally be simply pushed along, while the walking wounded could proceed under their own steam with a nurse in attendance for support. The number of casualties received at short notice often meant that improvisation was the order of the day.

A patient dressed in the 'hospital blues' uniform.
(Geoff Caulton, photodetective.co.uk)

Though many men would have arrived at the hospital in their muddy and often bloody uniforms, a hot bath and basic medical attention would soon clear the way to the issue of the hospital uniform for armed forces members, known as the 'hospital blues'. This consisted of a blue jacket and trousers, white shirt and red tie. Once a patient was admitted to the hospital, the duties of the nursing staff and doctors would be instantly recognizable to the modern-day reader. Patients would need to be woken and breakfasted, washed and perhaps helped to shave. Dressings would need to be changed, medication issued, physiotherapy completed and the patient made as presentable as possible for the ward inspection by the medical officer and other staff. Meals would need to be served, bedpans emptied and bedding changed.

Morale was very important and the nurses were expected to appear cheerful at all times, irrespective of the emotional strain of the work. There would be men who were broken in body, men who were broken in mind and some who were broken in both. Some would make almost full recoveries, while others would eventually succumb to their wounds. Others would survive but would possibly have to live the rest of their lives hampered by crippling injuries. Miss Sandbrook would have had to take all of these things in her stride.

She seems to have done well at it. In September 1915 she was promoted to sister and was later described as being 'a capable sister, devoted to her work & patients & well liked by the staff". Sister Sandbrook was placed in charge of a medical floor containing ninety-six beds. She was a good administrator, able to use her initiative when required and provided valuable help in the training of novices. Discipline was maintained under her direction but she was still 'agreeable to work with'.

In the summer of 1917, after almost three years of constant toil at the hospital, Sister Sandbrook suffered a decline in her own health. She attended several medical boards to ascertain her ability to continue in her work, where it was noted that she had been losing weight for several months and had on a few occasions lost her voice, while her breathing also appeared to be weak at times. By October 1917 she had been running a temperature for the preceding five weeks, a cough was present and migraines were frequent. It was thought that the cause was 'strain of nursing work and exposure to cold & wet in [moving] from quarters to duty.' In January 1918 it became obvious that Sister Sandbrook was suffering from pulmonary tuberculosis and she was despatched to a sanatorium for treatment. Though there were some signs of improvement, her overall health rendered her 'permanently unfit for further service' and she was discharged on 25 July 1918 with a gratuity of £38-11-6 and a pension of £50 per annum.[13]

During 1914–18 the main focus of medical work in Swansea was on treating military casualties. The effect of this was seen in a general reduction in the availability of hospital beds for the general population, due to the demands of the military. If that was not bad enough, just as it seemed that things might be about to improve as the allies pushed the Germans back on the Western Front in autumn 1918, another enemy arrived in Swansea. This was an enemy that did not wear a uniform or carry a gun and arrived unseen. It was the arrival in the town of the worldwide influenza epidemic and, surprisingly, instead of mainly

COUNTY BOROUGH OF SWANSEA

ADVICE TO THE PUBLIC ON PRECAUTIONS TO BE TAKEN AGAINST INFLUENZA.

INFLUENZA.

1. The golden rule is to keep fit, and avoid infection as much as possible.
2. The way to keep fit is to cultivate healthy and regular habits, to eat good food, and to avoid fatigue, chill and alcoholism. Healthy living does not of itself ensure against attack, but it makes the patient better able to withstand the complications which kill.
3. The early symptoms of influenza are usually those of a severe feverish cold. Though the actual cause of the disease is unknown, we do know that it is rapid in onset, that it is most infectious in its early stages, and that it is spread by discharge from the mouth and nose, and that it kills mainly by its complications. Every person suffering the disease, no matter how mild the form, is a danger to others.
4. It is not always possible to avoid infection, but the risks can be lessened by:
  (a) Healthy living.
  (b) Working and sleeping in well-ventilated rooms.
  (c) Avoiding crowded gatherings and close, ill-ventilated rooms,
  (d) Wearing warm clothing.
  (e) Gargling the throat and washing out the nostrils. The following may be used as a gargle:
    " A solution of common salt (one teaspoonful to a pint of warm water) to which a few crystals of potassium permanganate are added—enough to make the solution pink."
  (f) By wearing a mask and glasses when nursing or in attendance on a person suffering from influenza.
5. Do not waste money on drugs in the false hope of preventing infection.
6. Those attacked should
  (a) Go home, go to bed, and keep warm.
  (b) Call in a doctor.
  (c) Occupy, if possible, a separate bedroom or a bed that is screened off from the rest of the room.
  (d) When coughing or sneezing, hold a handkerchief in front of the mouth; the handkerchief should be boiled, or burnt if of paper.
  (e) Use a gargle as described.
  (f) Be careful during convalescence in order to avoid relapse or complications.
  (g) Avoid meetings and places of entertainment for at least one week after the temperature has become normal.

Advice on dealing with the influenza epidemic issued by the County Borough of Swansea. (Mumbles Press) affecting the young and the old as was often the case with influenza outbreaks, the infection and death rates were on this occasion highest among those aged between 20 and 40. The spread of the disease was made worse by the unusual conditions created by the war, with large numbers of men moving en masse to and from the front and often living in cramped and unsanitary conditions for lengthy periods of time in the front lines or in military camps in Britain.

In Swansea, increased numbers of influenza cases were noted in July 1918, although the severity did not cause undue concern at that time. However, in early October 1918 an outbreak at Danygraig School became apparent and seemed so serious that the school was closed on the recommendation of Swansea's Medical Officer of Health. As October 1918 drew to a close, further outbreaks of influenza were reported in the Brynmill and St Helen's schools, with an increasing number of cases becoming apparent in many other schools in the borough. For a short period of time all Corporation-run schools were closed in an attempt to halt the spread of the disease. Sunday schools were similarly treated, while children under 14 years of age were excluded from cinemas with the co-operation of the cinema proprietors. This was actually a half-hearted response as the cinema proprietors refused to close down completely for a period of time as might be thought advisable. Economic concerns were as much to the fore in their thinking as medical ones, it seems. They also declined to spray the interior of their cinemas with disinfectant, arguing, somewhat worryingly, that this practice merely replaced one smell with another. They did agree to cease the 'continuous' showing of films and to close between 5 pm and 6 pm, with two additional ten-minute intervals in both the afternoon and evening showings. Health concerns would have to be simply met by increased ventilation of the premises.[14]

The authorities attempted to provide advice on the best methods of minimizing the risk of contracting the disease, suggesting that patients be isolated as far as was practicable and contact with others kept to a minimum. Handkerchiefs, drinking vessels and any other items used by the infected should remain within the room to avoid the spread of the disease to other rooms of the property. Nurses were advised to wear overalls and a mask which should be removed before leaving the sickroom and hands should be regularly washed. Fresh air was important and windows should be opened to allow its free flow into the room. Tramcar attendants were instructed to ensure that their vehicles were adequately ventilated and the anti-spitting byelaw was more strictly enforced than was normally the case.

The hard-pressed local doctors were told that they could call on the services of the health visitors to nurse known cases, despite the risks that entailed. Severe cases had been removed to the isolation hospital at Fairwood, while it was noted that the only institutions in the town to escape the grip of the infection were the isolation hospital and the Bonymaen Industrial School. This was attributed to a prompt ban on the staff of those premises from using tramcars or visiting public places where crowds could be expected. Indeed, at the industrial school even the parents of the young attendees were prevented from visiting their offspring for a period of time.

Between 11 May and 21 December 1918 in Swansea there were sixty-one deaths in cases of patients aged up to 20, while in those aged from 41 upwards there were seventy-four fatalities. As was the case nationally, the largest loss of life occurred in the age group 21 to 40, with 121 fatalities recorded.[15] Mumbles was said to have had the epidemic 'raging', while at Fforestfach it was said to be very prevalent. Even Miss Amy Dillwyn, the well-known industrialist and local character, had been taken ill at a meeting of the Gower Poor Law Guardians and had subsequently taken to her bed at home in West Cross. Happily, she survived.[16]

One gentleman asked in the local press if the apparent immunity to the disease of the Swansea Jewish community might be ascribed to its avoidance of bacon and ham. Another businessman took out several advertisements for a product called Chymol, which he claimed helped people to build up a resistance to infection.[17] By March 1919 the Swansea Burial Board was reporting that demand for grave spaces was up by almost 40 per cent on the corresponding month for 1918.[18] Indeed, the annual statistics on deaths caused by influenza in Swansea showed a remarkable increase year on year. In 1915 there were twenty-one deaths attributed to influenza. The figure was only twelve for 1916 and a lowly ten for 1917. However, 1918, with the epidemic raging across the town, saw the figure increase to 273 and even in 1919, as the number of infections tailed off, it was still as high as 161. In March 1919 an unexpected rise in infections once again caused the temporary closing of Corporation-run schools in the town.[19] By 1920 things had thankfully calmed down somewhat, although the total deaths recorded were fifty-four, still a considerable increase on the years 1915–17 but far below the peaks of 1918 and 1919.

The 1918–19 influenza pandemic was a worldwide disaster and for the people of a Europe that had already seen four years of bloody conflict it was a very untimely and unwelcome visitor. Poorly-informed commentators in the modern-day media occasionally remark that the influenza pandemic caused more deaths than the Great War, as if to understate the scale of the tragic losses of that conflict. However, while the total number of influenza deaths worldwide did indeed exceed the total casualties of the Great War, it must be remembered that the pandemic affected people of many nations that had not taken a direct part in the war as well as those that had. It also affected those not in the military, such as children, the elderly and many women. The total deaths from influenza in Swansea for 1918 and 1919 amounted to 434, according to records of the time. The number of Swansea men killed in the war, however, amounted to around 3,000.

The war dead figure for Swansea is not easy to establish with precision, due to the manner in which records were kept (or not kept) in the pre-computer age. There is also the imponderable question of what actually constitutes a 'Swansea man' in terms of Swansea's war dead. Certainly someone who was born in the town and lived there all his life but what of a man who was born in Swansea but lived almost all his life elsewhere? Or the man who had arrived in Swansea from another part of the country as an adult, joined up, and was killed with a Swansea address as his last abode? The variations are almost endless. Even the recording of 'Swansea' as a man's address in the original records was subject to variation in the 1914–18 period, with 'Swansea' occasionally being omitted on a record and 'Oystermouth' or 'Gower' used instead. Those are just two examples of a great variety, making even a computer search of the digitized records fraught with difficulty.

What *can* be said of the Swansea figure for influenza deaths of over 400 in 1918/19, when compared to the figure for the Swansea war dead of around 3,000, is that clearly the Great War had a far larger impact on the people of Swansea than the influenza epidemic regarding fatalities. Many more Swansea families lost a relative to war than to influenza at that time. However, had the epidemic gripped the town for four long years, as had the war, then the story might well have been very different.

Notes

1. M. Fay Williams, *The British Red Cross Society: A History of the Swansea Division, 1910–70*. Undated.
2. *Cambrian*, 19 November 1915.
3. Hilda Conibear, contemporary scrapbook. Information provided by Eunice Conibear and Elisabeth Hill.
4. Ray Westlake, *British Battalions on the Somme*, p.146.
5. Wiliams, op. cit., pp.30-31.
6. T.G. Davies, *Deeds Not Words: A History of the Swansea General and Eye Hospital, 1817–1948*, p.155. *Cambrian*, 26 April 1915.
7. Davies, op. cit., p.161.
8. WGAS, D/D P 2652.
9. Commonwealth War Graves Commission.
10. WGAS, D/D P 2652.
11. *Gower Church Magazine*, September and December 1916.
12. *Cambrian*, 8 October 1915.
13. The National Archives (afterwards TNA), WO/399/14318.
14. *Cambrian*, 1 November 1918.
15. WGAS, HE/12.
16. *Cambrian*, 14 March 1918.
17. *Cambrian*, 14 March 1919.
18. *Cambrian*, 7 March 1919.
19. WGAS, TC/3/39.

Chapter Four

Industry and the War

In August 1914 the town of Swansea was still an industrial powerhouse, even if its crown as the world centre of metal processing that had earned it the title of 'Copperopolis' had slipped a little in the face of increasing world competition. Metal smelting on a large scale was still performed along the banks of the River Tawe, at places like the White Rock Works, at Middle Bank and at Upper Bank, at the Hafod and at the Morfa Works. Despite the fumes and the stink created by the smelting processes and the vast piles of polluted spoil that were produced, the town had nevertheless still acted as a powerful magnet for those from other parts who were seeking employment. In the nineteenth century they had flocked in from the surrounding countryside, from many parts of England, Ireland, Scotland and from much further afield in search of work. This was vividly reflected by the population of the town which grew from about 6,000 in 1801 to around 95,000 by 1911.[1]

The ready availability of a cheap coal supply had made it more economic for metal ores to be shipped to Swansea for processing rather than being smelted where they were mined, where coal might be in short supply and the industrial infrastructure available for its production inferior to that found in the bustling Welsh town. Because of the economically important metal and coal trades that were operated out of Swansea there was also a good transport system in place, provided by a mix of river, canal, road and railway links, and the vital funnel through which most imports and exports passed was, of course, the Swansea docks. Though the creation of the docks had been a long and tortuous process, by 1914 they were capable of handling vast amounts of incoming cargo

The busy docks at Swansea.
(Author's collection)

Dockside cranes at Swansea with a sailing ship in the background. *(Author's collection)*

One of the immense storage sheds on the dockside at Swansea. *(Author's collection)*

from all corners of the world, as well as being able to ship Swansea's huge industrial output in the opposite direction. The docks covered an area of over 131 acres and had 32,200 lineal feet of quays for the handling of cargo. The King's Dock was designed to accommodate the very largest ships, its deep lock being 875 feet in length and 90 feet in breadth. There were 27 fixed or movable coal hoists capable of shipping up to 700 tons of coal an hour, together with 100 hydraulic or electrically-powered cranes with a lifting capacity of up to 70 tons. For the storage of goods there was almost 750,000 feet of floor space. The fetching and carrying of goods to and from the docks was assisted by no fewer than five railway companies: the Great Western, the Midland, the London and North Western, the Rhondda and the Swansea Bay.[2]

In 1913 the docks at Swansea handled just over 1.1 million tons of imports and 6.1 million tons of exports. The imports included iron ore, zinc ore, copper, timber, bricks and slates, flour, grain, potatoes, fruit and hay. Exports included coal and coke, processed metals of many types, timber, alkali, wood and fire clay. Of the exports, some 5.4 million tons were shipped abroad, while the remaining 0.7 million tons were sent to other British ports. Trade was conducted with ships bound for Russia, Algeria, the West Indies, Australia, Africa, Bombay and Persia, among a host of other exotic destinations. A significant 10 per cent of the import and export trade was conducted with Germany, Holland and Belgium; therefore the outbreak of war would have a major impact on the trade of the docks.[3]

In fact in 1913 the Swansea Docks' trade with Germany and her Austrian ally, plus Belgium, had amounted to almost 508,000 tons. The figure for 1914, a disjointed trading

Another huge storage shed at the Swansea docks. *(Author's collection)*

year due to the outbreak of war in August, had been only 250,000 tons, while the figure for 1915, the first full year of the war, amounted to not a single ton, thus putting a hefty dent in the port's trade figures. As an island nation fighting a major war, it was inevitable that the trade patterns of Britain would be affected as production was diverted to military needs, thereby reducing the quantity and range of goods that would normally be available for export. On the import side, while British demand for supplies from other parts of the world to oil the military machine and to feed the population continued, there was the added problem of ensuring that shipping losses due to enemy surface vessels and submarines did not reach levels that had a critical impact on the economy and on the eventual winning of the war.

The Swansea Docks total trade figures for 1916 showed a 720,000-ton fall on 1915. The year 1917 saw a fall of over 900,000 tons on the previous year. While 1913 had seen total trade of 7.2 million tons, by 1917 the figure was down to 4.2 million tons; a dramatic fall largely occasioned by the wartime crisis.[4] Matters were not helped when in early 1915 the British government imposed restrictions on the export of tinplate, anxious that the material should not reach Germany or her allies by way of a neutral country. This naturally dampened the export trade even further at Swansea and matters were made worse when America shaped up to supply neutral countries with tinplate, thus impinging on what had traditionally been British markets.[5]

Tinplate production also suffered in another way. Steel was a key component in the tinning process and the heavy demands of the military for steel for munitions production naturally reduced its supply for other purposes. This had a knock-on effect on the tinplate

Fishing trawlers at Swansea. *(Author's collection)*

industry in Swansea and other places. In Swansea in late 1916 the supply of steel amounted to only about 42 per cent of what was required and it seemed likely that even this inadequate supply would shortly be further reduced in order to meet military requirements. The effect of this shortfall in material on employment in the metal-processing industries at Swansea was hard, with many long-serving men being laid off and finding it impossible to find work in other fields where their tinning skills were inappropriate. There was the added risk that certain neutral countries might step into the void in tinplate manufacture so that when the Swansea tinplate workers eventually returned from the trenches at the war's end they would find that the jobs they had left behind had largely vanished. The loss of a job would be a harsh reward, indeed, for risking life and limb while serving king and country.[6]

At the start of the war a substantial fishing fleet had operated out of Swansea. The Castle Steam Trawler Company was a Swansea business which found no fewer than twenty-two of its boats requisitioned by the Admiralty for military purposes. They were largely used in mine-sweeping operations, their civilian crews being mostly replaced by Royal Navy reservists. The loss of fishing craft at Swansea and the consequent impact on fish supplies was partly made good by the use of a small fleet of Belgian-owned and crewed trawlers, the boats and their crews having fled from their home country at the outbreak of war.

The enemy threat at sea, mainly provided by the German U-boat fleet, played a part in depressing the trade at the Swansea Docks with a knock-on effect on the people of the town. While the loss at sea of exported goods due to enemy action was a matter of great regret and inconvenience – although it could not be compared with the loss of life that often accompanied such sinkings – it was nevertheless true that it was the destination of the cargo that finally suffered the loss of material. It was the loss of a cargo that had been intended for import at Swansea that had a possible effect on the Swansea populace, of course. While Swansea acted as a distribution centre for other parts of the country, there would obviously be portions of many cargoes that would remain in the town for subsequent sale to the local industrial undertakings or, indeed, the local population. Reduced imports of ores and metals, whether due to a general trade depression or to the activities of the German U-boat fleet, had an adverse effect on the output of the numerous Swansea works that dealt with such items. Shortages could result in labour lay-offs and a consequential fall in demand in the local shops as families struggled to cope with a sudden drop in income but there was also an impact when foodstuffs came to be in short supply. The Swansea Harbour Trust reported that in 1915, for example, the importation of flour and potatoes fell by 17,000 tons, while sugar imports fell by 9,000 tons. This must have resulted in many Swansea families having to make do with reduced rations, food substitutes or, in the case of the worst shortages, simply having to go without. By 1917 food shortages had become commonplace in Swansea and elsewhere and rationing was not far away.

The South Wales Transport Company also encountered problems caused by the war. In 1914 the company was running twenty-six buses on passenger routes in Swansea. The business was doing well and was looking to expand its routes by the acquisition of additional vehicles. However, those ordered by the company shortly before the war were promptly requisitioned by the military, even while they were still under construction, thus stalling the company's expansion plans. To add insult to injury, fourteen of the

HMS *Nile* arrives at Swansea in 1912 to be broken up. The dock was easily able to accommodate her.
(Author's collection)

Tram transport in Swansea. *(Dave Westron)*

company's existing fleet were similarly requisitioned leaving the business to struggle to meet even its existing commitments, while any plans for expansion were of necessity put on hold.[7]

Another important aspect of the Swansea wartime economy was that of munitions production. The development of trench warfare on the Western Front had led to an unprecedented demand for weapons and explosives of all kinds. Existing military armaments factories had found it impossible to cope with demand and the government had concluded that the work must be spread among other factories that could be quickly adapted to produce military material. It made sense to make use of those areas of the country where engineering skills were readily available and there were existing factories where output could be quickly adapted for military purposes. Leeds was an early guinea-pig for this approach and Swansea soon came to the forefront of the thinking of those charged with identifying suitable areas for implementation of the new plan. A conference was held at Cardiff in June 1915 and was chaired by the Earl of Plymouth. He had been asked to look at the issue by Lord Kitchener, Secretary of State for War.

It was thought that to spread the work across a large number of fairly small engineering companies in a particular location would hamper the many other sorts of non-military engineering work that were still required in wartime. There would also be issues of having to place suitably-qualified and experienced personnel at numerous locations to supervise the complicated and potentially dangerous process of producing munitions. It would be far better, so it was believed, for the work to be concentrated in a single factory in each area so that supervision needs could be reduced and quality control improved. It was intended that those existing firms affected by the plan should provide their best co-operation and that this should extend to selling (or even lending) the government the tools already owned by the works that could be utilized for munitions production. Other machinery could be brought in from elsewhere if required.

It was agreed at the meeting that a committee be formed to consider how best to achieve the production of munitions in South Wales. Among those appointed to the committee were Mr Herbert Eccles, President of the Steel Association at Swansea, Mr T. Griffiths of the Steel Smelters Society and Colonel J.R. Wright of the Baldwin's Works at Swansea. A munitions plant was duly established at the Baldwin's Works at Landore, under what was known as the National Shell Factory plan. Manufactured there were 18-pound shells, 60-pound shell heads and 6-inch proof shots.[8] The Swansea Technical College offered assistance in the training of men for the production of munitions, though there was no question of the actual production of shells being carried out on the college premises.[9] The college was actually used by the government as a gauging and tool shop, although that work ceased in November 1915 when it was transferred to the Baldwin's Works. A new role for the college arose in the training in semi-skilled munitions work of men who were not of military service age and, increasingly, women.[10]

Recruitment of men to work in the new munitions factories, at Swansea and elsewhere, commenced in the summer of 1915 following a public advertisement. It was reported that enrolment at Swansea had been very satisfactory and a number of men had already received orders from the munitions office in London and had been briskly told where to report, their train ticket being very helpfully provided. Those selected were mostly skilled men including fitters, turners, mill-men, engine-drivers and mechanics, as well as platers, boilermakers, riveters and shipwrights. A number of unskilled men were also accepted, no doubt to assist with the requisite fetching and carrying of heavy items.[11] The Swansea Corporation had already been approached by a Local Government Board inspector to see how many men it could spare to assist with the production of munitions. The Corporation had baulked at releasing men who were engaged in refuse-collection or street-cleaning but nevertheless managed to identify thirteen men who could be spared in aid of the war effort. It was agreed that the Corporation would undertake to reappoint the men so released to their former positions once the need for their work in munitions production had abated.[12]

As the government was effectively directing the work of the new (and existing) munitions factories, it sought to ensure that the production of supplies vital to the war effort should proceed unhampered by any labour disputes. To that end, such factories were designated 'controlled establishments' and the Minister of Munitions reserved to himself the power to 'give directions as to the rate of wages, hours of labour or conditions of employment of semi-skilled and unskilled men employed in any controlled establishment on munitions work'. Another clause stated that if a particular worker had left employment in a munitions factory in the last six weeks, without the approval of the employer (as evidenced by a leaving certificate) or the approval of a munitions tribunal, then that man (or woman) should not be offered alternative employment by any other person. Having a settled workforce was an important priority and movement between jobs was to be discouraged in the present crisis. When working in a controlled establishment a worker was required to be sober, to follow instructions and to not take part in any disturbances or use abusive language. Workers were also required to attend at the workplace regularly, to work diligently and to be prepared to undertake a reasonable amount of overtime. In short, it was very much a 'stay here and do as you are told' approach in an area of work that was, of course, vital to the war effort. Despite these exhortations and the pressing national emergency, this requirement nevertheless proved difficult for some workers to satisfy.[13]

Mr Stait had worked at a controlled establishment in Swansea for several months, although it seems that the restrictions thus imposed on him had not been fully, if at all, explained to him by his employer. Subsequently, when Stait complained that the rate of pay he was receiving was less than that applicable at other works, the lack of a reply from management led to him leaving his employment and proceeding to Essex. Summoned before the munitions tribunal at Swansea, he failed to appear, claiming to have a throat infection. While the tribunal members were sympathetic to his circumstances, they

Munitions workers. *(Gwynne McColl)*

nevertheless thought that his unauthorized absence had retarded the important war work being undertaken at Swansea and accordingly fined him 10 shillings.[14] Another man was fined 10 shillings after missing a single shift, his plea of illness falling on deaf ears. It was stated at his hearing that a fall in steel output amounting to 25 tons had been occasioned by his unauthorized absence.[15]

The return home of a soldier from the front had resulted in a father and son absenting themselves from a controlled establishment for a week in order to spend some time with their returnee relative. On this occasion the tribunal took a sympathetic line and dismissed the case against each, while enjoining the pair to 'do their best in the future'.[16] A request for a leaving certificate based on the premise that the applicant felt he could earn better money elsewhere was simply refused. The tribunal stated that it had only the national interest in view, while the applicant was essentially only interested in lining his own pockets. He was quite entitled to do that in 'normal times' but not in the current difficult circumstances of a major war.[17] One worker absented himself from work for almost two hours and returned, according to his foreman, 'staggering drunk'; although the man denied this, claiming to have only consumed one pint of beer. The case was proven and as drinking while on duty was forbidden, a fine of £1 was imposed.[18]

Munitions work involved greater risks than merely falling foul of the authorities over time-keeping or sobriety, of course. Certain processes required the handling of picric acid (called lyddite in military applications) and this was:

A bright canary yellow powder...and comes to the factory in wooden tubs. It is then sifted. The house (windows, doors, floor and walls) is [sic] bright yellow, and so are the faces & hands of all the workers. As soon as you go in the powder makes you sneeze and splutter and gives you a horrid taste at the back of the throat.[19]

The yellow discoloration of parts of the body caused by picric acid led to munitions workers so affected being referred to as 'canaries'. It was not entirely a laughing matter, however, as picric acid was related to TNT and could be absorbed through a person's skin, digestive tract, or by the inhalation of fumes or dust. Once in the body, although many seemed to suffer no lasting ill health, some workers developed dermatitis, digestive problems, changes to the composition of the blood and liver degeneration (toxic jaundice). A number of munitions workers actually died during the war from liver problems and associated jaundice.[20]

A major hazard for those working in munitions was, of course, the possibility of death caused by an explosion. The explosive components of the artillery shells and other ordnance had to be handled with the greatest of care to minimize the risk of an explosion but, almost inevitably, given the scale of the undertaking up and down the country together with a largely unskilled workforce, accidents could not be totally avoided. A 1916 explosion at a munitions works near Leeds killed thirty-five women, while a 1917 accident at Silvertown in East London killed sixty-nine people, many of them women. A 1918 explosion at Chilwell near Nottingham resulted in a blast that was heard 20 miles away which killed 134 people, including over 30 women. Despite the tragedy, the surviving Chilwell workers were back at their jobs on the following day, fully aware of the importance of their work to the war effort.[21]

Although Swansea appears to have avoided any serious occurrences as regards munitions explosions, accidents were not unknown in other munitions works in the area. On 3 August 1917 the *Cambrian* laconically reported the deaths of six persons in a blast

Munitions production in an English factory, to which the scene in Swansea would have been similar.

With many men at the front, women stepped in to fill the gap in areas such as munitions production. *(WGAS D/D TAY PLA 7-12)*

'at a munition factory in South Wales'. A further three people were injured. Reporting of such incidents by the press was always vague regarding the precise location of a factory, lest any information so divulged should be of use to the enemy. That said, the location of the explosion was in all probability the shell-filling factory at Pembrey, near Llanelli. The dead comprised four men and two women. One of the women, Dorothy Mary Watson, was 19 years old and lived at Port Tennant Road in Swansea. The exact nature of the work performed was shrouded in secrecy but it was revealed that the men were engaged in mixing and stirring chemicals, while Miss Watson and another lady were charged with moving the product around on trolleys. This work was described as 'one of the least dangerous operations', although this seems not to have been borne out by events. The cause of the explosion remained a mystery, however. All the workers had been trained, supervision was apparently adequate, and a man who had left the area a mere three minutes before the explosion had noticed nothing amiss.[22] Another explosion occurred in March 1918, killing two people and injuring four.[23]

A tragic incident took place on 18 November 1918, a week after the Armistice came into effect. With the war essentially over (though it should be noted that hostilities could have recommenced in the event of any peace discussions coming to nought), the press was more able to freely report details than had hitherto been the case in relation to earlier accidents. The explosion again took place in the munitions factory at Pembrey and resulted in the deaths of three women with another two being injured. The deceased were all Swansea women: Mary Fitzmaurice of Sketty Crescent; Jane Jenkins of Washington Terrace, Landore; and Edith Ellen Copham of Matthew Street.

The women had been involved in disassembling 18-pound shells. Their supervisor had explained to them the difference between shrapnel and high-explosive shells but had, apparently, omitted to tell them to ensure that high-explosive shells utilizing a 106-type fuse also had a safety cap fitted. It seems that while handling a high-explosive shell that did not have a safety cap fitted over the 106-type fuse, the awkward and heavy projectile had slipped from someone's grasp and struck the floor. The lack of a safety cap resulted in an immediate explosion, killing the three female workers. The coroner's inquest decided that no blame could be attached to the management of the works as the foreman had been adequately instructed but he had simply failed to fully acquaint the workers with the risks involved.[24]

The unusual economic conditions brought about by the war led to price inflation that was not usually matched by a corresponding increase in a worker's wages. This was in turn exacerbated by local pockets of unemployment and the large number of families who found themselves less well-off due to a father, husband, son or brother being absent from home while serving with the armed forces. Though 'separation allowances' were paid to the families of serving men by the military, they did not always match the income lost. Those who were still in work also found that they had more to do due to the absence of men who had volunteered for, or from 1916 onwards, been conscripted into the armed forces.

To working-class families it often seemed that the sacrifices made in wartime were not being shared equally with, for example, locally prominent families being rather noticeable by their absence in the food queues and there was also an underlying suspicion that businesses were profiteering, largely at the expense of the working man. Many skilled men found their earnings being overtaken by unskilled workers who were able to perform simple, repetitive tasks in munitions production, for example, with their payment often being based on a piece-work rate rather than any special skill that was required. The more they completed, the more they were paid, and the traditional engineering skills of the qualified tradesman often came quite literally a poor second-best in the pay race. The

Not a man in sight! *(WGAS D/D TAY PLA 7-13)*

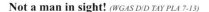

Hafod Copper Works. The railway carriages bear the initials of Vivian & Sons.
(Author's collection)

necessary 'dilution' of formerly skilled work so that unskilled men or, God forbid in the eyes of many craftsmen, even women, could perform a task previously reserved for a trained man also raised tensions among the skilled workforce. The admission of women into certain areas of work that had previously been the province of male labour actually proved a success and as a consequence increased the chances of a man who had possibly been previously exempted from military service due to the work he performed now being released and duly called up. It was hard enough for a man to accept that not only was a 'mere woman' now entrusted with his skilled work but that this meant he was also placed under the interested gaze of a military that was always keen to find a new recruit.

These factors caused a considerable amount of unrest as the wary worker, jealously attempting to guard his hard-won privileges, occasionally resisted the demands of government and employers for more effort while his workload increased but his pay failed to keep pace with prices, or he found his role undercut by an unskilled man or woman. Notwithstanding the fact that there was a war to be won, the unrest manifested itself in a large number of industrial disputes and strikes. While the figures are subject to debate, it does seem that between 1915 and 1918 there were over 3,000 strikes in Britain, involving in total some 2.6 million strikers and resulting in a loss of production equal to almost 18,000,000 days.[25] Swansea played an unhappy part in this unrest.

Where there was industrial unrest it was the role of the chief constable of Swansea to provide a police presence so that any violence which might ensue could be swiftly dealt with. His annual report for 1917, the year of the Passchendaele Offensive on the Western Front, gives an idea of the level of unrest experienced at Swansea in a single year, and this with the outcome of the war still in doubt. There were strikes involving drivers at the Weavers flour mill; among operatives at a number of wagon works; among the electrical and mechanical employees at the Dyffryn, Beaufort, Cwmfelin and Baldwin's Steel Works; among employees in the furnishing trades; workers at the Midland Bank Copper Works; the ships' carpenters at the Prince of Wales Dry Docks; the engineering staff at the Bristol

Channel Dry Docks; and among employees of the Co-operative Society shops.[26]

In May 1915 the men responsible for loading coal onto ships at the Swansea docks went on strike in a dispute over waiting-time pay, or rather the lack of it. It seems that the men were being required to attend at the docks at specific times, only to frequently find that either the coal had not arrived from the pits or, if the coal was indeed to hand, the ship it was intended for had not yet berthed. According to the standards of the day the employers declined to pay any waiting-time, the men being required to hang around on an unpaid basis. The dispute led to about 100 coal-tippers refusing to work, with another 600 men, whose work depended on that of the tippers, also being temporarily laid off. The employers eventually offered a war bonus of 12.5 per cent but this was rejected, the men arguing that such a bonus would expire at the end of the war, while waiting for work on an unpaid basis could recur at any time in the future. The dispute was still rumbling on sporadically in August when Roger Beck of the Swansea Harbour Trust bemoaned the action of the tippers in occasionally declining to work at a time of national crisis. He also made a patriotic appeal to the men's better instincts, while pointing out the adverse effect their inactivity was having on the funds of the Harbour Trust.[27] Referring to this dispute, the Swansea Chamber of Commerce later noted that 'several vexatious delays had occurred at the Swansea Docks...in practically every instance owing to disputes to which the shippers were not in any way parties, and in some cases owing to disagreements between the men themselves.' A war bonus of 12.5 per cent had, in fact, been accepted by the tippers but as the Chamber observed: 'the men do not adhere to this, but demand extras without any reason, except that of force, under threats of strikes, which under war conditions cannot always be resisted.'[28]

In July 1915 there was a short-lived strike in the South Wales coalfield that had the effect of temporarily depriving the local coal merchants of all supplies. With the employers unable to agree a deal with their employees and with threats from the government being ignored by the miners, it proved necessary for a deputation led by no less a personage than Lloyd George himself to rush to South Wales and twist the arms of the mine owners. The miners' demands were soon met and work resumed after six days of inactivity.[29]

It was not only the traditional heavy industries that were the subject of labour unrest. In September 1917 employees in the furnishing trades at Swansea came out on strike, pointing once again to the plain fact that wartime prices were far outstripping wages. It was claimed that the furnishing trade workers had received only a halfpenny an hour rise in both 1900 and 1913 (with nothing in between!), while 1914 saw wages rise by a

Cwmbwrla Tin Works. *(Author's collection)*

further halfpenny to 9d per hour. Although war bonuses of 5 per cent had been applied in both 1915 and 1916, it was felt that the cost of living had actually increased by about 50 per cent.[30] Bonuses themselves could be a matter of contention. In 1918 when the male employees of the Swansea Tramway Company received a nationally-agreed 5-shilling war bonus, their female counterparts, apparent victims of the male-dominated thinking of the time, received nothing. A brief strike ensued, with the coach drivers symbolically handing their vehicle starter-handles in to their managers.[31]

Swansea was not unlike many other towns and cities of Britain in seeing industrial unrest during the Great War. It must be remembered that many of the most basic employment rights had only comparatively recently been won from frequently stern-faced employers. The prospect of seeing those important gains diminished, even at a time of national crisis, naturally provoked a response from a predominantly male workforce that occasionally flared up in the form of often short-lived industrial action. However, despite the problems posed by the erosion of skilled wages in favour of largely unskilled piece-work and the introduction of women into previously unfamiliar workplaces, in the main the national interest was not allowed to suffer too much while employment troubles were briskly ironed out.

Notes
1. Ralph A. Griffiths (ed.) *The City of Swansea: Challenges and Change*, pp.113, 120.
2. *The South Wales Coal Annual 1919.*
3. *Swansea Harbour Trust, Annual Report, 1913.*
4. *Swansea Harbour Trust, Annual Report, 1918.*
5. *Cambrian*, 15 January 1915.
6. *Cambrian*, 15 December 1916.
7. *Cambrian*, 21 May 1915.
8. Information from members of the Great War Forum (1914-1918.invisionzone.com).
9. *Cambrian*, 11 June 1915.
10. *Cambrian*, 26 November 1915.
11. *Cambrian*, 9 July 1915.
12. WGAS, TC/3/35.
13. Munitions of War Acts, 5 & 6 Geo. V, c. 54 & c. 59.
14. *Cambrian*, 19 November 1915.
15. *Cambrian*, 25 February 1916.
16. *Cambrian*, 16 June 1916.
17. *Cambrian*, 20 October 1916.
18. *Cambrian*, 12 May 1916.
19. Diary of Miss G. West, Alphahistory.com
20. Great War Forum, op. cit.
21. Ian Beckett, *Home Front 1914–1918*, p.88.
22. *South Wales Daily Post*, August 1917, day unstated.
23. *Cambrian*, 8 March 1918.
24. *Swansea Herald of Wales*, 14 December 1918.
25. Beckett, op. cit., p.50.
26. WGAS, TC/3/37, Chief Constable's Report.
27. *Cambrian*, 14 May and 13 August 1915.
28. *Cambrian*, 4 February 1916.
29. *Cambrian*, 23 July 1915; Arthur Marwick, *The Deluge*, p.77.
30. *Cambrian*, 28 September 1917.
31. *Cambrian*, 23 August 1918.

Chapter Five

The Food Supply Problem

As an island nation at war, it was obvious that the continued supply of raw material imports to Britain would be crucial in meeting the growing needs of the military and also some of the essential material needs of the civilian population. The supply of foodstuffs was also of prime importance and although Britain was producing much of what was required in that respect, there was still an enormous amount of food importation, amounting to about 60 per cent of what was needed in order to meet demand in 1914. Any serious interruption to the food supply could lead to shortages and, ultimately, food rationing.[1]

As early as 7 August 1914 the Board of Agriculture in London had anxiously reassured the British public that wheat stocks, which were obviously essential for baking of all kinds, were at a level that would last for four months at the normal rate of consumption and without the need for imports. At that time many people expected the war to be of brief duration and in that case it was thought unlikely that a shortage of food would be a significant factor in the war economy.[2]

In Swansea the outbreak of war saw an early rise in food prices, possibly due to increased demand (as people laid in supplies of non-perishables on a 'just in case' basis), and perhaps because food wholesalers (and some shopkeepers) saw the chance of making a quick profit at a time of great uncertainty. Following representations from the Swansea grocers and provisions dealers, the mayor of Swansea wrote to the Local Government Board in late August 1914 pointing out that

The Weaver and Co. flour mill.
(Author's collection)

> ...certain firms are holding up large quantities of sugar which is in hand at the Swansea Docks warehouses, and also that certain millers who had large stocks of flour in hand prior to the outbreak of war had considerably increased their prices and further that large quantities of butter are stored in the Cwmbwrla Cold Storage premises in this town which commodities are apparently being held up with a view of further increased prices.[3]

It was not only the flour and sugar allegedly held in local stores that were causing problems in supply. The Hovis-

Bread Flour Company contacted the Corporation at Swansea to see if it would be interested in purchasing 130 bags of white flour, each weighing 220lbs, that were currently held in storage at the Swansea Docks as the planned export of the cargo to neutral Norway had been banned by the government. It was suggested by the company that the flour could be used by the local Swansea distress committees, which had been set up some time earlier, to provide practical assistance for the poorer elements in the town.[4]

The mayor also made an early appeal for shopkeepers to exercise restraint in setting prices, bearing in mind the hardships that the war was likely to bring, coupled with the existing high level of unemployment in the area.[5] By 14 August 1914 a list of 'official food prices' appeared in the local press at Swansea, setting out the Board of Trade approved prices for products such as butter, cheese, bacon, lard and margarine. It was noted that some food prices in Swansea were happily below the prescribed rates and it was suggested by those in authority that the businesses offering the lower prices should naturally be rewarded by increased custom.

Food prices remained an issue, however, and several meetings were held in the town in the early part of 1915 to discuss the problem. Labour leaders met to air grievances and to call for government action. Some thought that government links with business were a little too cosy and it was the serving, working or unemployed man and his family who were suffering from profiteering.[6] Anecdotal evidence suggested that the cost of living in Swansea had risen by 20 per cent since the beginning of the war and people were being forced to economize to remain within their weekly budget. It seemed that 'luxury' items such as biscuits and cake were no longer being purchased at pre-war levels, while tea and butter consumption was down, margarine often being used as a poorly-regarded butter substitute.[7]

The J-Shed in its original incarnation as a docks' warehouse. Today it houses a restaurant and other commercial enterprises.
(Author's collection)

A joint committee of Corporation members and grocery trade representatives set up in 1914 to monitor food prices was accused of having 'gone to sleep' on the issue at one of its infrequent meetings. While some Corporation representatives thought that certain traders were taking advantage of the situation to line their own pockets, the trade pointed to increased wholesale prices and their reduced profits. The meeting struggled to make any real progress in dealing with the issue, eventually wallowing in a plethora of claim and counter-claim. It was agreed, however, that strong representations should be made to the government on the matter.[8] The joint committee continued to meet erratically and without much obvious success as time passed by. Indeed, in July 1916 criticism of the grocery trade at a Corporation meeting led to the grocers declining to attend joint meetings in future unless the criticism was backed up by firm evidence.[9]

Some enlightened local employers, among them the Swansea Corporation and Messrs Vivian and Company, were paying certain employees a 'war bonus' that was intended to help alleviate some of the difficulties caused by higher food prices. In the case of Vivian's this worked out at 3 shillings a week extra (on a wage of less than 30 shillings a week) for a married man with dependants. Similarly-placed men earning more than 30 shillings a week received a weekly bonus of 2 shillings. That was fine for those who worked for well-intentioned employers, of course. For a great many others with less sympathetic employers or perhaps no job at all, a tightening of the belt remained the only practical option.[10]

A leaflet encouraging food economy.

Faced with food shortages, customers occasionally tried to shop around for the best prices but were frequently thwarted by shopkeepers only selling them, for example, butter on condition that other items were bought from their premises at the same time. Some suppliers were known to be happy to sell the much sought-after sugar but only if tea was purchased at the same time. This practice was frowned upon by the authorities in cases where tea could actually be bought elsewhere at a lower price, although the attraction of a supply of scarce sugar was often a powerful influence on the customer's final decision.

The Corporation attempted to use its in-house expertise for the benefit of the citizens of the town in an effort to ease the food supply problem. One idea was based on the work done by Mr Bliss, the Parks Superintendent, and his team at the Corporation nursery at Llangyfelach. At Llangyfelach cereals, vegetables and fruit were being grown and it was intended that the people of the town could usefully visit the site and bring away ideas and knowledge that would enable them to create their own food gardens. Mr Bliss thought that a Corporation food stall in Swansea Market would also attract attention and encourage participation in the scheme across the town. The idea was supported by Corporation members, providing the existing market stallholders were not disadvantaged by the Corporation's plans. Beyond that initiative, the Gower Peninsula was also touted as an ideal area for more intensive food cultivation. It had advantages of soil and climate that made it ideal for fruit-growing; no small matter when considering that on a single hot summer's day in 1915 no fewer than 10,000 baskets of strawberries had been brought into Swansea. Indeed, more than 80 per cent of the fruit and vegetables normally consumed in Swansea was actually bought in from England.[11] Removing the need for long-distance transportation of the often delicate produce had the added benefits of reduced delivery costs and improved freshness.[12]

In May 1916 one Swansea grocer had noted that while he could easily sell almost a ton of sugar per week, over recent weeks he had only been able to obtain a single ton and even that was of the less popular caster variety.[13] Indeed, prior to the war the firm of Walters, Jones and Company had been the only importer of sugar in Swansea. Up until the summer of 1916 the firm had been provided with its usual monthly quota of 50 tons of sugar but for August 1916, only 5 tons had been received. Walters Jones drew the matter to the attention of the mayor of Swansea, who in turn made representations to the Royal Commission on Sugar Supply, the body charged by the government with allocating the sugar supply as fairly and equitably as possible. The commission was quick to point out that Swansea was not being treated differently to any other comparable town. The supply of sugar was subject to fluctuation in quantity over time and in the summer of 1916 the demands of the military were being given some priority with a corresponding impact on the supply to towns and cities. The mayor's missive may have had some effect, or perhaps the supply position simply improved somewhat: in October Walters Jones received the grand amount of 10 tons, double that of their last delivery but still far short of the quantity required to meet the normal needs of a sweet-toothed Swansea population.[14]

A great scarcity of seed potatoes was expected in 1917 and this led the Corporation to consider ploughing up municipal parks in order to maximise the space available for crop-growing. The recreation ground, the Morriston, Victoria and Jersey parks as well as Park Llewelyn were all mooted as being suitable for cultivation, although it was thought best that existing floral displays should be left undisturbed whenever possible. It was hoped that if such land was parcelled up into allotments and let rent-free in the first year, the people of Swansea would welcome the chance of producing some of their own food.[15] There were some reservations on the part of the parks superintendent regarding the suitability of the soil at Victoria Park and the recreation ground, it being described as a mix of sand and ashes and unsuited to cultivation. Mr Thomas Morgan, Master of the Swansea Workhouse, begged to differ, stating in a newspaper article that simply applying a good layer of manure would bring the soil up to an acceptable standard.

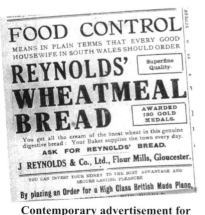

Contemporary advertisement for bread. *(Cambrian)*

Morgan had forty years' experience of potato-growing and he also thought that adding potatoes to flour was a practical method of increasing the bread supply with no major loss of taste or quality. This had been done at the workhouse and 'blind-tested' by some of the Guardians of the Poor with good results. However, Morgan's advice did not find favour with the majority of the Swansea bakers. Adding potatoes to the bread mix was a messy and time-consuming process and many bakers simply carried on with the more traditional bread-baking mix, even though this meant using more of the scarce wheat flour.[16]

Self-sufficiency was actually well advanced at the Swansea Workhouse where the paupers had 28 acres under cultivation; producing swedes, potatoes, parsnips, cabbage, wheat, oats and barley, among other things. The results met all the needs of 750 workhouse inmates for vegetables. In a telling comment on the prevailing economic conditions in the town, the workhouse master stated that he had recently sold a pig for £23, whereas the pre-war price would only have been around £7.[17]

The government became more actively involved with food supply problems in 1917 with the creation of the Ministry of Food and an important new post, that of Food Controller. It also took steps to guarantee minimum prices for wheat and oats for a period of five years in order to encourage their greater cultivation, while also fixing a minimum wage for agricultural labourers. Efforts were also to be made to improve the productivity of existing agricultural land while at the same time attempting to identify additional land that was suitable for crop cultivation.[18]

Wheat production was an important aspect of food supply and the newly-formed Glamorgan War Agricultural Committee met in May 1917 to consider how best to bring under cultivation for food purposes 30,000 acres of existing grassland. As far as the Swansea area was concerned it was planned to utilize 3,600 acres in Gower, 2,400 acres in the Swansea district and, in the Swansea Valley, a further 2,000 acres. Action taken in 1917 would obviously help the 1918 harvest and local farms were to be surveyed, hopefully with the co-operation of the farmers, so that land most amenable to wheat production could be identified. The committee also had potato production under its scrutiny and it was hoped to maximize yields by the use of potato-sprayers (300 would be provided for the entire county of Glamorgan) in order for potato disease and consequential loss of crops to be reduced.[19]

New potatoes were not subject to price control by the government's Food Controller and consequently the price fluctuated according to the normal laws of supply and demand. In June 1917 prices ranged from £3 5s to £5 per cwt [hundredweight] in a single week of wholesale trading. Jersey new potatoes were quoted at £5 per cwt compared to the 19s 6d per cwt of only a year earlier. The problem did not only revolve around price: one Swansea importer had agreed a price on 250 tons of Irish potatoes but then struggled to find a vessel on which to load them for transportation to Swansea.[20] An enterprising ship's

The Meat Question and its Solution

The staggering high prices of meat, bacon and bread are making people THINK–and WORRY

The increasing sales of Quaker Oats prove that thoughtful housewives know that Quaker Oats is the most economical food—as well as the most nourishing. Even with meat at ordinary prices you had to pay 3/6½ for strength and energy which Quaker Oats would supply for 2½d.

Nothing else can compare with Quaker Oats as the family's war-food.

By order of the Food Controller.

"QUAKER OATS is imported to be sold under license of the Food Controller at a price not exceeding 9½d. for the 2-lbs. (gross) packet or 5d. for the 1-lb. (gross) packet throughout the United Kingdom."

It is requested that any cases where higher prices are charged be reported to ——
The Secretary, QUAKER OATS Ltd., Finsbury Square, London. E.C.2

Substitutes were sought for scarce foods and suppliers were keen to promote the claims of their own products.
(Cambrian)

captain had filled some spare space in his hold with 10 tons of Irish potatoes but not having met the prescribed formalities and being under suspicion of profiteering, he found that his edible (and perishable cargo) was impounded at the port. Happily for the Swansea population for whom the potatoes were intended, they were eventually released by HM Customs before they had spoilt, the regulations having eventually been met.[21]

As the availability of meat also became more problematic it was decided that the local bye-laws controlling the keeping of pigs could be relaxed. While a large institution like the Swansea Workhouse had the space available to prevent pig-keeping becoming a public nuisance, more care was needed in allowing pigs into a domestic setting where garden space might well be more limited and in close proximity to neighbouring properties. Nevertheless, given the emergency situation, it was agreed that pigs could be kept domestically subject to an application being made to and approved by the Corporation's Health Department.[22]

The government, via its Board of Agriculture and Fisheries, had provided that where a parcel of land was not rated under the Poor Rate it could simply be taken over by the Corporation with no rent payable and handed over to any society willing to undertake its cultivation. Plots of land already under the control of the Corporation were also identified and earmarked for the use of those willing to cultivate them. A number of local ward ratepayers' associations came forward in response to this opportunity.[23] One initial sticking-point arose around the length of tenure granted for the working of an allotment. Those keen to cultivate a plot provided to them by the Corporation thought that a letting period of perhaps ten years might be a suitable reward for the effort required to bring such barren plots into use. However, the Corporation felt that in the case of its land at Hill House, for example, it should revert back to the Corporation in 1920. It might, after all, become valuable building land in the coming years and an overlong letting period would inhibit the prospects of the Corporation getting a good return on its holding.[24]

The proposed rush to the allotments did not meet with full approval in all quarters. Several reverend gentlemen representing the 'Christian community of Swansea' understood that allotment-ploughing was to be carried out on Sundays and thought that this move, even at a time of national crisis, should not be entertained as Sunday should be a day of rest. The Allotments Committee of the Corporation made it clear that it had given allotment-holders no such permission but accepted that there was nothing in the allotment-letting rules to actually prevent Sunday working. It was agreed to leave the matter to the individual consciences of those involved and the general feeling was that little such work would actually be undertaken on a Sunday.[25] This seems not to have been the view of many allotment-holders as the local press was soon reporting that many plots were indeed being dug over on the Sabbath which, for many working people, was probably the only free day that they had each week.[26]

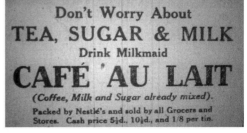

Shortages in one area offered commercial opportunities in others. *(Cambrian)*

Though the Corporation was keen to encourage the bringing into cultivation of plots of wasteland in and around the town, it received one suggestion with which it was unhappy. A sub-committee of the Glamorgan War Agricultural Committee had its eye on 2.5 acres of land at the Corporation-owned Morriston Cemetery. The Corporation pointed out that the land identified was habitually used to graze the horses used for haulage by the Corporation and, as such, was required for that ongoing purpose. The agricultural sub-committee wanted to see the plot ploughed up so as to be suitable for sowing with corn, ready for the 1918 harvest. With the decision going against it, the Corporation decided to appeal to the full committee.[27] It is unclear whether or not their appeal succeeded.

Despite the best efforts of the Corporation and others, in the short term potatoes remained in short supply. In April 1917 while swedes, parsnips and sprouts were on sale in Swansea, it was stated that about five out of every six people who were asked had not eaten a potato in the previous two weeks.[28] If food production could not meet the demand for a product, another option for those in authority was to try to reduce that demand. With meat in short supply, the government introduced 'meatless days' in restaurants and hotels in order to reduce demand for a relatively scarce foodstuff. The first of these days took place in April 1917 and apparently passed off successfully in Swansea. Meatless days were set on Wednesdays and Fridays and on those days potatoes could be served in the absence of meat. That was fine in theory but as several Swansea catering establishments simply had no potatoes available, it proved necessary to substitute rissoles made from butter beans for the absent tubers. There were other restrictions on those who ate away from home. Hotels were required to provide guests with just two slices of bread at breakfast, although if the customer was also due to take lunch at the establishment he could opt to have his bread allowance for that meal with his breakfast, if preferred. Sugar was restricted to one lump per cup with only one cup per meal.[29]

By May 1917 it proved necessary, despite all the ad hoc efforts at food economy, to provide practical advice that would help the people of Swansea to make best use of the foodstuffs actually available. To this end the Swansea Ragged School building was converted into the 'Swansea War Kitchen', the aim being to provide the people of the town with practical food preparation demonstrations. How to use barley and oatcake were among the topics to be explained. Assuming the scheme was successful, it was planned to open similar kitchens in other parts of the town.[30] Early demonstrations at the Ragged School premises included the 'Preparing of Wartime Dinner for Four Persons' by the aptly-named Mr Ham of the Hotel Metropole; 'Bread, Wheat Substitutes and Wartime Cakes' by the Misses Martin and Thomas; and 'Savoury Dishes' by the Misses Evans and Jones.[31] Mr Ham (who was a chef at the Hotel Metropole) offered up soup and vegetable cream with onions, braised beef, rice fritters and flaked maize pudding as his contribution to the proceedings.[32]

With the town Corporation keen to assist its citizens the mayor, in collaboration with Parks Superintendent Mr Bliss, managed to obtain 3 tons of potatoes at £14 per ton in May 1917. These, he stated, had been obtained for the poorer classes in Swansea rather than for those of greater means who could afford to buy the more expensive, albeit often less palatable, substitute products. The potatoes were duly bagged in quantities of 4lb weight and the distribution day was set for a Saturday.

Mayor of Swansea, Ben Jones. He acted as mayor for the latter part of 1917 due to the illness of incumbent David Davies and then took on the full role until November 1918.
(WGAS TC/19/10)

Though the distribution was to commence at 10.15 am, as early as 7 am an eager crowd had started to gather in the vicinity of the Tunnel Hotel. By 8 am the number had reached the hundreds and less than two hours later it had grown into thousands. The queue was five deep in places and many who arrived a little later than the mass of those queuing promptly turned away, seeing a protracted wait as a fruitless, and probably potato-less, exercise. The bags were sold at 7d each and the names and addresses of those receiving them were carefully checked and recorded to avoid anyone obtaining more than one bag per family. The distribution proceeded efficiently, well-marshalled by Chief Inspector Hill and several of his officers with the bags being doled out by Corporation members, no doubt with one eye on the wellbeing of the people and the other on the future local elections. It was apparent that many people had tramped in from the outlying districts, such was the appeal of the scarce potato. A number of those present confirmed that they had not tasted a potato for several weeks. When supplies finally ran out a large number of people were disappointed, although their apparent good humour disguised their obvious regret.[33]

The actions of the government's Food Controller began to have an impact both nationally and locally. Under the Cheese (Requisition) Order of 1917, all cheese imported into Britain from America, Canada, New Zealand and Australia had to be handed over to the Food Controller who would renegotiate the terms of sale before setting the retail price and then passing the product on to the grocery trade. Prices were also set for items such as butter beans, haricot beans, lentils and split peas, where such items were intended for human consumption. Mr William Lewis, an officer of the Swansea Grocers' Association, found the actions of the Food Controller to be 'not British'. He claimed the price restrictions being imposed meant that he was being made to trade at a loss, quoting Welsh oatmeal and Japanese peas as examples. Lewis thought that once current stocks of the loss-making items had been exhausted, local grocers should refrain from re-stocking them in order to make the Food Controller realize the folly of his policy.[34]

Beer also came to the attention of the Food Controller and in October 1917 it was a cause of concern to the Swansea licensed victuallers that the government was setting a price of 5d per pint for sales of beer in public bars, although smoke-rooms, railway refreshment rooms and theatres were free to

When you've got them, tell the people! An advertisement for the often-rare potato.
(Cambrian)

charge higher prices. As with the grocers and food prices, the brewers were concerned that the set price would not allow much room for a sustainable level of profit in respect of some types of beer. Drink was seen in some quarters throughout the war as almost as great an enemy as Germany, its overindulgence resulting in drunkenness and lost production. The king had 'signed the pledge' early in the war, hoping to act as a beacon for others to follow his lead although the results were mixed at best. The price and strength of beer were adjusted over time and public house opening hours restricted in an effort to control what was seen as a major problem. A 'no treating' order was also introduced in many areas, making the buying of drinks for others (soldiers were often 'treated' by civilians) an offence.[35]

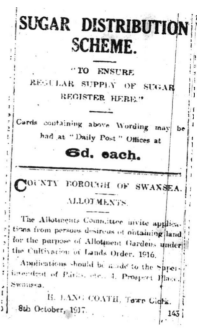

The Corporation became involved in both sugar supplies and allotments. *(Cambrian)*

In August 1917 the Local Government Board directed local authorities to form their own local food control committees, at first to deal with the thorny issue of the sugar supply and with the prospect of other produce eventually coming under the purview of the committee as matters progressed. The Swansea Parliamentary and General Purposes Committee decided that, as well as the obligatory councillor representatives, there should also be a labour representative, a female and someone from the co-operative movement. The Corporation was allowed to incur some expenditure in setting up and staffing an executive office for the purpose of food control and it was decided that those responsible for administering the scheme would be housed in offices provided at the Free Library on Alexandra Road.

The Free Library on Alexandra Road.
(Author's collection)

Under the new arrangements for the sugar supply, every Swansea household was required to first obtain a sugar registration card from the local food control office. This process would initially require about fifty members of staff to administer it in Swansea, although that number should reduce to about twenty once the cards had been successfully distributed. Each household would then need to present the sugar registration card to the grocer of its choice. The grocer (who would have also needed to register with the local committee as a sugar supplier) would have to accept all cards proffered. Sugar could then be provided to the grocer in quantities that matched the needs of the registered customers of that business, assuming that supplies were always plentiful enough which was by no means a certain proposition.

That measure would prevent families calling at more than one grocer's shop to lay in supplies of sugar in excess of their short-term needs, as well as ending the practice of a grocer turning away non-regular customers as had often happened under the unregulated arrangement. It was later reported that applications in respect of registration for sugar supplies had been received from 27,517 Swansea households, comprising 110,939 persons.[36] Approximately 12,000 other persons from Swansea were said to be serving with the colours. All issues of sugar still rested on the premise of an adequate supply being available in the first place, a situation that could not be guaranteed in wartime.[37]

By the end of October 1917 the Swansea Food Control Committee was considering bringing other foodstuffs within its remit, specifically meat, milk and butter. Indeed, such was its desire to get things right and minimize the risk of criticism that with regard to meat, some carcasses were especially cut up under the committee's direction and scrutiny so that a more informed approach could be taken when accounting for wastage and an appropriate price level for particular cuts of meat.[38] Fish seems not to have been in short supply at Swansea during the war, although it was subject to price control. Swansea was, of course, already an established fishing port and the availability of Belgian trawlers based at the harbour compensated at least in part for the loss of Swansea trawlers requisitioned by the military.

COUNTY BOROUGH OF SWANSEA.

FOOD CONTROL COMMITTEE.

Defence of the Realm (Ministry of Food).

The Meat (Maximum Prices) Order, 1917.

The above Food Control Committee prescribe until further notice the following scale of Maximum prices for sale of meat by retail within their area:—

BEEF.	Best English. ported. s. d.	Imported. s. d.	PORK—	Best English. ported. s. d.	Imported. s. d.
FOREQUARTER—			Belly	1 7 ... 1 5½	
Shin beef—with bone	0 6 ... 0 4		Head	0 6 ... 0 4½	
Shin beef—without bone	1 0 ... 0 10		Leg	1 6 ... 1 4½	
Brisket—best end	1 0 ... 0 10		Fillet	1 10 ... 1 8½	
Brisket—back end	0 10 ... 0 8		Loin	1 8 ... 1 6½	
First Five Ribs	1 6 ... 1 4		Loin chops	1 10 ... 1 8½	
Flats	1 0 ... 0 10		Neck	1 5 ... 1 3½	
Blade Ribs	1 4 ... 1 2		Shoulder—with hock	1 2 ... 1 0½	
Leg of Mutton cut	1 5 ... 1 5		Shoulder—without hock	1 4 ... 1 2½	
Chuck—with bone	1 5 ... 1 5				
Neck—with bone	0 6 ... 0 4		LAMB AND MUTTON—		
Neck—without bone	1 0 ... 0 10		Breast	1 0 ... 0 10½	
HINDQUARTER—			Leg	1 4 ... 1 2½	
Sirloin	1 7 ... 1 5		Loin	1 5 ... 1 3½	
Three Wing Ribs	1 6 ... 1 4		Loin chops	1 9 ... 1 7½	
Pinbone	1 5 ... 1 5		Neck	1 0 ... 0 10½	
Pinbone steaks	1 9 ... 1 7		Shoulder	1 4½ ... 1 5	
Bowl bone	0 6 ... 0 4				
Whole rump	1 5 ... 1 1				
Rump steaks, joints	1 5 ... 1 5		VEAL—		
Topside, no bone	1 7 ... 1 4		Leg	1 4 ... —	
Thick Flank	1 5 ... 1 5		Fillet	1 10 ... —	
Silverside—whole	1 4 ... 1 2		Loin	1 4 ... —	
Silverside—cut up best end	1 7 ... 1 5		Chump end	1 3 ... —	
Silverside—back end	0 11 ... 0 9		Shoulder	1 0 ... —	
Leg bone—with bone	0 6 ... 0 4		Breast	1 0 ... —	
Leg bone—without bone	1 0 ... 0 10		Neck—best end	0 10 ... —	
Thin flank	0 10 ... 0 8		Scrag end	1 6 ... —	
Aitchbone	1 5 ... 1 3		Cutlets		
Suet	1 2 ... 1 0				
Kidney	1 2 ... 1 0				

N.B.—THE PUBLIC ARE URGED IN ALL PURCHASES TO ASK FOR VOUCHER (in cases of doubt), STATING NAME, WEIGHT, AND PRICE OF JOINT BOUGHT, AND THEREBY ASSIST THE FOOD COMMITTEE IN PREVENTING ANY CONTRAVENTION OF THE ORDER.

H. LANG COATH,
Hon. Executive Officer.

Maximum prices were set to avoid profiteering. *(Cambrian)*

Swansea Market. A scene of occasionally-raised tempers when food supplies were scarce.
(Dave Westron)

Butter was often in short supply and when supplies did become available it was not always possible to sell it in an orderly manner due to the high demand. In early November 1917 some stallholders at Swansea Market attempted to retain what limited butter stocks they did have for the benefit of their regular customers, while another market trader insisted on customers buying a rabbit from the stall before being allowed any butter. The market stalls were soon surrounded by irate would-be butter customers (with female munitions workers well to the fore) and it was only a swift intervention by the police that prevented matters getting out of hand. The butter was swiftly parcelled up into half-pound packs and sold to those who simply had the money to pay. Therefore a number of 'regular' customers lost out in this process, apparently having grown used to preferential treatment, and arriving at a leisurely pace only to discover that all the packs had been sold.[39]

Things had improved slightly within a few weeks, even though some prominent suppliers still had no butter for sale. Those that were able to sell did so under the watchful eyes of a small police presence to ensure that any further outbreaks of unrest were avoided.[40] The issue of queuing for lengthy periods was regarded as particularly problematic for expectant mothers and women with infants in hand and it was agreed that supplies of certain basic foodstuffs should be provided at a set location and distributed on the authority of the Food Control Office to the appropriate ladies, subject to a medical certificate being produced where required. This would eliminate queuing and the possibility of the jostling of ladies who were in a 'delicate' condition.[41] Mr Victor Evans, an officer of the Swansea Food Control Committee, stated that 4oz of butter per person per week was the best that could be expected in the current situation and he believed that

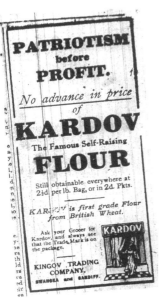
On occasion flour prices rose more than the flour itself! Kardov claimed to have kept its prices stable. *(Cambrian)*

sufficient quantities of butter were being received in the town but he stated: 'I attribute the unequal distribution largely to the greed and gluttony of many in the queues, who seem to desire to want to get...three times their shares.' One woman had queued for butter for six hours, while one young lad initially gained great sympathy after outlining a heartrending tale in his attempt to obtain some butter before it was noticed that his basket already contained 2lb of margarine.[42]

The Swansea Food Control Committee had taken a further tentative step towards exercising greater control over butter and margarine supplies in the town by sending its proposed distribution scheme to the central authority for consideration. The Swansea proposal would see butter and margarine dealt with in a similar way to sugar. Households would obtain a card that constituted their entitlement to butter and margarine for each three-month period and would then obtain their weekly allowance from the registered supplier of their choice. This would enable specific amounts to be provided to suppliers based on the number of persons listed on the cards that they had received. Allowance would have to be made for supplying travellers and itinerants, of course.[43]

A subsequent meeting between Corporation representatives and Lord Rhondda, the minister in charge of food control, was not an unqualified success. The proposed Swansea scheme was essentially judged to be inferior to that brought in for London and Lord Rhondda urged the Swansea delegation to adopt that scheme for the sake of uniformity. He advised that the London scheme would actually form the basis of a national scheme that it was hoped would be brought in very soon. His Lordship also

Tea-rationing required registration by the customer. *(Cambrian)*

SUGAR, POTATOES, MEAT, FLOUR,

HANDY TIME-TABLE FOR THE HOUSEWIFE.

The following useful information is given in the first issue of "The National Food Journal," published by the Government:—
Sept. 15.—Sugar: Last day for retailers' application for registration.
" 15.—Potatoes: Free sale of home-grown 1917 crop ends. Return of stocks required for prescribed varieties.
" 15.—Meat: Butcher's first fortnightly average of profits may be checked.
" 17.—Bread: The 9d loaf procurable.
" 17.—Flour: Factors seeking registration apply to Ministry of Food or miller.
" 18.—Flour: Bakers and factors seeking compensation for stocks apply to Food Offices.
" 20.—Sugar: Last day for issuing form of application to the public.
" 22.—Sugar: Last day for issue of registration certificates. Manufacturers, caterers, and institution to apply.
Oct. 1.—Flour: Licenses for factors in force.
" 1.—Milk: New wholesale and retail maximum prices.
" 6.—Sugar: Last day for receiving application for sugar cards.
" 9.—Sugar: Manufacturers', caterers' and institutions' vouchers issued.
" 26.—Sugar: Last day for issue of sugar cards.
Nov. 1.—Oats: Home-grown winter oats released for sale or use.
" 4.—Sugar: Manufacturers', caterers' and institutions receive authority to obtain.
" 5.—Sugar: Last day for retailers to receive cards from public.
Dec. 30.—Sugar: Distribution by card begins.
Jan. 1.—Rye: Home-grown rye released for sale or use.

Hints for housewives on the rationing process. *(Cambrian)*

OXO

makes other foods go farther.

By the judicious use of OXO many delicious vegetable dishes can be prepared which will economise rations.

For instance, OXO with potatoes and other vegetables can be made into satisfying, nourishing dishes to take the place of a meat course.

Besides being a nutritious food in itself OXO enables the system to obtain more nourishment from other foods. Thus when OXO forms part of the diet less food is required.

A cup of OXO and a few biscuits form a sustaining light lunch.

OXO Limited, Thames House, London, E.C.4

Making what you have go further: Oxo outlines its versatility. *(Cambrian)*

advised against an over-ambitious approach, suggesting that tea, butter, margarine and meat be brought under control in the first instance with other items being added as the situation required. The suggestions were duly accepted by the Corporation.[44]

As the war dragged on, the approach of Christmas 1917 brought little cheer. Food shortages were still much to the fore in Swansea, despite the efforts made by the authorities to tinker with supply and demand. Poultry was in very short supply as birds were apparently being held back from the market to ensure that the festive demand could be better met. Red meat was in evidence, although bacon was scarce. Butter was again a great cause for concern, no delivery having reached the traders at Swansea Market. One shop that did have a quantity of butter for sale was quickly subject to a queue of people six or eight deep in places and extending for 30 yards in Oxford Street and a further 50 yards up Goat Street. A number of shops had no butter, margarine or lard for sale, with new deliveries not being expected for almost a week. To round off a miserable day's shopping for many, both cheese and tea were also hard to track down. It was apparent that the queues contained a higher than normal proportion of men but if the hope of particular families had been that a little extra 'muscle' might prove useful in a shopping scrum, such hopes were often dashed by the simple absence of the much-wanted items from the shop shelves.[45]

As 1918 got under way the butter situation had happily perked up somewhat, although the supply of meat in the town had by then become critical. Although the Swansea slaughterhouse had killed 109 cattle, 600 sheep and 120 pigs in the first week of the New Year, that proved inadequate for the needs of a town of 100,000-plus citizens, especially when the meat subsequently sent for sale outside the district was taken into account. The local food controller commented that if the farmers did not help by sending their animals to market in a timely manner, he would not baulk at commandeering them and getting them to market himself in a more brisk fashion. In response to this threat the farmers pointed to a new and complicated selling and grading arrangement for meat which delayed the despatch of animals to market while the unfamiliar pricing on the various cuts was being worked out.[46]

Several market stalls that normally sold meat had failed to open on occasion early in the New Year,

NOTICE TO THE PUBLIC.

THE RETAIL BUTCHERS OF SWANSEA hereby give notice to the Public that, in consequence of the increase in the prices of Cattle and Sheep, and the Local Food Committee having declined to increase the retail price lists, they will be compelled to close their Shops until such times as the prices of Wholesale Cattle and Sheep are controlled or the Local Food Committee grant an increase of the present retail prices.

Swansea, December 19th, 1917.

Swansea butchers feel the pinch and claim that they are being made unprofitable by the setting of maximum prices. *(Cambrian)*

while those that did often endured a siege by their customers. It was reported that, once given the requisite power, the local food controller planned to target the Gower rabbit population as an additional food source. Rabbit-trappers would be employed to that end once the relevant landowners had been contacted and access to their land agreed.[47] Reports that horseflesh was being offered for sale in the town were condemned by the Corporation Health Committee, stating that it 'cannot in any way countenance the sale of horseflesh' and instructing its officers to ensure compliance with all legal enactments regarding the matter.[48]

With the supply of foodstuffs to the town still being erratic it fell to the forces of organized labour to speak up, not only for its members but also for those in the all-too-frequent food queues whose voices otherwise went largely unheard. Representatives of several branches of industry attended a meeting with the Swansea Food Control Committee in January 1918 to air their grievances. The scarcity of essential foodstuffs had an exacerbated effect on, for example, certain railway workers who might leave Swansea and stay at several different addresses over a week in the course of their work before returning home. This caused problems as the worker was often staying in towns during the course of his weekly shift where he had only limited authorized access to food. The labour representatives thought that many food items needed to be rationed so that everyone got a fair share of what was actually available. While sugar rationing was working smoothly, it was claimed that cases were known where butter was being obtained by certain persons in larger than necessary quantities. It was also claimed to be very noticeable that the regular food queues around the town usually contained no representatives of the 'better' classes of Swansea, implying that that class was being well provided for with foodstuffs obtained from other quarters. However, this may well have been simple points-scoring by the workers' representatives as it is unlikely that the 'better classes' would trouble themselves with queuing; they would probably simply have despatched a domestic servant for this task.

Mr Dupree, a railwaymen's representative, noted that '...while the people were going short, yet there was a banquet at the Royal Hotel, where Sir A. Mond and the Mayor and

A Swansea food-rationing card as reproduced in the local press. (Cambrian)

the "nibs" had as much food as they wanted. Sir A. Mond got the best of everything....' It was stated that some Great Western railwaymen had recently refused to complete long-distance runs, ending instead at about the halfway mark in order that they could return home to their own limited food supplies rather than having to scrounge around in unfamiliar towns. Other workers were in similar straits and the risk of labour walk-outs was high, in which case it was claimed that the town would grind to a halt. Councillor Wilson noted that the amount of foodstuffs typically available to manual workers was now insufficient to maintain the strength and energy needed to perform a physically demanding job.

The meeting, which was occasionally very animated, came to the general conclusion that, in the interest of fairness, other foodstuffs needed to be distributed under a rationing scheme similar to that already pertaining to sugar. It was clear that some were receiving more supplies than they needed, while others went short or even totally without. Some of the recent queuing had resulted in very unpleasant scenes, with margarine on one occasion being distributed in larger packs than had been planned since, as the food control officer told the meeting: 'It was done because the people concerned were in fear of their lives, and they were glad to get rid of it.' Within a few weeks matters had progressed to the point where rationing cards covering supplies of meat

Food choice becomes more limited: potatoes and gravy are suggested as a main course. *(Cambrian)*

and tea, as well as butter and margarine, were about to be issued in Swansea, with bacon and possibly jam soon to follow suit.[49]

On occasion difficulties in the supply of food arose not from a simple shortage of the product but from problems in the production process. By August 1918 the continual demand for more men for the armed services had led to a 'combing out' of men whose occupations had previously been judged to be important enough to the war effort to preclude their being called up. One such class of men was those of military age who were employed in bread-making. When three more baking operatives from the Morriston and Landore districts were 'combed out' and rendered liable for military service, the situation reached crisis point. Mr Palmer, President of the Master Bakers' national association, stated that Swansea now had only eighty-five bakery operatives left; half the pre-war number. Those remaining could not work any harder than they already were; operatives were putting in as many as fifteen hours a day while Palmer himself had worked ninety-six hours in a week, having had only five Sundays off in five months. The nature of the work, which included moving heavy sacks of flour, was considered unsuitable for women, while the training of discharged soldiers for the role would be a very lengthy process, always assuming that a soldier used to the open spaces and fresh air could be

DEFENCE OF THE REALM. E.P. 6.

MINISTRY OF FOOD.

BREACHES OF THE RATIONING ORDER

The undermentioned convictions have been recently obtained:—

Court	Date	Nature of Offence	Result
HENDON - -	29th Aug., 1918	Unlawfully obtaining and using ration books -	3 Months' Imprisonment
WEST HAM -	29th Aug., 1918	Being a retailer & failing to detach proper number of coupons	Fined £20
SMETHWICK -	22nd July, 1918	Obtaining meat in excess quantities - - -	Fined £50 & £5 5s. costs
OLD STREET -	4th Sept., 1918	Being a retailer selling to unregistered customer	Fined £72 & £5 5s. costs
OLD STREET -	4th Sept., 1918	Not detaching sufficient coupons for meat sold -	Fined £25 & £2 2s. costs
CHESTER-LE-STREET	4th Sept., 1918	Being a retailer returning number of registered customers in excess of counterfoils deposited - - - -	Fined £50 & £3 3s. costs
HIGH WYCOMBE	7th Sept., 1918	Making false statement on application for and using Ration Books unlawfully - - - - - - -	Fined £40 & £6 4s. costs

Enforcement Branch, Local Authorities Division,
MINISTRY OF FOOD.
September, 1918.

The Ministry of Food publicizes what those who breach the food rationing order can expect.

tempted into a hot and dusty bakery. The bakery operatives were prepared to carry on, provided no further military call-ups were made from among their number. Contact had been made with the central food controller so that he was aware of the problem and representations were also to be made to the regional recruiting officer for the army.[50] Matters were not helped during the autumn of 1918 when the worldwide influenza pandemic hit some of those working in the baking trade at Swansea, causing them to be absent from their places of work for a time.[51]

The local fruit trade was also not immune to the pressures of rising prices in wartime. It was stated that before the war it was routine for many English fruit-growers to visit the Swansea fruit merchants with a view to obtaining orders for their produce. Matters had been reversed with the advent of war, however. One Swansea merchant had toured the Worcester, Evesham and Hereford areas in search of produce but had returned to Swansea empty-handed, being unable to obtain as much as a single crate of apples. The 1918 summer fruit crop had been poor by normal standards, so demand exceeded supply and prices rose sharply as those prepared to pay a higher price than their competitors somewhat reluctantly produced their cheque books. In what was becoming a familiar refrain, the fruit merchants thought that the farmers were taking advantage of the situation to reap excessive profits. One variety of apples had had a typical pre-war price of 3d per pound; they were now selling at a shilling per pound. It was also noted that in the case of wild bilberries, the pickers did not even have to first grow their crop; they merely picked it as it grew wild in the hedgerows but this 'windfall' crop produce still attracted what were seen by some as unnecessarily high prices when brought to sale.[52]

The end of the war naturally eased the problem of food supplies, albeit to a limited degree at first. At least the shipping that brought food supplies to Britain was no longer

Swansea fish market. *(Author's collection)*

under risk of attack by the enemy submarine force; nevertheless, there was no immediate increase in the availability of certain produce. In November 1918 came the cheery news that a large cargo of apples, nuts and oranges was on the way from overseas, scheduled to arrive just in time for the Christmas festivities. At the same time, shortages of both butter and potatoes remained an issue for many. In the spring of 1919 fruit was expected from Tasmania and California.[53] A relaxation in the setting of prices for fish at

Swansea saw an immediate jump in cost to the customer, leading the food controller to threaten to re-impose price controls if it was felt that advantage was being taken of the situation by the fish merchants.

In 1919 the local food control committee was still at work, threatening several local bakers with prosecution for producing bread that did not meet the requirements of the food control regime, while additionally several butchers were taken to court for selling meat at prices that were above the permitted maximum.[54] It was 1920 before the food controls were finally allowed to lapse and normality could gradually return.[55]

Fish prices increased greatly. *(Cambrian)*

Notes

1. Ian Beckett, *Home Front 1914–18*, p.112.
2. *Cambrian,* 7 August 1914.
3. WGAS, TC/27/18.
4. Ibid.
5. *Cambrian*, 14 August 1914.
6. *Cambrian*, 5 February 1915.
7. *Cambrian*, 12 February 1915.
8. Ibid.
9. *Cambrian*, 14 July 1916.
10. *Cambrian*, 26 February 1915.
11. *Cambrian*, 11 August 1916.
12. *Cambrian*, 23 June 1916.
13. *Cambrian*, 19 May 1916.
14. WGAS, TC/27/31.
15. *Cambrian*, 15 December 1916.
16. *Cambrian*, 12 October 1917.
17. *Cambrian,* 29 December 1916.
18. Beckett, op. cit., p.248.
19. *Cambrian,* 1 June 1917.
20. *Cambrian,* 15 June 1917.
21. *Cambrian,* 2 July 1917.
22. *Cambrian,* 19 January 1917.
23. *Cambrian,* 5 January 1917.
24. *Cambrian,* 19 January 1917.
25. *Cambrian,* 26 January 1917.
26. *Cambrian,* 30 March 1917.
27. WGAS, TC/3/37.
28. *Cambrian,* 6 April 1917.
29. *Cambrian,* 20 April 1917.
30. *Cambrian,* 18 May 1917.
31. *Cambrian,* 5 June 1917.
32. *Cambrian,* 6 June 1917.
33. *Cambrian,* 18 and 25 May 1917.
34. *Cambrian,* 15 June 1917.
35. Marwick, *The Deluge*, pp.64–5; *Cambrian,* 26 October 1917.
36. *Cambrian,* 2 November 1917.
37. *Cambrian,* 24 August 1917.
38. *Cambrian,* 26 October 1917.
39. *Cambrian,* 23 November 1917.
40. *Cambrian,* 14 December 1917.
41. WGAS, TC/3/38.
42. *Cambrian,* 18 January 1918.
43. Ibid.
44. WGAS, TC/3/38.
45. *Cambrian,* 21 December 1917.
46. *Cambrian,* 18 January 1918.
47. *Cambrian,* 11 January 1918.
48. WGAS, TC/3/38.
49. *Cambrian,* 15 February 1918.
50. *Cambrian,* 19 July 1918.
51. Ibid.
52. *Cambrian,* 9 August 1918.
53. *Cambrian,* 22 November 1918.
54. *Cambrian,* 7 March 1919.
55. Beckett, op. cit., p.139.

Chapter Six

The Role of Women

With many men being away at the front it was inevitable that women would be called upon to play a larger part in the daily life of the country than had hitherto been the case. A range of opportunities arose that would not normally have been considered suitable use of a woman's time in the pre-war days when male-dominated views on the role of women were entrenched in everyday society. One of the simplest ways in which women could get involved in activities that aided the war effort was by simply opening their purses. This had the benefit of being an option that was available to all women, irrespective of age or health. It did, of course, require the lady in question being able to afford to offer some funds in aid of the war effort without pushing herself into financial hardship. As such, it is likely that a number of the poorer women of Swansea would have been unable to contribute in cash, although other possibilities were open to them.

An early manifestation of fund-raising for the war effort was a local appeal for the women of Swansea to 'do their bit' by raising money for the purchase of an ambulance for use at the front. The sum of £400 was required to achieve this and such was the response that the appeal fund had to be closed in October 1914 and the surplus cash sent to Lord Rothschild's appeal fund, to be applied in helping to meet the running costs of the Swansea Women's motor ambulance. As might be expected, the headline donations came from Swansea's most well-known and respected families. Mrs John Glasbrook contributed £50 and that was supplemented by £25 from Mrs Benson of the Fairyhill family. Other donors included Mrs Heneage, Mrs J.T. Pascoe, Mrs Gilbertson and Mrs Moxham.[1]

Apart from domestic service, nursing, certain clerical or secretarial positions and several other forms of employment that typically came with low pay and prestige, the role of women in 1914 was largely confined to the home, with the possibility of some

Many pre-war jobs for women revolved around domestic duties. *(Cambrian)*

The National Shell Factory (Landore) ladies football team. *(Leighton Radford)*

sewing or laundry work helping to boost a meagre income. Indeed, it was the practice in some areas of employment (for example, jobs with the Swansea Corporation) for women to resign their positions upon marriage so as to free up the position for another, while their new husband provided for them in the time-honoured way. As is well-known, the demands of war and the subsequent departure of huge numbers of men to the front placed significant pressure on the economy. It was inevitable that in a major war the traditional role of women in the workplace would need to be enlarged and expanded in order to free up men for military service. This was not achieved without opposition, however, as working men who had only recently been able to wrest basic concessions in the workplace from their employers viewed such innovations with deep suspicion.

The military, being short of men and prior to the advent of conscription in 1916, were conscious of the large number of civilian men who could be released from their work if only women could be placed in jobs in their stead. Major Anderson, the chief recruiting officer at Swansea, raised the issue directly in April 1915 and the mayor of Swansea was happy to convene a meeting so that the issues surrounding the question could be fully aired. The meeting was held at the Swansea Guildhall and among those present were representatives of the Swansea Improvements and Tramway Company, Ben Evans and Co., the Borough Stores and the Swansea Co-operative movement. Though very welcome, this small group of attendees must have actually represented only a small proportion of the entire Swansea workforce. The mayor chaired the meeting and Major Anderson was also in attendance to state his case.

The mayor was pleased that the town of Swansea had reacted well to the need for recruits by already seeing many men join the forces. However, in the present emergency the government wanted every available man and the mayor thought that if women could take over some of the jobs currently performed by men who were eligible for military service, for example by working on trams or in shops, then it would be of great assistance to the military. There would, of course, be the need for a man whose job was identified as being capable of being performed by a female to then actually enlist in the forces. That was quite a different matter as coercion could not yet be used in the absence of conscription, which did not arrive until 1916.

Major Anderson pointed to the high casualty figures relating to the recent attack at Neuve Chappelle. Losses in officers and men had occurred on an unprecedented scale and, given the nature of modern warfare, there was no immediate likelihood of a reduction in casualties as further attacks were made. He noted that the railway companies and the Post Office were doing well with recruitment and he now looked to other employers to follow their lead.

Mr David James of the Swansea Improvements and Tramway Company pointed out that 102 men, being about 27 per cent of his workforce, had already joined up and had been encouraged to do so by the company. It was now their company policy not to appoint men who were of a suitable age for recruitment. He added that further reductions in manpower would undoubtedly have an effect on services which would, in turn, have an impact on transport for the working man (by September 1915 the company was employing female conductors with the approval of the Corporation).[2] Mr Barrett of Ben Evans and Co. added that every effort had been made to replace eligible men with female labour, although a shortage of suitable women workers actually meant that it was not always an easy process. The meeting broke up with an agreement that local employers should do everything possible to use female labour in order to free up men who were eligible and willing to serve in the armed forces.[3] The Corporation itself was able to help in some respects. In order to replace male teachers who had volunteered, the rule on married women not being employed was relaxed. Sixteen married ladies returned to their former teaching roles and provided cover at numerous schools, often 'rotating' so that they served at more than one school to meet demand wherever it appeared.[4]

On Christmas Eve 1915 the Swansea Chamber of Commerce debated the issue of women in the workplace. There were certainly by that time shortages of men in roles that could possibly be performed by women in the town. It was noted that

A postwoman. Before the war this role was typically the domain of men.
(Geoff Caulton, photodetective.co.uk)

in London there were about 6,000 women receiving training in clerical work. Once trained and employed in suitable roles, the gaps left by men who had enlisted or wished to do so could be filled by a previously largely untapped source of female labour. The Chamber thought that any training provided in Swansea should be aimed at 'young women of leisure' as it would not be desirous to simply attract women who were already employed in other well-paid roles. That would be an unnecessary dislocation of the jobs market. Even where women were usefully employed in previously unfamiliar roles, it was thought best that after the war they should return to their 'ordinary life'. A list of local ladies who were prepared to come forward for employment was being compiled and employers were being asked to detail their requirements so that suitable matches could be made.[5]

By 1917 things had moved on apace, at least as far as the employment of girls was concerned. A January 1917 report to the Swansea Corporation Juvenile Employment Committee revealed a growing number of girls working in roles that had previously been largely the domain of boys. It was noted that while there were two errand girls in 1915, by the end of 1916 the number had risen to a remarkable forty-three. Errand boys employed saw a fall in numbers from 254 in 1915 to 156 in 1916. Girls were also being employed as telegraph messengers and printers' helps, while one girl had even found employment in gas appliance work. The effect of the war on available manpower also had an effect on what were termed 'abnormal' employments, with juveniles taking on roles that would not normally have been offered to them. For example, eight boys were

Managers and workers at the Baldwin's munitions works, Landore. John Thomas is on the left: he lived at Cecil Street, Manselton while working at Baldwin's but later moved back to his home town of Neath. *(Leighton Radford)*

being utilized in potentially dangerous munitions work; a relatively small number given the importance of the resultant output to the war effort. Girls were also placed in munitions work, although no girl under the age of 18 was so employed. Some boys were working at the local tinworks, as were a small number of girls. The figures reported to the committee concerned only those juveniles passing through its hands; no doubt others had gained similar employment by the more traditional methods of appointment via interview or even benevolent nepotism.[6]

Another avenue open to Swansea women in helping with the war effort was involvement in the Women's Army Auxiliary Corps (WAAC). By late 1916 the demands for manpower for service abroad were still increasing as the casualty lists lengthened. It was realized that in the same way as, in certain areas of the domestic economy, women were taking the place of their absent menfolk, it was possible for them to perform a similar role overseas. Though there were highly-placed doubters in the establishment, the Women's Army Auxiliary Corps was approved and created in early 1917. Members of the corps (affectionately called WAACs) could serve at home or abroad, replacing men in certain roles and thus potentially freeing them up for a more militaristic role. WAACs worked in clerical positions, as cooks, telephonists, drivers and storekeepers, to name but a few of the numerous roles undertaken.[7]

In October 1917 a meeting held at St James' Hall, Swansea attracted a large number of women keen to see how they could become involved. It was reported that the War Office hoped to recruit a further 40,000 women as WAACs before Christmas 1917. These recruits would take the places of men who could therefore be released for active service in the defence of the country. Swansea, it was claimed, had already provided more than its fair share of women volunteers compared to any other town in Wales. The organizers of the meeting hoped that mothers would encourage their daughters to play a part in the war, just like their fathers, husbands and brothers. There were opportunities both at home and abroad to provide useful service in the war effort and those present had no doubt that Swansea women would not be found wanting.[8]

One Swansea woman who did volunteer for service as a WAAC was Vera Mason. Vera had been born in Swansea in 1894 and was living at 9 Marlborough Road, Brynmill, in 1917. She lived with her parents, her father having formerly been employed as a steamship agent. Miss Mason was prepared to offer her services as a WAAC general clerk. To that end she had visited Cardiff in May 1917 for a medical examination which she duly passed, with the proviso that certain dental work needed immediate attention. Vera was at that time employed at a private school located in Alexandra Terrace, Swansea and run by Miss Bonnett. Vera was eventually enrolled into the WAAC on 18 June 1917.

This was not without difficulty, however. Vera claimed that Miss Bonnett had agreed that she (and another school employee, Lillian Hopkins) could leave her employment to enlist in the WAAC. However, as the day of departure grew closer, Miss Bonnett sought to retain their services until the end of term and appealed on that basis to the authorities. Vera felt that her employer had made little real effort to appoint a replacement and determined that she would in any event leave as planned. The authorities were eventually able to smooth the passage in some way and Vera was eventually released.

There is minimal information in Vera's service record to show what she did or where she went during her service in the WAAC. She did, however, proceed to France as a general clerk and she actually remained in the service until April 1919, some months after the Armistice of November 1918. Away from the front lines there was a plethora of clerical tasks required to help keep an army in the field. The typing of reports, the filling out of forms and the writing of letters were all matters that could be performed by either male or female labour and it is likely that Vera would have had a busy time while not necessarily being too close to any fighting. Her friend Lillian from the private school in Swansea had also become a WAAC and Lillian wrote to the local newspaper in September 1917, mentioning Vera and outlining their early experiences in France:

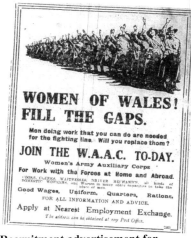

Recruitment advertisement for service in the WAAC. *(Cambrian)*

My friend Vera Mason and myself have been out in France two months, and the life is great. We happen to be situated in a very healthy spot, and are billeted in an hotel. We have every comfort, and the hotel has been fitted out to suit the girls...there are 180 girls and we are all very happy. We have to be up at 7 o'clock, roll call at 7.5 a.m., then we have breakfast at 8 o'clock. We have to be at the office at 9 o'clock and the work is very interesting...[9]

A WAAC recruit.
(Geoff Caulton, photodetective.co.uk)

In April 1919 Miss Mason attended a medical board in Bristol where it was discovered that she was suffering from tachycardia: a heartbeat rate that exceeds the normal resting heart rate for the patient's age group. This could result in a heart that worked inefficiently with the consequence of a reduced flow of blood within the body. While sometimes benign, tachycardia increases the risk of stroke or heart attack and, as such, would have been a cause for concern for the WAAC hierarchy. It was also found that Vera was suffering from general debility and she was granted four weeks' leave in an effort to aid her recovery. She was then re-examined but with little sign of improvement. A final medical board held on 28 April 1919 recommended her discharge from the WAAC on grounds of neurasthenia, a condition that had been recognized since the 1800s and was characterized by fatigue, anxiety and depression, among other things.[10]

Another wartime development was the appearance in Swansea (and elsewhere) of so-called 'lady patrols' that were intended to act as extra pairs of eyes and

A group of WAACs take a photo call. *(Geoff Caulton, photodetective.co.uk)*

ears for the local police force, especially in parts of the town where impressionable females might have easy contact with military men. This was essentially a continuation of what many males would have seen as an encroachment by women into areas of work that had previously been populated entirely by men. As such it often met with resistance from inside the police force and from the man in the street, as well as from those who walked the corridors of the Swansea Guildhall or other business premises. In 1915 the Women's Freedom League was agitating for the introduction of women patrols in Swansea, although the prospect was abhorrent to most members of the Swansea Corporation. One member thought that the women were trying to usurp the role of the men, while the chief constable was adamant that only offers of assistance that had the backing of the Home Office should be entertained. Despite these reservations it was agreed that a deputation of ladies should be received by the Corporation, if a request was actually made.[11]

Some months later a deputation was duly received. It was led by an official of the National Union of Women Workers and that lady was supported by several notable local ladies including Lady Llewelyn and Mrs Talbot Rice. These eminent personages spoke in a manner that revealed the distinct moral attitudes of the time. They wished to 'get hold of the giddy young girls who were about the streets so that they might be prevented from drifting into questionable paths'. It was thought that many impressionable girls were simply 'infatuated' with the military and its unavoidable presence in the town had increased the risk of potentially unhealthy associations.

Lady Llewelyn of Penllergaer.
(Cymru1914.org)

The ladies involved knew of Swansea's 'undesirable streets where women and soldiers congregated'. Those were the streets that the lady patrols would visit and their mere presence had usually produced an uplifting effect on behaviour on similar streets in other towns. The troublesome Swansea streets were listed as 'the Mumbles-road, Recreation Ground, parts of Sketty and Oxford-street'. The ladies had heard stories of soldiers being unable to walk the streets without the unwanted attention of young women. It was those females who found themselves attracted to soldiers who were the ladies' main concern. The docks area and also the Strand, with its many visiting foreign sailors, would not be patrolled as it was deemed to be too much of a risk for the ladies, with one councillor commenting: 'We should have to organise special rescue parties to save you down there (laughter).' There would be no powers of arrest but the ladies, working closely with the local police, would be able to act as a brake on immoral behaviour. If arrests were required, it was the police who would make them. Additionally, there were no plans for the patrols to attempt to 'rescue' women of a certain character from their lowly positions; there were other agencies in the town that were better placed to perform that role.[12]

The YWCA appealed for funds to assist in setting up wartime canteens etc.

In the ensuing discussion it was agreed that, if women patrols were introduced, no extra costs would fall on the police authority. Additionally, the number of patrols and the areas of the town to be covered were to be submitted for the approval of the relevant committees, while the chief constable would have overriding control over the activities of the patrols. There was some concern that the patrols might interfere with what were legitimate friendships and those girls who merely wished to befriend soldiers who were separated from their homes and families might be discouraged from doing so, to the detriment of the soldiers.

The idea was eventually accepted on an experimental basis and must have proved a success since, in July 1917, it was reported that there were eighteen women patrols operating in Swansea and doing very useful work to assist a sometimes overstretched constabulary. The patrols were, in effect, still working without the benefit of full and official endorsement by the Swansea Corporation. Those ladies who had dedicated themselves to the patrol work, despite the icy official reception often afforded them, considered it only a matter of time before women police constables became the norm.

This deployment of women on ladies' patrols was seen by its advocates as a natural progression from the movement of women into unfamiliar work territory in support of the war effort to other areas of employment where pure physical strength was not a prerequisite for the job. The aim was not to supplant the role of men but rather to supplement it. There were, after all, some instances where women could play a more useful role than policemen; for example, in dealing with sensitive situations involving other women or children. The ladies worked a six-day week of eight hours a day on duty. Training was deemed advisable but not essential and bursaries were available in certain cases where finance would otherwise be an issue for the prospective recruit. After completion of training, a proficiency certificate was issued to demonstrate that the candidate had met the required standard.

In the industrial parts of Wales it had long been the practice for working men to 'club together' by paying a few pence out of their weekly wages in order to eventually fund and build a working men's club. These had traditionally been based in the coal-mining communities and, in some cases, were indeed solely working men's clubs where females were not even allowed membership. While the original aim of the clubs had been educational as well as social, it was the social aspect that was usually much to the fore with facilities for games such as darts and snooker often being provided. In Swansea in 1917 some recognition was made of the enlarged role played by women in the wartime economy. The Young Women's Christian Association had been active in other parts of the country in providing social facilities for members of the female workforce and it was planned to open a club and hostel in Swansea where

> a good hot dinner will be obtainable for a few pence, and soup, tea, coffee, and light refreshments will be provided at cost price. There will be a rest room where in their little leisure time, tired women and girls may spend their well earned rest, and reading, writing, and club rooms will also be provided.[13]

An appeal for funds from the people of Swansea was also made for this purpose.

The employment of women in roles formerly held by men did not proceed without incident. In August 1918, despite the war approaching a critical phase with a major allied offensive under way, the Swansea tramway workers became involved in a national dispute over pay differentials between men and women. In Swansea about 350 employees ceased work, although it was reported that many of the men were largely disinterested in the treatment of their female colleagues. However, when a group of female conductresses refused to work it led to the drivers ceasing work as well. It was noted that while male drivers usually received well over £3 a week, the pay for women was only about seven shillings a day, amounting to just over £2 a week if six days were worked. Efforts to provide a reduced tram service for the benefit of munitions and other workers during the strike failed, with a consequential effect on essential war output.

As a result of the war a great many Swansea women, in

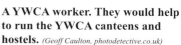

A YWCA worker. They would help to run the YWCA canteens and hostels. *(Geoff Caulton, photodetective.co.uk)*

A female conductress.
(Geoff Caulton, photodetective.co.uk)

common with women in other parts of the country, had experienced work of a quite different nature than had hitherto been the case. Working in perhaps a munitions or tinplate factory in a war situation had provided good pay plus the chance of well-paid overtime. Skills were learned and confidence had grown among the female workforce. This had a lasting effect in the post-war situation when women, many of whom had worked in domestic service before the war, declined the chance to go back into such service which they knew offered low wages, frequent drudgery and minimal respect. Basic unemployment benefits were being paid at that time, dependent on the recipient accepting any reasonable offer of employment via the local employment exchange, and this afforded a rudimentary safety net for those without work in the short term.

In January 1919 there were over 2,200 women in Swansea who sought employment but could not find a suitable position. Many of these simply declined the readily-available offers of domestic work in the homes of the better-off inhabitants of Swansea and held out for a better position in other sectors of the economy. When these were not forthcoming, unemployment benefits were frequently stopped, meaning that some difficult decisions had to be faced by the unemployed women. Swansea was, in fact, in a better position than some other areas. Many South Wales women had moved to the Midlands where British engineering skills were put to good use in the innumerable small factories in support of the war

A Land Army woman. A white uniform was indicative of work on a dairy farm.
(Geoff Caulton, photodetective.co.uk)

effort. These women subsequently proved reluctant to move back to Wales at the war's end when there were fewer job opportunities available in their home town.

The authorities were nevertheless keen to see women back in what were regarded as their 'usual' employment roles, although it seems that the women were, in many cases, not quite so happy. A May 1919 meeting held at the Albert Hall saw a large number of women in attendance and it was emphasized from the chair that women needed 'to answer the call of peace and reconstruction, as they had that of the war, and now that the time of trial was over, their duty was to take up once more their pre-war occupations as soon as possible'. Domestic service was strongly recommended to the gathering.[14] In September 1919 the Juvenile Employment Committee of the Corporation was suggesting that girls aged between 14 and 15 should, as a matter of compulsion, be given training in 'house management' and be regarded as 'home helps'. It was considered 'that the status of home helps should be raised and girls taught to feel that there was as much dignity in sweeping a floor as serving a yard of ribbon [in a shop].'

Another important aspect of the work of women during the Great War was the effect that their exertions had on those who exercised power and had previously deemed them unworthy of the right to vote. The pre-war agitation of the suffragettes had actually caused a lot of resentment among powerful men in the land, with many of them feeling that to create what was to them unnecessary friction actually undermined their cause.

Swansea had experienced some suffragette activity as early as 1910 when Mrs Mary Cleeves of Chez Nous, Sketty, a leading Swansea suffragist, refused to pay for a carriage licence. Her explanation was simply that as she had no vote and therefore no say in what licence fees might be set by those in elected authority, she would not regard herself as bound to pay any fees that had been set by a system that essentially ignored her. The issue certainly created a stir in Swansea with several public meetings being held to lend support to the embattled lady. However, in 1914 with the

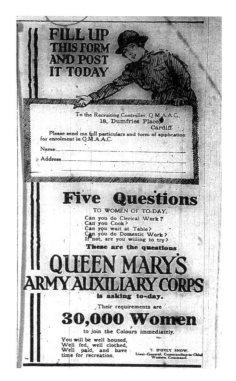

A recruitment poster for Queen Mary's Army Auxiliary Corps.
(Cambrian)

advent of war the suffragette movement had essentially ceased its confrontational activities to give its full support to the war effort. Indeed, when Mrs Pankhurst visited Swansea in February 1918, it was not to state the case for the enfranchisement of women but rather to encourage the replacement of men by women at work in order to free up more men for service at the front.[15]

The war had brought with it an inevitable expansion of the types of work undertaken by women and many people began to look a little more kindly on their role in society and future expectations. Additionally, when certain women performing medical roles at the front or toiling in potentially dangerous munitions works carried out heavy or dangerous work without complaint or were killed or performed feats of heroism, the male argument that women were unsuited to any work involving physical strength or exposure to danger began to look a little weak. This was an argument that had frequently been deployed in defence of the idea that 'fragile' women could not earn the right to vote. It had also become apparent that the war effort was harnessing the hitherto latent power of the women of Britain to the great advantage of the country across a range of industries. With some thought already being given to post-war reconstruction, it was becoming obvious that to ignore the possibility of an increased role for women in many areas of work would be to sell the country short. The large losses of manpower occasioned by a brutal war could not be made good overnight and, if women were not given a freer rein than had previously been the case, the recovery from a damaging war would take all the longer. Those in authority duly took note and in February 1918 the Representation of the People Act 1918 was passed, granting the vote to all women over the age of 30 who also met a minimum property qualification.[16] It was not a total victory for women but it was an important step along the road.

Notes
1. *Cambrian*, 30 October 1914.
2. WGAS, TC/3/35.
3. WGAS, TC/26/26.
4. WGAS, TC/3/35.
5. *Cambrian*, 24 December 1915.
6. *Cambrian*, 26 January 1917.
7. Marwick, *The Deluge*, pp.85–8.
8. *Cambrian*, 19 October 1917.
9. *Cambrian*, 28 September 1917.
10. TNA, WO/398/145.
11. *Cambrian*, 26 February 1915.
12. *Cambrian*, 19 November 1915.
13. *Cambrian*, 26 January 1917.
14. *Cambrian*, 16 May 1919.
15. *Cambrian*, 22 February 1918.
16. Marwick, op. cit., pp.103–05.

Chapter Seven

Home Front: Relief Efforts in Swansea

The war naturally brought with it a great amount of disruption, with some industries booming while others struggled to remain in their traditional line of business. For example, many of the Swansea-based fishing trawlers were promptly requisitioned by the Admiralty for military use and were subsequently manned by Royal Navy reservists and that must have meant that many trawlermen were suddenly left without a job with a consequential effect on the availability of fish at Swansea. Even where a Swansea sailor was able to retain his employment at sea, he had to then be prepared to risk the attentions of an unseen and malevolent enemy in the form of the German U-boat fleet to whom a slow-moving trawler was a very tempting target.

Financial hardship was not new to Swansea or similar towns, of course. Indeed, even before the commencement of hostilities Swansea had established a local 'Distress Committee' in accordance with the requirements of the Unemployed Workmen Act of 1905.[1] This committee could make small cash grants or provide temporary work for those of essentially good character, who did not have a criminal record and who had not previously claimed relief from the Poor Law Guardians in Swansea. In 1914 the Poor Law Guardians still ran the Victorian-era Poor Law system that included the Swansea Workhouse. Funding for the distress committee came largely from the government but

A knitting group making woollen items for Welsh troops at the Babell C.M. Church, Cwmbwrla. The Rev. John Richards is on the right, while his wife Lucy is second left in the second row. *(Noel and Alan Cox)*

also from private donations. It was considered preferable for the unemployed to be given some work to do, to avoid them becoming wholly dependent on a handout or dole for which nothing was done in return. Such work that had been provided in the past had included preliminary tasks in relation to the widening of the Neath and Penfilia Roads. There was always a fear among local officials that providing what was essentially 'free' labour to assist a business would possibly result in the employer lowering the wages of those who were employed or delaying the employment of more workers in the hope that the distress committee would eventually send someone along on the cheap. Work on publicly-funded Corporation schemes was deemed somewhat more acceptable but even then there was the possibility that a man who was required to work on publicly-funded projects in return for the support he had received was indirectly denying another man a 'real' job with the Corporation.[2]

In the year ending 31 March 1915 almost 2,800 men applied to the local distress committee at Swansea for assistance. The claims also encompassed just over 1,700 women, being the wives of the applicants, plus another 6,500 other dependants, mostly children but also including mothers, fathers or other relatives of the principal claimant. Some of those claims were actually rejected, while others may have been referred to the Poor Law Guardians as being a more suitable avenue of relief. Successful claims might well be of short duration, perhaps only until a breadwinner gained new employment. Not all the claims would have been war-related, of course, but the war certainly would not have helped an already difficult economic situation.[3]

In many working-class Swansea families the wages brought home by a wife or daughter could be a very useful addition to a stretched household budget. The Corporation did its best to monitor employment levels for women and girls, although it accepted that it did not possess the full picture, labelling one of its reports 'approximate' when it came to the accuracy of the numbers of females involved. On 1 February 1914 the Corporation had recorded ninety-two ladies having registered as unemployed. The corresponding figure for 1915 was a hefty 230. The situation was no better for unemployed 'young girls' with the initial figure of 44 rising to 116 in the same period. It was the lady tailors, dressmakers and seamstresses who saw the biggest increase in unemployment, from five in February 1914 to fifty-eight in February 1915. This was probably the result of many young men being fitted out in uniforms provided under army contracts that had been arranged centrally, the work being carried out away from Swansea. This removed much of the need for making new or altering civilian working clothes in Swansea and therefore affected the employment of those involved in the town's tailoring trade. The Corporation planned to lobby the relevant authority so that hopefully some contracts for the making of army uniforms could be awarded locally, while the Watch Committee of the Corporation was to be asked to consider the appointment of female police officers, with unemployed seamstresses and the like being potential candidates.[4]

At the start of the war military reservists and Territorial Force men were called up for duty, while a large number of Swansea men promptly volunteered for military service, leaving their families behind. The sudden absence of a family's main breadwinner brought immediate problems in terms of their income as the separation allowance paid by the military did not always match a man's peacetime earnings. In the absence of any real alternative it was then likely that the newly-impoverished family members (some of whom would sadly soon become war widows) would have to fall on the mercies of the Poor Law Guardians, with the prospect of a shameful admission to the dreaded workhouse being a real worry.

In Swansea in November 1914 another group experiencing financial difficulties due to the onset of war was that of the local landladies. These mostly elderly ladies had previously eked out a living by letting rooms to young men who, upon gaining employment, had decided to leave their often overcrowded family home and strike out on their own account. Similarly, many young men moving to the area in search of work frequently sought out a room to rent from a Swansea landlady. With many young men joining the army in the autumn of 1914 and thus being accommodated elsewhere at the army's expense, the Swansea landladies' principal source of income had simply dried up with the result that applications were made by some of them to a number of local bodies for funds to help them out. The possibility of billeting men who had been recruited into the newly-formed Swansea Battalion was one avenue that received consideration, although that could at best be a temporary solution as at some point the new battalion would have to leave the town for further training followed by active service abroad.[5]

A likely increase in poverty and distress across Britain as a result of the war had been noted by Edward, Prince of Wales. He made an immediate appeal for the establishment of a 'national relief fund' with the aim of donations received being applied to assist the wives, families and dependants of soldiers, sailors, reservists and members of the Territorial Force, as well as helping to prevent and alleviate any distress among the civilian population that arose as a result of the war. The appeal was a huge success, with over £1,000,000 being pledged in the first week. It was thought that a national fund would allow a more equitable distribution of aid than if each locality were required to raise its own funds, with wealthy areas having large resources but little need while the poorer areas had scant resources but greater distress. Before the fund became fully operational, a number of impoverished families had actually been forced to turn to the Poor Law Guardians for relief. This could often be by way of a cash payment, meaning that the recipient was at least spared the ignominy of having to enter the workhouse. Once the fund was working properly, all such monies paid out under the Poor Law were in any event repaid by the fund to the Poor Law Guardians, with the added requirement that the names of those who had received such temporary payments be expunged from the relevant records. It was felt that as they were not responsible for the hardship they had endured, their menfolk having loyally answered the call of duty, it was only right that their names should not be indelibly linked to the stigma of pauperism.

To ensure that the national funding for relief measures was directed in appropriate ways a local 'representative committee' was established in each county, borough and urban district council across the country. Those committees would examine local claims for relief and determine their worthiness or otherwise. They would liaise with other local charitable organizations to try to ensure that multiple claims were not submitted by devious individuals. The Swansea local committee was headed by the mayor and included a number of other councillors as well as representatives from the Board of Poor

Law Guardians, the Chamber of Commerce, the Labour Association, the Swansea Metal Exchange and sundry other organizations, a host of church nominees of various faiths and denominations, as well as a number of the local 'great and the good' including Miss Amy Dillwyn.

The dependants of soldiers and sailors who required assistance from the fund were required to apply in the first instance to the local branch of the Soldiers' and Sailors' Families Association or the local representative committee. The information received would be shared by both bodies when deciding on the merits of a claim in order to minimize the possibility of both bodies being asked to assist in a particular case, to the benefit of the applicant who might then receive help from both. The proverbial right hand needed to know what the left hand was doing if mendacious claims were to be avoided. In its own turn, the local representative committee could apply for grants from the National Fund for application in local cases. The money accrued from local fund-raising initiatives could also be processed via the National Relief Fund apparatus where it made sense to do so.[6]

A number of local businesses and individuals donated to the National Fund via the local committee. Employees of the Swansea Gas and Light Company had made monthly contributions to the fund since its institution, having an accrued amount of over £200 by the end of October 1915, although at that point they decided to cease further contributions and simply let the fund accumulate. The company also donated 50 tons of coke, a practical gesture designed to help the Swansea poor through the winter. William Thomas and Sons were timber importers based at Cambrian Place, Swansea and at the onset of war the firm had donated to the Prince of Wales' Fund a considerable quantity of pitprop ends that could be used as firewood by those in need. Disappointingly, eight months later the props still mouldered in a Corporation yard, leading the company to suggest that they be sold to other local timber merchants with the proceeds of sale going to the fund.

Since the beginning of the war local organizations had offered practical help to the Corporation via the office of the mayor. The National British Women's Temperance Association offered to visit or investigate cases where an application for assistance had

The premises of the Swansea Gas and Light Company (the modern-day Tesco site in the city centre). *(Author's collection)*

been made. The manager of the Empire Theatre offered to stage a special fund-raising matinee show, while one gentleman offered the use of an empty house at Gwydr Crescent for recruiting or Red Cross purposes. The Union of Operative Bakers and Confectioners offered their labour in bread-making free of charge as long as the Corporation could provide a bakery, the equipment and the much sought-after flour.[7]

Others made direct financial contributions to the fund. Colonel J.R. Wright donated £250 and Sir Alfred Mond did likewise, indicating that this was an initial payment and more was to follow. The Graigola Merthyr Company handed over £1,000, while the Morfa and Middle Bank Copper Works donated £500.[8] These sums provided a useful boost to the funds for assisting those genuinely in need.

However, then as now, efforts were made to ensure that there were no unjustified claims and that duplicate claims were not made on more than one body, a task that was much more difficult in the pre-computer age.

Fund-raising in aid of Welsh prisoners of war. *(SWDP)*

In January 1915 the list of existing applicants in each electoral ward was closely examined and a considerable reduction was made in the number of cases and the amount of relief awarded, principally from doubt over the reduced circumstances of the applicants actually being war-related as opposed to some other circumstance. In some instances the applicant's resources appeared to be sufficient without requiring the fund's assistance. Each electoral ward had a small committee whose role included recommending suitable cases for relief. After the lists had been scrutinized and reduced by the distress committee, one ward committee disputed matters with some success, while another declined to send up any more cases to the full committee as it felt that its actions had been undermined. Matters were swiftly smoothed over, however; the mood probably being lightened by a lively discussion over which body should meet the cost of the fodder provided for the horse that pulled the local coke delivery cart.[9]

Towards the end of 1915 the level of distress within Swansea seems to have subsided, at least for the time being. In May 1915 there had been 14 men and 57 women claiming on the National Fund while, by the end of November 1915, the figures had fallen to 9 men and 24 women. Many of the men were soldiers who had been discharged, some due to wounds, some due to ill health, and others due to their unsuitability for service life. Employment opportunities had been boosted by a number of Swansea men taking work on the construction of the munitions factory at Pembrey. It was likely, however, that once that was completed a surge in new applications for assistance could be anticipated.[10]

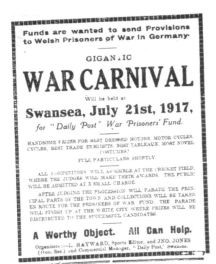

Funds are wanted to send Provisions to Welsh Prisoners of War In Germany·

GIGANᴛIC

WAR CARNIVAL

Will be held at

Swansea, July 21st, 1917,

for " Daily Post" War Prisoners' Fund.

HANDSOME PRIZES FOR BEST DRESSED MOTORS, MOTOR CYCLES, CYCLES, BEST TRADE EXHIBITS, BEST TABLEAUX, MOST NOVEL COSTUMES'

FULL PARTICULARS SHORTLY.

ALL COMPETITORS WILL ASSEMBLE AT THE CRICKET FIELD, WHERE THE JUDGES WILL MAKE THEIR AWARDS. THE PUBLIC WILL BE ADMITTED AT A SMALL CHARGE

AFTER JUDGING THE PROCESSION WILL PARADE THE PRINCIPAL PARTS OF THE TOWN AND COLLECTIONS WILL BE TAKEN EN ROUTE FOR THE PRISONERS OF WAR FUND. THE PARADE WILL FINISH UP AT THE WHITE CITY WHERE PRIZES WILL BE DISTRIBUTED TO THE SUCCESSFUL CANDIDATES.

A Worthy Object.   All Can Help.

Organizers :—L. HAYWARD, Sports Editor, and JNO. JONES (Hon. Sec.) and Commercial Manager, " Daily Post," Swansea.

A fund-raising carnival in aid of those held as prisoners of war in Germany. *(Cambrian)*

The issue of duplicate claims came under even closer examination as time went on. A comparison of families helped by the National Relief Fund found that five families in the Brynmelyn ward were also getting relief from the Poor Law Guardians. This was severely frowned upon by the Local Government Board; it had to be one or the other, and most certainly not both. The Local Government Board inspector also noted that the National Relief Fund was providing support to people 'whose continued distress must be regarded as due to their physical unfitness, age or inadaptability rather than to the war.' Such cases were to have their National Fund assistance withdrawn and their circumstances referred to the Poor Law Guardians. Funding was also likely to be withheld where a man failed to report for the work that had been found for him, or where he was judged to be 'no good' by the employer.[11]

Though there had been an understandable flurry of relief-based activity in the early days of the war it seems that, very commendably, there was little abatement of this during the entire course of the war as the citizens of Swansea continued to 'do their bit' for the men at the front as well as those who had returned home with wounds. Towards the end of 1914 use had been made of a minor hall at the Albert Hall for the establishment of a soldiers' and sailors' free club. Entry to the club was free of charge to all soldiers and sailors and it was open six days a week, from 10 am to 10 pm. There were newspapers, games, a piano, a gramophone and writing materials, as well as the provision of refreshments for which a small charge was made.[12] In a similar vein the Swansea YMCA opened a free canteen in the guards' waiting room at High Street train station for the benefit of travelling soldiers and sailors. The Great Western Railway Company had provided the room free of charge, while heating was similarly provided gratis by the Swansea Gas and Light Company. Volunteer ladies provided the staffing during the day, while during the night men of the Volunteer Training Corps stepped in.[13] By November 1916 some 20,000 men had availed themselves of the facility by day, with another 10,000 doing so by night. The enterprise had cost the YMCA nothing as all the supplies consumed had been generously donated by the businesses and people of Swansea.[14]

There were also plans, led by Mrs Lloyd George, to mark St David's Day in 1915 by selling Welsh flags; the proceeds of this would go towards helping to provide comforts for Welsh soldiers at the front. Over 90,000 flags had been ordered. Although Swansea servicemen were already well provided for, there were many at the front from the more rural parts of Wales who did not have the benefit of an efficient support mechanism back home and this initiative would help them greatly.[15] Similarly, an Irish flag day was held in March 1916; both to raise funds and to recognize the sacrifices of Swansea's

Irish contingent, a list of the fallen being pinned to the door of St Joseph's Church. On sale were 80,000 flags, 6,000 rosettes and 2,400 sprigs of shamrock.[16]

Fund-raising concerts, fêtes, whist drives and bazaars were regularly held with a view to raising funds to assist those at the front or the needy at home. The Swansea Chamber of Commerce sent almost 600,000 cigarettes to the front in 1916, a popular move that must have received a rather wheezy three cheers from the happy recipients.[17] The Theatre Royal proposed holding charity concerts on Sundays: a move that, notwithstanding the war, was bound to raise the hackles of Swansea's religious community. Despite that fact, the Swansea Watch Committee agreed to the request, subject to the accounts being subsequently submitted for examination. The proceeds were to be split between the Mayor's War Fund (set up to provide comforts for the troops), the *South Wales Daily Post* Prisoners of War Fund, the Red Cross and the Swansea Hospital.[18] The *South Wales Daily Post* fund for prisoners of war had, by September 1916, raised well over £4,000 and had sent almost 10,000 parcels of

One of the many lists published naming contributors to the Welsh prisoners-of-war fund. *(Cambrian)*

provisions to Welsh prisoners of war who were being held, often in poor conditions, in prison camps inside a blockaded Germany.[19]

At a 1916 Swansea Red Cross jumble sale and auction a ram was bought and then generously sold on again on no fewer than six occasions, producing a healthy £6 for the fund, while several calves and a pig also changed hands more than once, each additional sale adding to the balance of the fund. Other items that fell under the hammer included fourteen eggs (sold for 2 shillings), a pair of fowls and, rather oddly, 10 tons of basic slag, a gift from Messrs Gilbertson and Company.[20]

A war relief fund was set up in Morriston and among the contributors in 1915 were a number of well-known businesses whose employees were contributing small sums on a regular basis. These included Vivian and Sons, the Dyffryn Works, Graig Brickworks and the Bowen's Mineral Works. There were also contributions from various Corporation employees, the Morriston teachers and the local shop assistants and tradesmen.[21] Ben Evans' department store, Swansea's best-known shop, had a great interest in the war with 102 of its staff serving with the colours. At a concert held in the shop's costume department, an audience of over 600 was entertained by a number of artistes with the proceeds to be shared among the local war charities, £200 having already been donated.[22] The Lady Mayoress of Swansea had established a garments fund so that clothing could be recycled or new items knitted and tailored for the benefit of those at the front or those who remained at home. By the end of November 1915 the ladies had sent 400 parcels to soldiers serving at the front, totalling 1,766 items of clothing. On the home front some 800 parcels had been given to local families and Belgian refugees. Even after this intense activity there were still 1,500 garments remaining in the stock of the garments fund for use in future parcels.[23]

Practical efforts were also made to assist servicemen who had returned from the front, possibly with life-changing injuries making them unable

The interior of the Ben Evans store, ladies department. *(Author's collection)*

to follow their previous callings. It was obviously beneficial to help such men acquire the skills they would need if they were to obtain employment in a new field, as this would help restore their self-esteem and reduce their need to call on the state for financial assistance should they remain unemployed. At Swansea special facilities were granted to ex-servicemen where they desired to attend classes at the Technical College.[24] By December 1917 there were twenty-one disabled soldiers studying full-time at the college and, over time, classes were offered in the painting of coach and motor bodies, as well as picture frame-making. As 1918 neared its end and the conclusion of the war drew closer, it was reported that in the year ending September 1918 126 ex-servicemen had applied to follow courses at the college. These included 101 potential motor mechanics, 16 dental mechanics, 7 engineering draughtsmen, 1 laboratory steward and 1 steel-works chemist.[25]

Before the Great War the financing of military conflict involving Britain had largely been achieved by the government borrowing from financial institutions or well-off individuals. Such loans were gradually repaid with interest, much to the benefit of the original lenders. However, earlier wars had been fought on nowhere near the scale of the present conflict and by a purely volunteer army and navy but this all changed during the Great War. To use the modern phrase, after conscription was introduced in 1916 they really were all 'in it together' and this led to different thinking about how the war might be funded.

NEXT WEEK

is the Last week of

NATIONAL WAR BONDS

If you have not yet secured all the War Bonds or War Savings Certificates you intend to buy, now is the time. After one more short week the opportunity to put your money into the World's finest investment will have passed for ever.

Thanksgiving Week provides your big chance—to give your patriotic support to the local effort and to buy National War Bonds on the exceptionally generous terms which will never again be offered by a future Government.

Check up your savings now. Look to your Bank Balance and decide the urgent question. "How much more can I invest in War Bonds before it is too late?"

Buy the biggest Bond you can or put every shilling you can into War Savings Certificates. Let this be your practical tribute to the heroic valour of our Soldiers and Sailors and Airmen—your share is helping to bring them back to the homes they love—your contribution to the great task of Reconstruction which confronts us all to-day.

Pushing the sale of war bonds.
(Cambrian)

NATIONAL

War Savings Week

JULY 16th to JULY 22nd, 1916.

Mayor of Swansea's Appeal

WHY all should save
WHAT to do with your savings

"The Nation needs to pay for the war increased production and reduced consumption not only now but also when peace returns." CHANCELLOR OF THE EXCHEQUER.

PLEASE READ THIS PAMPHLET AND KEEP FOR REFERENCE.

An appeal by the mayor of Swansea in support of war savings week. *(WGAS D 27/2)*

It also seemed churlish to restrict the ultimate benefits of war borrowing (that is, the interest paid to the lenders) to only the more wealthy layers of society when all levels of society were now making great sacrifices on a daily basis. With that in mind, 1916 saw the appearance of war savings certificates which could be bought for a modest outlay up to a maximum of 500 certificates per person. This allowed the proverbial 'man in the street' to not only help the war effort with what little money he had to spare but also promised him interest payments in the coming years, assuming he was still around to receive them, of course.[26]

As the war dragged on, the need for yet more money to fuel the wartime economy was unrelenting and regular efforts were made at national and local level to reinvigorate the savings issue by way of patriotic appeals. In January 1917 a 'war loan barometer' was installed at the Labour Exchange in Castle Bailey Street, Swansea. This was a device that was graduated up to £1,000,000 and which was periodically topped up with liquid to indicate the new level of war savings in Swansea. On its launch the carefully-measured red-coloured liquid was ceremoniously poured in and rose within the gauge to a remarkable level of £900,000.[27] Additionally, the Swansea Patriotic War Savings Association reported that, in a fifteen-month period ending in June 1917, it had opened over 3,200 accounts and taken in almost £30,000.

November 1917 saw the start of a war savings' week designed to increase publicity and boost funds. Twenty-one local branches of the Swansea Patriotic War Savings Association had been established including those at the Dyffryn Works, Danygraig School, Mannesmann Tube Company and the St Andrew's Church Sunday School, to name but a few. The branches encompassed almost 5,500 account-holders with deposits amounting to £51,000. Despite some satisfaction with these figures, it was noted that the number of depositors amounted to only one in twenty-four of the Swansea populace. The Ben Evans department store was even selling war savings certificates to its

The Ben Evans store at Swansea. Described as 'the Harrods of Swansea', it was totally destroyed in the 1941 'Three-Day Blitz'. *(Author's collection)*

clients, along with the more usual items of clothing and household goods.[28]

The *Cambrian* at Swansea published a table in February 1918 showing the amounts paid into war bonds per head of population in the principal towns of Wales. Swansea stood proudly at the top of the table with £16 5s 1d per person, beating Cardiff, which could only boast £14 11s 8d per person, into second place. Carmarthen, Llanelli, Neath and Newport followed, with poor little Maesteg lying bottom of the table in eighteenth place with only 3s 5d collected per head.[29]

A popular and effective form of fund-raising was the sending of a military tank to particular towns and cities to act as the focus for fund-raising efforts with a vivid link to the front-line activity. The tank was, of course, regarded at that time as a novel and wonderful machine and its mere presence on the High Street of a town was guaranteed to draw a large crowd of potential depositors, many of whom would hopefully be gripped by patriotic fervour resulting in the rapid extraction of their wallet or purse. A tank was due to arrive at Swansea in the second week of July 1918 and an added carrot for investors and for the town was the undertaking that should £250,000 be raised, a tank at the front would be named 'Swansea' in honour of the town.[30] War savings figures were indeed impressive: a single week in September 1918 saw war bonds to the value of almost £369,000 being bought in Swansea. The local press reported that Cardiff had only managed £50,000 and Newport £4,000, while the residents of Neath chipped in £8,000. Some of the figures for other towns probably need to be treated with caution, lest a little inaccurate 'crowing' on the part of the Swansea press was taking place![31]

Civic dignitaries at Swansea make an address from a tank. *(WGAS P/PR 34/3/4)*

The tank trundles down High Street with the Lewis Lewis store in the background (left).
(WGAS P/PR 34/3/9)

The efforts of the numerous relief funds that were set up to support those at the front or those who remained back home but in reduced circumstances due to the loss of a wage-earner were not the only kind of aid available. Relief, essentially in the form of very welcome relaxation, could also be made available in a non-financial way to the benefit of the hard-pressed general population of Swansea. An important aspect of keeping up morale on the home front was the availability of recreational or leisure pursuits that could take a person's mind off the often depressing war situation, at least for brief periods. It must be remembered that the press of the time was filled with war news, albeit much of it censored and always very optimistic, irrespective of what was actually happening at the front. More depressing but unavoidable was the daily listing of the names of local servicemen who had been reported killed or missing, often featuring a photograph of the man concerned and a very brief biography. This was a constant reminder to those at home of the dangers faced by absent husbands, fathers and sons at the front. So it was only natural that many would take advantage whenever possible of any activity that temporarily deflected attention from the weightier matters relating to the war.

Sport was available to watch, although with problems in its top-class incarnations. The Swansea rugby club, the famous 'All Whites', cancelled all rugby fixtures for the duration of the war so play did not resume until the 1919–20 season. A non-cap match between players of Wales and England was staged at Cardiff in April 1915 with all the players (including three from the Swansea club) being servicemen. Proceeds were to be passed to the *South Wales Daily Post* Prisoners of War Fund. It is sobering to reflect that during the war no fewer than twenty-four members of the club, officially

Football matches for Christmas, 1917. *(Cambrian)*

known as the Swansea Cricket and Football Club, were killed while on active service.

The Swansea Town Association Football club, however, took a rather different tack and continued playing matches until April 1915. After that time a decision to 'close down' for the duration of the war came into effect across the country in respect of the first-class game. This must have come as a relief to the Swansea directors since it was reported that gate takings were 50 per cent down on the previous season. Matters had not been helped by elements of the local press boycotting the games as it was considered by some that at a time of war there were matters of far greater concern than mere football matches. An additional complication arose from the absence of key players due to their having joined the armed forces. As conscription was not introduced until 1916, in 1915 they would have enlisted on a purely voluntary basis, although it is possible that some men were territorial soldiers or, having served previously, had been recalled to the colours from the reserve. Of those who did remain with the club, it was noted that many were engaged in munitions work and as such were often unable to be released to play due to the importance of their work.[32]

Second-class sport continued through the war; a smaller number of games than would typically take place were completed. *(Cambrian)*

Swansea Town Association Football Tournament.

Table up to and including Nov. 10th, 1917.

Division A.

Club.	P	W	D	L	Goals F	Goals A	PTS.
Shropshires	3	3	0	0	19	2	6
Mannesmann	4	3	0	1	16	5	6
St. Paul's	3	1	2	0	3	2	4
Skewen U.	4	2	0	2	5	8	4
Pentre Villa	3	1	1	1	4	4	3
Cwmfelin U.	2	1	0	1	2	5	2
Llansamlet U.	3	1	0	2	4	5	2
Clydach U.	3	1	0	2	2	8	2
Ynys U.	3	0	1	2	2	19	1
Forest S. Wks.	2	0	0	2	1	3	0

Division B.

Club.							
East Side U.	4	4	0	0	26	1	8
Hafod Villa	4	3	1	0	20	1	7
Hillside	4	3	0	1	15	1	6
Burrows	3	1	1	1	5	11	3
Hawthorne Villa	4	1	1	2	2	11	3
Templars	4	1	1	2	4	7	3
Belgrave	3	1	0	2	5	9	2
Gas Works	4	1	0	3	3	8	2
Excelsiors	4	1	0	3	5	15	2
Whitcliffe R.	4	1	0	3	6	24	2

Division C.

Club.							
St. Catherine's	4	3	0	1	23	4	6
Shropshires II.	4	3	0	1	15	5	5
Mysydd	4	2	1	1	16	13	5
Morriston Villa	4	2	0	2	18	12	4
Mynyddbach	2	2	0	0	5	10	4
Montana	2	1	1	0	4	2	3
Glais	3	1	1	1	9	10	3
Llansamlet II.	4	1	0	3	10	16	2

As with the rugby, the odd representative football game was staged at the Vetch Field for the entertainment of the locals. One example is that of a match involving a Royal Flying Corps team versus Swansea Town that was played on 1 April 1918 before an enthusiastic crowd of about 6,000 people. Again the takings were presented to a charity, on this occasion the Mayor of Swansea's Sailors' and Soldiers' Comforts Fund.[33]

Throughout the war, even if professional sport was somewhat scarce as a spectacle, there were no such problems in relation to the cinemas or theatres in Swansea. Programmes varied widely and, at least in the case of the Swansea Empire, included a regular feature entitled 'Latest News and War Films'. Some still-familiar names appeared on some of the advertisements including those of Charlie Chaplin and Mary Pickford, while most of the films or the

The war apparently saw an upsurge in the purchase of pianos. Two Swansea companies compete for the attention of the piano-buying public. *(Cambrian)*

theatre artistes are now long forgotten. What was shown was a probably typical-of-the-time mix of comedy, drama, variety and a weekly serial, together with the occasional show that had a more direct link to the war. *Oliver Twist* featured in 1917, as did *A Tale of Two Cities*. A more martial air was apparent in *Pathé's History of the War*, *The Ten Tommies*, *In the Trenches* and *A Munitions Girl's Romance*. Documentaries were also in evidence, such as the unexciting-sounding *Some Tropical Birds*, *Some Fish* and finally *Beauty Spots in Southern France*, the last of which must have appeared in stark and sobering contrast to the battered terrain of much of northern France at that time.[34]

It might seem odd to observe that so much cultural activity carried on almost as usual in Swansea and elsewhere, despite the country being involved in what could be construed as a life-or-death struggle over four long years. The fact is that much of the entertainment, especially that presented in cinematic film, frequently featured foreign actors and technical staff who were not (or not yet, in the case of America) involved in the war. Local amateur dramatic productions could usually survive with a mix of 'old stagers' and those who had

The show must go on...despite the war. Advertisements for Swansea's palaces of pleasure. *(SWDP)*

not yet attracted the attention of the military or had served but had then been returned to Britain as unfit for further active service due to wounds or other issues. Given the often depressing news about losses coming back from the front, the constant worry about loved ones, economic problems and the frequent food shortages, it would be wrong to begrudge those who lived through the war years a little respite from their daily woes.

Notes

1. The Unemployed Workmen Act, 5 Edw. VII, c. 18.
2. *Cambrian*, 14 August 1914.
3. WGAS, TC/50/1/31.
4. WGAS, TC/27/10.
5. Ibid.
6. WGAS, TC/27/4.
7. WGAS, TC/27/17.
8. WGAS, TC/27/1.
9. WGAS, TC/27/10.
10. *Cambrian*, 26 November 1915.
11. WGAS, TC/27/10.
12. *Cambrian*, 20 November 1914.
13. *Cambrian*, 10 December 1915.
14. *Cambrian*, 10 November 1916.
15. *Cambrian*, 12 and 26 February 1915.
16. *Cambrian*, 24 March 1916.
17. *Cambrian*, 26 January 1917.
18. *Cambrian*, 25 February 1916.
19. *Cambrian*, 15 September 1916.
20. *Cambrian*, 31 March 1916.
21. *Cambrian*, 23 April 1915.
22. *Cambrian*, 6 April 1917.
23. *Cambrian*, 26 November 1915.
24. WGAS, TC/3/37.
25. WGAS, TC/3/38.
26. Arthur Marwick, *The Deluge*, p.130.
27. *Cambrian*, 26 January 1917.
28. *South Wales Daily Post*, 12 November 1917.
29. *Cambrian*, 15 February 1918.
30. *Cambrian*, June 1918, page undated.
31. *Cambrian*, 27 September 1918.
32. *Cambrian*, 23 April and 16 July 1915.
33. http//:scfcheritage.wordpress.com
34. *South Wales Daily Post*, 6 and 30 June, 4 July, 14 and 17 September, 1 October, 2 November, all 1917.

Chapter Eight

Swansea's Victoria Cross Winners

Even members of the public with little or no interest in military matters will nevertheless usually be aware of the significance of the Victoria Cross. It is, of course, the highest British award for bravery in time of war. The award dates back to 1856 when the young Queen Victoria was disappointed to find that, although bravery awards for officers were within her gift, there was no corresponding award for the common soldier. The queen desired the creation of an award for brave conduct that could be granted irrespective of the arm of service or the rank of the recipient. The result of her interest in this area was the institution, by Royal Warrant in 1856, of the Victoria Cross.

The Victoria Cross.

The warrant was precise in what was required in order to gain the award of the Victoria Cross. It stated that '...the cross shall only be awarded for most conspicuous bravery, or some daring or pre-eminent act of valour or self sacrifice or extreme devotion to duty in the presence of the enemy.'[1] Being 'in the presence of the enemy' was a key point. Outstanding valour in, for example, a naval shipwreck would not qualify for an award of the Victoria Cross as the enemy would not (usually) be present.

The first awards were made in 1857 to sixty-two officers and men who had performed heroic feats in the Crimean War. Since that time there have been 1,358 Victoria Crosses awarded, with just three men winning it twice: Surgeon Captain Arthur Martin-Leake, Captain Noel Chavasse and Captain Charles Upham. An award was also made to the American Unknown Soldier of the Great War. During the Great War the Victoria Cross was awarded 628 times, to 627 recipients (Noel Chavasse winning the award twice). Only two awards during that time were made to men with strong links to Swansea. Those men were William Charles Fuller and George Prowse.

William Charles Fuller was born in 1884 in Laugharne, Carmarthenshire and had moved with his family to Swansea by about 1888. His education had not been without issues and for a time he attended the Industrial School at Bonymaen. This type of school was intended for those under the age of 14 who had perhaps been found begging or wandering, were homeless and frequenting with thieves, or those whose parents simply could not control them. Those under the age of 12 who had committed an offence for which the usual punishment was imprisonment were also provided for. At this distance in time it is not clear into which category the young Fuller fell.

In 1914 the adult Fuller was living at Charles Place, Swansea with his wife and two young children; one aged 4 years and the other just 13 months. Prior to leaving for the front he had worked as a watchman at the Elysium in the High Street, having previously been employed by Messrs John Lewis and Sons, timber merchants, in the role of a timber-haulier. Fuller's father was a successful butcher in Swansea with premises at both Wassail Square and St Thomas. At one time his father had also kept the Tradesmen's Club in St Mary Street.

William Fuller had already seen army service prior to the Great War. Indeed, he had served in the Second Boer War of 1899–1902. Fuller, as an experienced soldier, was recalled to the colours to help meet the crisis of 1914. He was posted to the 2nd Welsh Battalion which was a regular army battalion. As such, it comprised professional soldiers rather than enthusiastic but untrained volunteers such as the men who answered Lord Kitchener's 1914 call for recruits. The 2nd Welsh was mobilized for action as early as 4 August 1914 and being below strength at that time was augmented by almost 600 men recalled from the reserve, Fuller among them. By 12 August 1914 the battalion was at Southampton where it boarded the *Braemar Castle* for the trip to Le Havre, that port being reached at 6 am on the following day. The battalion arrived in France conscious of the edicts regarding the standards of behaviour expected of British troops in a foreign land as laid down by the Secretary of State for War, Lord Kitchener, which ended with the stern injunctions 'Do your duty', 'Fear God' and 'Honour the King'.[2]

As the British Expeditionary Force marched to the support of its French allies, it neared the town of Mons and it was here on the morning of 22 August 1914 that shots were exchanged between a detachment of the 4th Dragoon Guards and a group of German soldiers. Apart from the battles in the Crimea, these were the first shots fired by British soldiers on mainland Europe since the Battle of Waterloo in June 1815. By 23 August 1914 the Battle of Mons was raging with around 80,000 British soldiers being assailed by the 250,000 men of von Kluck's German First Army. With its French allies in retreat, even the fighting spirit and skill of the British army could not hold back the massed ranks of the German infantry, although a heavy toll was exacted by the accurate and rapid rifle-fire of the men of Sir John French's command. The retreat from Mons had begun.

William Fuller, VC. *(Mark Butler)*

Fuller and his comrades in the 2nd Welsh were not heavily involved in the early fighting, although a German cavalry patrol was encountered on 23 August 1914 and sent back to its own lines minus several horsemen.[3] Days of gruelling marches followed in the August heat as the battalion was forced to fall back, passing Le Cateau, Guise, Soissons and Meaux, among other places. By 5 September 1914 the 2nd Welsh was south of Coulommiers. Captain H.C. Rees, an officer of the 2nd Welsh, stated:

> The determination of the men during the Retreat passed all belief. The reservists, as I remarked before, were not in any way fit for such a terrific test of endurance.

Between 22 August and 5 September, we marched about 240 miles, and only on one day did we have any semblance of rest. The men were absolutely tired out before the actual retreat began on 24 [August]. At the end of some of the marches it was impossible to maintain our formation, and the column became merely a crowd flowing very slowly along the road, the men looking as if they neither saw nor felt anything. Almost without exception their feet were raw and bleeding, and many marched with puttees wrapped around their feet. Their one desire was to halt and fight the enemy and not being allowed to do so was the cause of bitter complaint.[4]

If the British were having a very hard time during their retreat it must be remembered that the Germans were also enduring long, hard marches in pursuit of their prey; a pursuit that was punctuated by some sharp fighting exchanges. Supply issues grew worse as the advancing German troops marched past the remains of deliberately-destroyed railway lines. Gradually the German soldiers simply marched further and further away from their nearest supply depots, the speed of repair of the damaged rail tracks failing to keep up with the pace of the marching soldiers. Essential matériel had to be manhandled from railway wagons to motor vehicles or horses, which then promptly added to the already tangled congestion on the roads.

With the Germans approaching Paris and the British so fearful of the loss of the Channel ports that far-off St Nazaire might have to become their prime base on the continent, the time for a fighting riposte was ripe. The French General Joffre provided it; telling his men (over 1,000,000 of them plus the British force that following reinforcement now stood at about 125,000) that:

> At the moment when the battle upon which hangs the fate of France is about to begin all must remember that the time for looking back is past; every effort must be concentrated on attacking and throwing the enemy back. [Troops that could not advance] must at any cost keep the ground that has been won, and must die where they stand rather than give way.[5]

The 'Miracle of the Marne' was about to begin as, on 5 September 1914, the allied armies finally fell on their antagonists and began to force them back. The 2nd Welsh was soon on the move, finally heading north after thirteen days of retreating south, reaching the vicinity of Bourg on 13 September 1914. On the following day the now Lance Corporal Fuller would earn his cherished place in the history of the Victoria Cross.

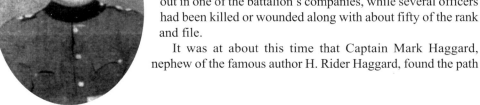

On 14 September 1914 the 2nd Welsh was advancing near Chivy on the River Aisne when it became involved in an action with the retreating German rearguard. Some of the Germans were dealt with at the point of a bayonet while a German field gun battery was surprised in its gun pits; its subsequent fire forcing the British to hug the ground for safety. Ammunition was running out in one of the battalion's companies, while several officers had been killed or wounded along with about fifty of the rank and file.

It was at about this time that Captain Mark Haggard, nephew of the famous author H. Rider Haggard, found the path

Captain Mark Haggard.
(Cymru1914.org)

of his advance blocked by a German machine-gun position. He immediately decided to attack it and set off followed by three of his men, one of whom was William Fuller. Haggard advanced at a fast pace and by the time his three followers had reacted, he was some 30 yards in front of them and firing his rifle at the enemy position. Despite several Germans being shot, Haggard's fire was returned by the enemy and he soon fell to the ground, severely wounded in the stomach. Of the three men who had followed his advance, one lay dead while another was badly wounded. Fuller, however, had surprisingly not been hit. He quickly approached the stricken officer who cried out: 'I'm done, get back.' Fuller initially did as ordered but looking towards Captain Haggard and seeing the bullets snapping into the ground near to where he lay, he made the decision that, notwithstanding the great risks involved, he would have to try to move his officer to a safer place. He quickly left his cover and dashed to Haggard's side. As he later told a reporter from the *Cambrian*:

> It became necessary for me to carry Captain Haggard back to cover. This was done by him putting his right arm round my neck, while I had my right arm under his legs and the left under his neck. I was only from ten to twenty yards behind him when he was shot, and as he fell he cried 'Stick it, Welsh'.[6]

Having carried the officer back to some protective cover, Fuller then bandaged Haggard's wounds as best he could before quickly realizing that it was impossible to move any further due to the heavy fire from both sides that was passing close by. Haggard was still conscious and after an hour or so it was agreed that a safer place must indeed be sought, irrespective of the risks. Fuller was advised to remove his kit, which was bulky and inhibited easy movement. A little later, as the duo waited for an opportune moment to fall back further, a soldier managed to reach them and with the help of another officer, Haggard was finally carried to a farm about three-quarters of a mile away for further assistance. Sadly, he died the following day.

Fuller, meanwhile, who had the good fortune to emerge from his heroics unscathed, resumed his duties with the 2nd Welsh. The battalion was withdrawn to the Vendresse Ridge, a position that was not as exposed to enemy fire as that previously held.[7] The Germans were now attempting to regain lost ground and the battalion had to deal with several attacks of varying intensity as trench warfare became established and severely curtailed the movements of both sides. By 22 October 1914 the men of the 2nd Welsh were forced to watch helplessly as German shellfire destroyed the town and church of Langemarck. In just four hours it was reduced to ashes and rubble.[8]

On 29 October 1914 a German attack near Gheluvelt was aided by the presence of early-morning fog. As the Germans had advanced unseen on some parts of the front (which at that time was not a continuous trench line) they had been able to penetrate into the rear areas and it proved necessary to launch an urgent counter-attack. The 2nd Welsh took part in this, entering the village of Gheluvelt as its defending troops fell back, warning others that the Germans were advancing in force. Undaunted, the 2nd Welsh entered the village, dealt with its enemy occupiers and even advanced beyond its boundaries into open country.[9]

At about this time William Fuller, who later gave the location of this incident to a press reporter as 'Dixmude', stopped to bind up the wounds of a comrade named Tagg.

While doing this Fuller was hit by a burst of shrapnel, the metal hitting him 'on the right side, and the bullet travelled right up to behind the neck'.[10] He was invalided home to a hospital in Manchester. It was only after he was sent for treatment to Swansea on 11 October 1914, however, that it was discovered that a shard of shrapnel was still present in his body and this was removed by Doctor Isaac, a surgeon at the Swansea General and Eye Hospital. Fuller, possibly being somewhat suspicious of new-fangled medical procedures, declined the administration of chloroform. He later recalled that the resultant pain of the operation was, therefore, understandably severe.

Fuller's heroic action in going out under heavy fire to bring Captain Haggard back had not gone unnoticed and he was in due course awarded the Victoria Cross by the king. The Army Order of 25 November 1914 stated:

> For conspicuous gallantry on 14th September near Chivy on the Aisne, by advancing about 100 yards to pick up Captain Haggard who was mortally wounded, and carrying him back to cover under very heavy rifle and machine-gun fire.[11]

William Fuller, VC, with his arm still in a sling.
(Cymru1914.org)

While William Fuller and the residents of Swansea were initially oblivious of the fact, the *London Gazette* duly published his Victoria Cross citation. On that November 1914 evening Fuller was spending some time at the newly-opened Free Soldiers' and Sailors' Club at the Albert Hall in Swansea. As a wounded soldier he proved to be the centre of attention, so much so that his bandaged right arm was slightly hurt again as a crowd of well-wishers thronged around him. No doubt the pain was eased when the matter of his award became common knowledge. He received his Victoria Cross from the hand of the king at Buckingham Palace on 13 January 1915. The Industrial School at Bonymaen that Fuller had attended planned to erect a brass tablet in his honour in the school dining room.[12]

The injuries sustained by Fuller meant that he was unfit for active service and he was duly discharged from the army on 30 December 1915. He did some useful work as a recruiting sergeant and also received occasional gifts, such as when he was given just under £100 in Exchequer Bonds by the grateful people of Tenby in April 1916.[13] At that Tenby event Fuller stated that although he had completed thirteen years in the army and reserve, he had apparently not qualified for a pension, other than the £10 a year that was granted to all holders of the Victoria Cross.

Post-war William Fuller VC at one time sold fresh fish around the streets of Swansea and also served as an air-raid warden in the Second World War. He lived in Swansea for the remainder of his long life, dying in December 1974 at 90 years of age.

William Fuller was not the only Swansea man to win a Victoria Cross during the Great War. Fellow Victoria Cross recipient George Prowse had actually been born in Gilfach Goch, near Llantrisant in 1886 but later moved to Camerton, near Bath at around the turn of the century. Like his father before him, he found employment in the mining industry. Prowse certainly did not fit the popular image of a coalminer in being short and stocky. Indeed, he was a full 6 feet tall with an expanded chest measurement of 39 inches.

In due course George Prowse was attracted to Wales by the abundance of employment opportunities available in the South Wales coalfield and he found employment in the mines near Gorseinon, Swansea in 1907. By 1913 he was settled at Pentre-Treharne Road, Swansea in the family home of his new wife, Sarah.

The war, of course, broke out a year later and Prowse volunteered to join up, apparently expressing a preference for the navy. An imposing physique would have done him no harm at the recruiting office and he was duly accepted for service, initially in the Royal Naval Volunteer Reserve, entering it on 26 February 1915. There was a problem, however, although it was not of Prowse's making. The rapid influx of volunteers for all branches of the armed services meant that by happily taking on all who met the recruitment criteria, the navy soon found that it had far more men than were actually required to crew the available ships. Therefore Prowse and a great many like him found themselves sailors without a ship and were accordingly restricted to operations on land.

Indeed, even before Prowse had joined his unit, many of the excess reservists and new recruits had been hastily brought together in August 1914 to form three brigades (including one of marines) of what were essentially supposed to be sailors but who actually served as infantry. They were deployed to Belgium to assist in what turned out to be the unsuccessful defence of Antwerp, their efforts hampered by the issue of obsolete equipment and a total absence of artillery and other support units. Although many of the men were withdrawn to Britain after the fall of Antwerp, over 1,000 were forced to cross the border into neutral Holland where they were promptly interned. The men who did manage to get back to Britain were reorganized on arrival and received the official designation of the 63rd (Royal Naval) Division a little later. A number of its battalions were named after famous admirals, including Nelson and Benbow, with Prowse being assigned to Drake Battalion.

As a raw recruit it was inevitable that Prowse would not see immediate action as he was subjected to a training regime designed to instil military discipline, familiarity with infantry weapons and an appreciation of his unfamiliar role in any engagement with the enemy. Thus, although a couple of battalions of the Royal Naval Division were deployed to Gallipoli, landing with the 29th Division on 25 April 1915, Prowse and his battalion were not among them. Indeed, Prowse embarked on a sort of mini 'Grand Tour' of the Mediterranean as he was shipped around it without seeing any action. He developed jaundice in October 1915 and was hospitalized on Malta. On his release from hospital he promptly went down with a stomach problem, requiring further medical attention. By the time Prowse had partially recovered from that setback the stalemated Gallipoli campaign was being wound

Recruiting poster for the Royal Naval Division.

down and the troops readied for a secret evacuation from under the noses of their Turkish opponents. Prowse was therefore despatched back to Britain via Alexandria, Mudros and Marseilles, before rejoining Drake Battalion which was by then in France, in September 1916.

If George Prowse had been frustrated by his inability to see any significant action, that situation was soon to change. On 13 November 1916 the Royal Naval Division was part of a force that was to make an attack in the very last phase of the long-drawn-out and bloody Somme campaign. It became known as the Battle of the Ancre and ran from 13–18 November 1916, though Prowse was fated only to take part in the first day of the attack. Drake Battalion was placed behind the Hood and Hawke battalions, on a forward slope facing the lower end of the Beaumont Hamel spur. The Royal Naval Division had never participated in an offensive on the Western Front before and steps had been taken to provide the best possible briefing for the men. The leading battalions were to take the German first-line trenches, while the battalions behind them were then to 'leap-frog' through the first attackers and capture a high bank that was a prominent feature of the terrain. Further leap-frog movements would follow so that an important enemy trench and the village of Beaucourt could also be captured.

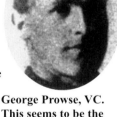

George Prowse, VC. This seems to be the only published photograph of him.
(Cambrian)

Things did not begin well. Even before the starting-positions were reached by the attacking troops, the commander of Anson Battalion was killed by German shellfire. As Drake Battalion moved forward (following Hood Battalion), enemy machine-gun fire came in from the flank, mortally wounding Prowse's commanding officer. Despite these setbacks the German front-line trench was stormed and several hundred prisoners taken, although fighting continued on both flanks. An attack on the next objective was then staged, led by Lieutenant Colonel Bernard Freyberg of Hood Battalion but with elements of Drake Battalion assisting. This objective was achieved after some brisk fighting. Once again Freyberg rallied a mixed contingent of Hood and Drake men to attack the village of Beaucourt. Though the edge of the village was quickly reached, the artillery fire of both sides began to fall dangerously close to the attackers, causing a quick retirement to a slightly safer position. They then dug in amidst a landscape littered with shell-holes and simply held their position.[14] This was essentially the end of the battle for George Prowse. Although Freyberg was again prominent in the subsequent day's action (and received four wounds and a Victoria Cross for his trouble), Prowse did not take part, having received a serious gunshot wound in the left thigh on the first day of the attack. Precisely when this occurred and under what circumstances is not known.

After initial treatment at the 14th General Hospital in France, Prowse was conveyed back to Britain via the hospital ship *St David* for further treatment at Epsom Hospital.

HMHS *St David.*

SS *Cambria.*

It was 28 March 1917 before Prowse went back to his old battalion, having recovered from his wounds. Drake Battalion was soon in action and once again George Prowse seems to have been in the thick of the fighting. From 23 April 1917 his division was engaged in the Second Battle of the Scarpe; an attempt not simply to gain ground but also, very importantly, to take German pressure off the ailing French army, many units of which were on the brink of mutiny following the failure of the French General Nivelle's offensive at Arras. The Royal Naval Division moved to attack Gavrelle and managed to secure the village before being brought to a halt by heavy German artillery fire. It is likely that George Prowse was a victim of this bombardment as he was reported as being wounded by shrapnel on the left side of his body as well as his left shoulder. The wounds were categorized as 'slight to severe' and after initial treatment in France, he was sent back to Britain for further treatment, this time aboard the hospital ship *Cambria.*

While back in Britain Prowse was awarded his first Good Conduct Badge and also seems to have attended a training course of some description at the Military School, Tidworth. He was assigned to the 2nd Reserve Battalion at Aldershot and it was not until the spring of 1918 that he rejoined the Royal Naval Division in France. He was appointed Acting Chief Petty Officer and confirmed in that rank on the same day (the Royal Naval Division retained its maritime rather than army ranks, despite being deployed as infantry).

Apart from periods of holding the line (a dangerous business in its own right) and a small-scale trench raid, the Royal Naval Division did not take part in another offensive until 21 August 1918. By that time the allies were beginning to reap the rewards of their 8 August 1918 counterstrike at Amiens; an attack that German General Erich Ludendorff described as 'the black day of the German Army'. This was not due to the ground lost but to the fact that some elements of the German army, having seen their great March 1918 offensive brought to a halt by determined allied resistance, were now demoralized and prepared to capitulate where before they would have tenaciously fought on.

The Royal Naval Division was asked to drive towards and beyond Logeast Wood, near Miraumont and despite coming under heavy fire, this was achieved although at the cost of a number of casualties. George Prowse distinguished himself by winning a

Distinguished Conduct Medal, the citation for which reads:

On 21st August 1918, at Logeast Wood, he led his men with great gallantry against a machine gun that was holding up the advance of the flank of his company, and in spite of difficulties of heavy mist he captured it, disposing of the crew. On a subsequent occasion he held a position against repeated counter-attacks which were supported by an intense bombardment for twenty-four hours. His courage, leadership, and cheerful disposition had an invaluable effect on his men.[15]

At the beginning of September 1918 the German army was still in retreat and the Royal Naval Division was advancing steadily in its wake. Prowse set such an example of bravery and leadership at that time that he was awarded the Victoria Cross. From his citation it seems that the award was made for several acts of courage displayed over several days rather than for a single act of gallantry. The citation reads:

For most conspicuous bravery and devotion to duty when, during an advance, a portion of his company became disorganised by heavy machine-gun fire from an enemy strong point. Collecting what men were available he led them with great coolness and bravery against this strong point, capturing it together with twenty-three prisoners and five machine guns.

Later, he took a patrol forward in face of much enemy opposition, and established it on important high ground. On another occasion he displayed great heroism by attacking single-handed an ammunition limber which was trying to recover ammunition, killing three men who accompanied it and capturing the limber.

Two days later he rendered valuable services when covering the advance of his company with a Lewis-gun section, and located later on two machine-gun positions in a concrete emplacement, which were holding up the advance of the battalion on the right.

With complete disregard of personal danger he rushed forward with a small party and attacked and captured these posts, killing six enemy and taking thirteen prisoners and two machine guns. He was the only survivor of this gallant party, but by this daring and heroic action he enabled the battalion on the right to push forward without further machine-gun fire from the village. Throughout the whole operations his magnificent example and leadership were an inspiration to all, and his courage was superb.[16]

A little after these events Prowse must have been told that he had been recommended for the award of a Victoria Cross as he wrote to his wife warning her:

But don't set your mind on my getting the V.C. But to know I have been recommended I must have done something very great. You say I shall not be half 'swanking' now but you know there is not much 'swank' attached to me.[17]

Drake Battalion continued with its work at the front and on 27 September 1918 it approached the ruins of a sugar-beet factory close to Anneux that was being defended by the Germans. The factory was bombarded before the infantry attack went in. It was during this encounter that George Prowse was apparently hit by a bullet, his death being described as 'instantaneous', although this term was regularly used to conceal a more painful truth from grieving relatives. With little time to bury the fallen and the ground being subjected to incessant bombardment, Prowse's body was not recovered and he therefore has no known grave. He is commemorated on the Viz-en-Artois memorial in France, as well as on the Swansea Cenotaph.[18]

There seems to be no other civic recognition in the form of a central plaque or statue relating to George Prowse VC in Swansea, as is also the case with William Fuller VC. Both men seem to have been largely forgotten in the post-war period and even the British government's recent announcement (in 2013) that it will provide the birthplace of every VC winner with a suitably-inscribed 'paving stone' will not help. In the case of the Swansea VCs, one will go to Laugharne and the other to Gilfach Goch. Contemporary press reports refer to about 15,000 Swansea men serving, of whom only two won the Victoria Cross. While all played their part in the eventual victory, many laying down their lives for the cause, it would be a great disservice if Prowse VC and Fuller VC were not to receive even some sort of belated recognition in Swansea, especially in light of 'their' Victoria Cross paving stones being destined for other parts. Perhaps it is time for the present-day council at Swansea, the successor to the Swansea Corporation, a body which was itself active on a multitude of fronts in aid of the 1914–18 war effort, to now take the lead and arrange some sort of permanent memorial in the city for two men who should count among its most famous sons, even if it was by way of 'adoption'.

Notes
1. Max Arthur, *Symbol of Courage: A Complete History of the Victoria Cross*, p.xi.
2. T.O. Marden, *History of the Welch Regiment*, p.277.
3. Marden, op. cit., p.293; Martin Gilbert, *First World War*, p.55.
4. Marden, op. cit., p.298.
5. Gilbert, op. cit., p.70.
6. *Cambrian*, 27 November 1914.
7. Marden, op. cit., p.308.
8. Ibid., p.313.
9. Ibid., pp.315–16.
10. *Cambrian*, 27 November 1914.
11. TNA, WO/98/8.
12. WGAS, TC/3/34.
13. *Cambrian*, 14 April 1916.
14. Miles, *Official History*, pp.485–89.
15. *London Gazette*, 16 January 1919.
16. *London Gazette*, 30 October 1918.
17. *South Wales Daily Post*, 31 October 1918.
18. Gerald James contributed a very informative article on George Henry Prowse, VC, DCM, to *Morgannwg: The Journal of Glamorgan History*, volume LIV (2010). The service record for George Prowse VC is at The National Archives, reference ADM/339/2/3741.

Chapter 9

Tales from the Front

Exactly how many Swansea men saw active service in the Great War is open to debate, although contemporary press reports quoted a figure of 15,000 with the majority apparently finding their way into the navy. However, how a 'Swansea man' was defined by the press is not clear and the figures must be treated with some caution. What is certain is that when the cenotaph was unveiled it displayed the names of around 2,200 Swansea men who had fallen in the conflict and it is very likely that several hundred others were 'missed off' the memorial for a variety of reasons. Application had to be made to the Corporation for a name to be inscribed on the cenotaph and in some cases there was simply no family member available to make the Corporation aware of a particular man's claim. Some families may have simply decided not to apply, still heartbroken at the loss of a loved one.

It is certainly true to say that in almost every significant event in the Great War, a Swansea man was there, with the largest number of casualties occurring among those who served on land. Indeed, only two weeks after the outbreak of war Private Owen Owen of Albert Place, Swansea, a member of the 6th Welsh, Swansea Territorial Battalion, died in Britain during training and was buried in Danygraig Cemetery. He was aged just 17 and qualified to be counted among the war dead as a serving soldier, even though the first British bullet was not fired in Belgium until 22 August 1914. On the infamous 'First Day on the Somme' on 1 July 1916 no fewer than fourteen Swansea men were listed among the fallen, eight of them serving with the Devonshire Regiment. The men of its 2nd Battalion had advanced into no-

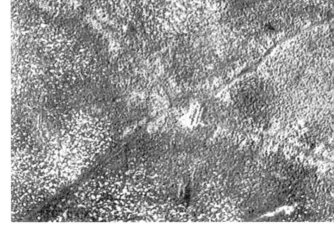

An artillery war: the village of Passchendaele before and after bombardment.

David Hitchings. *(Gwynne McColl)*

man's-land under fire and were at first
thought by onlookers to be lying down,
awaiting a chance to move forward again
when the enemy fire lightened. It was soon
realized that they were, in fact, almost all
casualties.

Although it could not match the Western
Front for the scale and intensity of the
fighting, the British campaign against the
Turks in Egypt and Palestine certainly
captured the imagination of the British
public. This was especially so when
Jerusalem was captured in 1917 and the
Mount of Olives also featured in the
actions of the British forces. The capture
of Jerusalem returned it to Christian
control for the first time since the
Crusades. David Hitchings from Horeb
Road, Morriston played a part in those

**Greetings card sent from Morriston to
David Hitchings.** *(Gwynne McColl)*

actions, serving with 266th Brigade of the Royal Field Artillery. He had previously served in France and kept up a brisk correspondence with his wife Beatrice back in Swansea. Naturally the attentions of the wartime censor did not allow him to elaborate on military matters and he was largely confined to family news. Happily, unlike so many other Swansea men, he returned home at the end of the war.[1]

Losses among Swansea men continued to be suffered throughout the war, of course. Private D.C. Weston of the Swansea Battalion fell in action on 7 November 1918, a mere four days before the Armistice was signed. He was 23 years old. That was not the end of it: between 11 November 1918 and 28 July 1921 almost eighty Swansea men died of wounds received in action or in accidents or as a result of illness that occurred while they were still under arms. The last Swansea man officially judged to be a war casualty seems to be Company Sergeant Major John Boland DCM of the Swansea Battalion who died on 28 July 1921, apparently of wounds received some years earlier (the government decreed a cut-off point in 1921 as the latest that a former serviceman could die of injuries received and still be regarded as a casualty of war).

While naval casualty numbers were understandably less than those of the army, there were still Swansea men aboard a number of ships that fought and occasionally blew up, with disastrous consequences, as at the Battle of Jutland. Swansea men were also aboard the armoured cruiser HMS *Hampshire* when she sank after hitting a mine, taking Lord Kitchener down with her. William Rogers, whose parents lived at Stepney Street, Cwmbwrla was lost along with Lord Kitchener, as was Michael Veale who also lived in Swansea.

Air Force casualties were few but still tragic, of course, due to the relatively small numbers involved in aerial operations. Nevertheless, at least one Swansea man fell under the guns of the deadly 'Red Baron' of the German Air Force, while several others were lost in combat or in flying accidents.

In the Merchant Navy Richard Gaul and James Simpson were both originally from Swansea but had moved to Liverpool to ply their trade as seamen in the huge port there. They had the misfortune to be taken on to the crew of the passenger liner RMS *Lusitania* and were lost along with almost 1,200 others when she was sunk by a German submarine in 1915.

RMS *Lusitania*, sunk by a German U-boat.

These are just some of the remarkable stories of the Swansea men (and the occasional woman) who saw active service on land, on sea or in the air during the Great War. With fatalities approaching 3,000 it is, of course, impossible to tell the story of each and every individual, even if the records still existed (many have simply not survived the passage of time and the effects of a Second World War bombing raid). What follows in the next three sub-chapters are small vignettes of the actions and fate of a number of soldiers, sailors, airmen, doctors and nurses who had a link to Swansea and who gave service during the Great War. They are not in any way representative of the vast majority of those who fought or died but I hope they will give the reader some insight into the varying fortunes and experiences of some of Swansea's brave forebears during a mighty conflict.

Notes
1. Information provided by Gwynne McColl.

Chapter Nine (a)

The War on Land

Despite over 5,000,000 men and women serving in the British armed forces during the Great War, only a relatively tiny number actually left a written record of their experiences. One member of the Swansea Battalion (the 14th Welsh), John Stanley Strange, did not actually complete a written memoir as such but he did leave behind over 200 documents relating to his wartime service. This archive, which remains in the care of his family to this day, consists of his Field Service Pocket Book (which contained his day-to-day orders and reports made while at the front), copies of certain orders given or received, letters from his family, friends and comrades, telegrams, postcards and other memorabilia. It is a remarkable treasure trove and, used in conjunction with other official records and histories, gives a vivid insight into the wartime experiences of a prominent member of the Swansea Battalion.

John Stanley Strange was born in 1884 in Bradfield, near Aldermaston, where his family owned the Aldermaston Brewery. He attended Charterhouse School in Godalming, Surrey from 1899 until 1904, during which time he captained the school football team, while also making an occasional appearance in the first team at cricket. He also became head of his house at the school.

After his time at Charterhouse it seems that Strange was keen to embrace the brewing trade as a means of employment, helped no doubt by his father's expertise in that area. At some point prior to the outbreak of the Great War he found himself living and working in Swansea, managing a local brewing concern while his wife initially remained at home in England.

Charterhouse School.
(Charterhouse School Archives)

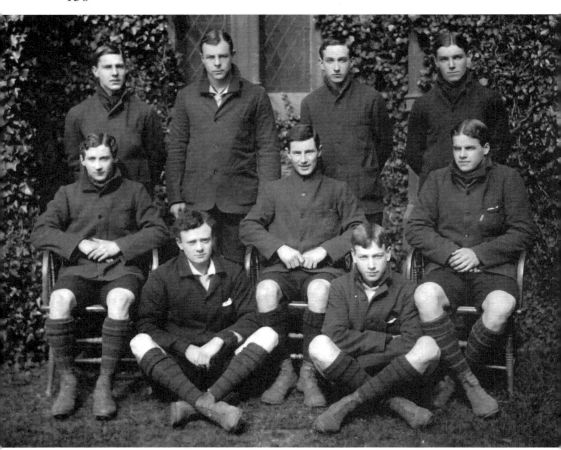

John Strange (centre of image) at Charterhouse School. *(Charterhouse School Archives)*

Following the declaration of war on 4 August 1914 the Swansea Corporation (the forerunner of today's city council) deliberated over how best it could help the war effort. After communicating with the War Office in London it was decided that the best course would be to try to raise a 'town' battalion by way of a public appeal for volunteers. It was natural that the focus for such an effort should rest with the town's mayor for 1914, Alderman Thomas Taliesyn Corker, and he duly took the lead in arranging a public meeting to gauge the level of likely support for the formation of a battalion from the people of the town. A packed meeting at the Albert Hall in Swansea on 16 September 1914 enthusiastically endorsed the mayor's proposal for the formation of a town battalion and it is worth noting that the mayor's oldest son, Frank, was an early recruit, soon being commissioned as a second lieutenant.

Another early recruit was John Stanley Strange who, the day after the public meeting, put himself forward as a volunteer. In terms of physique, Strange was very much a man of his time, being only slight in build. Aged 29, he was almost 5 feet 7 inches tall and weighed just 9 stone 7lb. His chest measurement was usually 34 inches but increased to 38 inches on expansion. His complexion was described as 'fresh' and he had brown eyes and black hair. As time would tell, what Strange lacked in physical build was more than made up for by his bravery and calm-headedness.

The detailed history of the Swansea Battalion has been told elsewhere.[1] Regarding John Strange, he was enlisted into it as a private in September 1914. In March 1915 he was recommended and subsequently approved for a commission in the Swansea Battalion as a second lieutenant; aided, perhaps, by his cut-glass accent and public school background. These factors would have tended to mark him out, by the standards of the time, as a man of authority who was very capable of leading others. Attendance at an officers' training course at Camberley helped

John Strange in 1915.
(Author's collection)

the erstwhile brewery manager master the mysteries of bombing, musketry, range-finding and fire-control.

With the training of the Swansea Battalion having been completed at Rhyl and Winchester, it departed for France and the Western Front in early December 1915, in company with other units that helped form the 38th (Welsh) Division. Although the Swansea Battalion was soon serving in the front-line trenches it was also frequently out of the line and so a little further back from the attentions of the enemy, even though the risk of danger from artillery fire or sniping was often present.

By the summer of 1916 the German strategy on the Western Front was to simply hold on to the land it had conquered, its anticipated total conquest of France and Belgium having foundered in a maze of fortified trench lines and barbed wire. It thus fell largely to the allied forces to undertake offensive action while the enemy simply strengthened its positions and awaited events. The British generals believed that a man's 'fighting spirit' needed frequent agitation lest it should simply settle into the seat of his army trousers. To this end the practice of 'raiding' the enemy trenches assumed great importance. Raids were intended to be short, sharp incursions into the defences of the enemy with the aim of bringing back prisoners, equipment and information while also keeping the men busy. In the harsh reality of war, if the chance also arose to kill a few Germans, that was all to the good.

The night of 4 June 1916 was earmarked for raids on the German lines by two units of the Welsh Division. Men of the 10th Welsh Battalion were to cross no-man's-land and bomb (hand-grenade) the enemy trenches before quickly returning to the safety of the British lines. A party of men from the 14th Welsh Battalion (the Swansea Battalion) was to undertake a similar enterprise nearby. All did not go to plan, however, and the 10th Welsh raiding party found the German barbed wire mostly uncut by the British trench-mortar barrage and thus impenetrable. With the enemy alerted, the raid was abandoned but not before three men had been killed and thirteen others wounded.

The raid by the Swansea Battalion men was more of a success although, as was always the case in such enterprises, successes came at a price. Forty-two men took part in the raid, including officers John Stanley Strange, Frank Corker (the mayor's son) and

Arnold Wilson. It was planned that, under cover of darkness, Corker and Wilson would approach the German trenches before jumping in and, hopefully, surprising the sentries. The chance would then be taken to kill or capture enemy soldiers and grab any booty that might be close at hand before withdrawing. John Strange, meanwhile, would wait in no-man's-land with a nine-man reserve, plus two signallers and two stretcher-bearers.

On quietly entering the German trench, Wilson's party initially found no enemy present but this soon changed and a sharp exchange of fire occurred. Corker's men entered the German trench and came into immediate contact with its defenders and bombs were quickly thrown by both sides. It was noted that Frank Corker was wounded and a hasty withdrawal was ordered. This withdrawal meant that those enemy soldiers who had previously been engaged with Corker's group could now move down the trench and into the rear of Wilson's party and this forced Wilson to get his men out of the immediate danger and into no-man's-land.

The raiders joined with Strange and his men in a ditch before making their way back to the British lines. It was then realized that Frank Corker, the son of the mayor of Swansea, had not returned and Strange and two others went out to search for him. There was no trace of Corker, although the body of Private William Williams of Morriston was recovered. Williams seemed to have been struck by a machine-gun bullet and killed as he made his way back to the British lines. The following night Strange and Wilson went out again in what proved to be a dangerous but eventually fruitless search for Frank Corker which attracted a great deal of enemy machine-gun fire. Corker's body was never found. His father, by then the ex-mayor of Swansea, had died suddenly some months earlier. For his part in this sad affair John Strange was awarded a Military Cross. The citation read:

> For conspicuous gallantry when reconnoitring the enemy's position prior to a raid, and later commanding the covering party to the raiders. He also displayed great courage when searching for a missing officer under machine-gun fire. Both the men with him were wounded, but he brought them both in after two hours under heavy fire.[2]

The next major event in the experience of the Swansea Battalion on the Western Front took place on 10 July 1916. The British offensive on the Somme had opened with the disaster of the attack on 1 July 1916. Further attacks on other parts of the line had followed, partly carried out at the request of the French, to prevent German troops being transferred to the heavy fighting at Verdun. By 10 July 1916 the Welsh Division (and with it the Swansea Battalion) found itself staring at the dark mass of Mametz Wood, part of the German system of defence on the Somme. A couple of earlier small-scale attacks against the wood had petered out without success and so it was decided that the whole of the Welsh Division would be flung at the wood on the morning of 10 July.

After a tremendous bombardment, the smoke and dust from which hid the wood from the eyes of the attackers, the Welsh infantry advanced towards its objective. With the Germans firing from the fringes of the wood, it proved difficult to gain entry through the torn and tangled undergrowth although this was eventually achieved. The scene inside the wood was one of chaos and confusion, with the dead of both sides being strewn about among the discarded detritus of war.

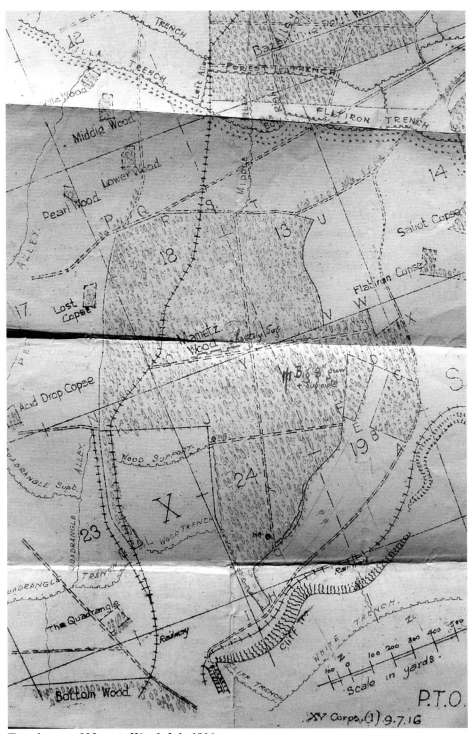

Trench map of Mametz Wood, July 1916. *(Sue and Andy Thorndycraft)*

John Strange was seen in the wood by Private Charles Mew, barking orders at any troops within earshot as he tried to impose order on a chaotic situation. Indeed, when Mew was wounded by an exploding shell it was Strange who emerged through the smoke and dust to bind his wounds and send him out of the wood for treatment. With Swansea Battalion officers being wounded or moved on to other more pressing duties, command of the battalion devolved temporarily onto John Strange. It was while he was still fighting his way through the wood that he was wounded and forced to retire. After three days of hard fighting and a great many casualties, the wood was finally secured.

Strange had actually suffered a shrapnel wound to his right shoulder. It was a light wound with no serious bone or tissue damage and he was treated in France before being sent home on the hospital ship *Western Australia*. He soon rejoined the Swansea Battalion which had since been moved north, to the dreaded Ypres Salient, towards the end of 1916. The battalion had suffered heavily in the attack on Mametz Wood; incurring almost 400 casualties, about 100 of whom were either killed or later died of their wounds.

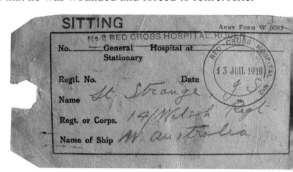

Embarkation tag for John Strange. He came home on the hospital ship *Western Australia* for a brief period of recuperation after being wounded at Mametz Wood. *(Sue and Andy Thorndycraft)*

Though the Swansea Battalion carried out a very successful and large-scale raid on the German trenches in November 1916, it seems that Strange was not a participant. His next significant involvement was with the battalion in the Third Battle of Ypres, which opened on 31 July 1917 and is better known today as the Passchendaele Offensive. By now promoted captain, Strange led 'C' Company of the Swansea Battalion as it crossed the start-line for the attack.

While initially successful, the attack was soon severely hampered by a deluge of rain that transformed the already torn-up battlefield into a quagmire. Nevertheless, John Strange again demonstrated his leadership, as shown by the citation that accompanied his award of the Distinguished Service Order:

> Having led his company with great ability and determination to its final objective, he took over command of the front line, and held it for three days until relieved. He personally reconnoitred his whole front and sent back very valuable information, setting a fine example throughout to all ranks under most trying circumstances.[3]

The Swansea Battalion remained at the front in 1917/18, enduring the danger that was always present in trench warfare. A significant event took place on 10 May 1918 when the 15th Welsh (the Carmarthen Battalion) undertook an attack at Aveluy Wood on the Somme. Due to a ranging error in the British guns, 'friendly' shells began to fall among the attacking infantry of the 15th Welsh, causing casualties and confusion. As the attack broke up in disarray it was John Strange who led a small number of his men forward to try to stabilize the flanks of the advance.

Telegram advising that John Strange is a prisoner of war. *(Sue and Andy Thorndycraft)*

He took six men forward but four of them rapidly became casualties. He sent back his runner to bring up more men and posted a Lewis-gunner in a strong position, while he himself continued to probe for the enemy's positions. He was observed to enter the German positions alone where he found an enemy post that contained five men and he wasted no time in shooting three of them, killing the fourth and overpowering the fifth. He attempted to bring the fifth man back as a prisoner but the German escaped his grasp and set off down a communication trench, pursued by Strange. In the cruel 'kill or be killed' environment of the Western Front, Strange promptly caught and killed his reluctant prisoner.

He then regained his bearings, only to find that he was by now behind the enemy front line. As he moved cautiously forward in an attempt to get back to his own lines, he was confronted by numerous German soldiers, several of whom had their guns pointed at him. Left with little option, he was forced to surrender but only after he had managed to safely dispose of his secret maps and orders.

The capture of John Strange did not mark the end of his wartime activities, however. After an arduous journey he was imprisoned in Graudenz prisoner-of-war camp. In 1918 Graudenz was part of the German Empire and was situated in West Prussia. It was a former army barracks and had been adapted to contain about 600 prisoners of war. It had the usual mix of guards, tall walls and barbed wire to prevent escape.[4]

John Strange, however, was not daunted by the security arrangements at the camp. On the night of 6/7 September 1918 Strange and fifteen other prisoners (Captain Clinton,

Graudenz prisoner-of-war camp.

John Strange (seated, middle row, right) at Graudenz, apparently surrounded by those with whom he escaped (before being recaptured). *(Sue and Andy Thorndycraft)*

six Australians and eight pilots) emerged from the tunnel they had dug under the camp walls and melted away into the surrounding woodland. Unfortunately their success was short-lived and within fifteen days all had been recaptured, Strange being picked up by a dog patrol near the Polish frontier. Fourteen days in solitary confinement was the penalty for his misdemeanour.

Clinton and Strange were determined to try to escape again and on 4 October 1918 Captain Clinton escaped by 'shimmying' on utility wires across the prison walls from the upstairs window of a building. The camp walls were in places traversed by utility wires of varying kinds and Clinton saw the escape potential of grabbing a couple of wires by hand while resting his feet on two others. He would then be able to support his weight across the four cables as he shuffled across the walls to the outside world before making a run for it. By this precarious method Clinton did indeed manage to escape. John Strange, who was poised to follow his lead, had to abort the plan when it became apparent that the astonished camp guards had seen Clinton's escapade and were poised to shoot the next man to attempt it.

With the German army in retreat on all fronts, there was still time for one more escape attempt by John Strange before the war ended. The first part of the plan involved the successful bribing of a guard who was encouraged to look the other way at the opportune moment. This having been agreed (and paid for), Strange and two others somehow secured access to a sturdy plank of wood which was taken into the upper floor of the mess room. The plank was then fed through an open window onto the top of the barbed wire, after which the three men rushed across and jumped to freedom. Strange was shot at and narrowly missed by the soldier guarding the exterior wall of the camp as he made off. Recapture of the three men followed shortly afterwards.

With the ending of the war John Strange was released from Graudenz and in December 1918 returned to Swansea. He had been a brewery manager at the outbreak of war, had enlisted as a private, ended up as a captain and had been awarded a Military Cross and a Distinguished Service Order. He was presented with his medals in 1921 by King George V at Buckingham Palace.[5]

Though born in Neath in 1893, Richard Charles Russell's employment on the railways frequently brought him to Swansea where he reported to the District Manager at Landore, Swansea. He had started work at Neath railway station selling newspapers and later worked in the refreshment rooms. He then moved to work on the buffet car of the Cork express train, which ran between Cardiff and Fishguard. When the war broke out he spent some time regularly travelling to the train stations at Swansea, Cardiff, Pontypool, Hereford and Birmingham simply to assist in feeding troops who were on the move, as well as those being brought back from the front on ambulance trains. He recalled that the latter resulted in him seeing some heartbreaking scenes as the badly-wounded were carefully brought off the trains.

Richard Charles Russell.
(Jean Morgan)

Russell tried to join up several times but for some unknown reason was not accepted. On 12 April 1915 he was handed a white feather, a mark of cowardice, by a stranger at Cardiff railway station: this increased his determination to join up and he finally enlisted into the 1st Battalion, Welsh Guards. This was a new regiment, formed under the authority of a Royal Warrant on 26 February 1915. Russell and the rest of the Welsh Guards sailed for France on 17 August, landing at Le Havre on 18 August 1915. St Omer was reached two days later and the men were then billeted in Arques.[6] Training in both well-established and some new techniques of warfare continued apace with long marches, trench-digging, scouting and instruction in the effective use of barbed wire all being undertaken. Some of the training was performed under war conditions in no-man's-land in the presence of the enemy, with all the risks that that entailed.

The British attacked towards the town of Loos on 25 September 1915, hoping to break through the German line and release its reserves for a further advance. It was hoped that the nearby town of Lens would become untenable for the enemy if the attack on Loos succeeded. Also planned was the first use of poison gas by British forces. The battle raged for two days before the Welsh Guards were committed to the fray. Russell recalled the fighting as being 'hell itself'. The Guards' objective was the recapture of Hill 70, a prominent landmark and a tactically-important position. They marched into the ruined town of Loos, which had been wrested from German control, before attacking towards the hill. Enemy strongpoints that had supposedly been captured were, in fact, still in enemy hands and a storm of machine-gun fire met the attackers as they approached the crest of the hill, forcing them to take cover. The deployment of poison

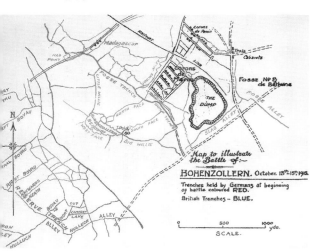

Map of the area around the Hohenzollern Redoubt, 1915.

gas by the British met with only mixed success as the erratic wind blew some of the discharge back onto the British lines. Russell recalled that this was made worse by the fact that his unit did not have any gas masks to hand.

The Welsh Guards eventually got back to the comparative safety of their lines but were soon committed to another attack which was to be made on 13 October 1915. The objective this time was the Hohenzollern Redoubt, a well-defended German position. Although some progress was made, the attack was ultimately unsuccessful. Russell noted that he had actually managed to get close to the German trenches named 'Little Willie' and 'Big Willie', probably so named by the British in a mocking reference to the Kaiser. However, the trenches could not be taken at that time.

By December 1915 Russell found himself back in Britain after having undergone an operation at Merville. While still in France it seems that he had developed what was probably rheumatic fever and he was therefore sent back to England. He rejoined his unit in February 1916 but by December of that year he was a patient at the Guards' Hospital at Caterham, remaining there for about three months, again with rheumatic problems that were affecting his heart. His heart was found to be enlarged and weak in certain places and he was advised not to lift heavy weights, nor to exert himself or experience avoidable excitement; a list of restrictions that obviously made him unsuitable for further active military service. He nevertheless appears to have remained in uniform, probably training new recruits, and he seems to have spent some time on garrison duty at the Tower of London.

He was released from the army in August 1919 and even though a medical board had attributed his health problems to military service, it was decided that as his disablement, which was normally expressed in percentage terms, amounted to 'nil', no pension was payable. He was simply regarded as being fit enough to resume his old line of work. In fact he had been found to be A1 regarding fitness on enlisting in the army and only B3 upon discharge. He duly queried the rationale of the decision and later obtained a small pension from the military.

Despite having being promised his old railway job at the end of the war, this did not actually happen. Instead he spent

Captain H.E. Allen. The Allen family still lives at Cresselly.
(Hugh Harrison-Allen)

a short period as butler-valet to Captain H.E. Allen at the Allen family seat at Cresselly in Pembrokeshire. Captain Allen had served as an officer in the Welsh Guards until being invalided home in May 1917. On 3 August 1915 he had had the honour to kneel before the king to receive the colours on behalf of the Guards. After finishing his role with Captain Allen, Russell finally returned to work on the railways at Port Talbot. He spent the rest of his working life in various posts on the rail network before retiring in 1958. He died in 1971.[7]

Less than one month after the outbreak of war Thomas Loveridge, who later in the war became involved in recruiting at Swansea, attested for military service at Cardiff. He completed the requisite form and declared that he had previously served with the Royal Warwickshire Regiment but had bought himself out. In 1914 he was 32 years of age, a collier and lived at Nelson, Glamorgan with his wife Lily and their two children. He was 5 feet 6 inches tall with a fresh complexion, brown hair and brown eyes. As an 'old soldier' he was already well-acquainted with the ways of the military and, unlike

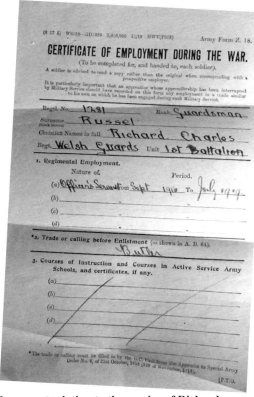

Document relating to the service of Richard Charles Russell. *(Jean Morgan)*

raw recruits, did not need a lot of training. Indeed, he reported to the Royal Warwickshire depot on 5 September 1914, was promoted lance corporal on 9 October and went overseas for active service on 26 October 1914.

The 2nd Royal Warwickshire Battalion had been overseas since 6 October 1914 when it had landed at Zeebrugge. It was part of the 7th Infantry Division, a unit that noted Great War historian Cyril Falls described as 'one of the greatest fighting formations Britain ever put into the field'.[8] It is likely that Thomas Loveridge joined his unit at about the time that the Germans launched a massive assault on Ypres, starting at 5.30 am on 29 October 1914. The Germans left their trenches, advanced towards the British positions and were met with what was known by the British infantry as 'the mad minute': sixty seconds of rapid rifle fire that saw each British soldier fire at least fifteen aimed shots at the enemy.[9] This hail of shot had a devastating effect on the German infantry who, nevertheless, pressed on against many parts of the front line. The 1st Royal Welch Fusiliers, who were positioned close to Thomas Loveridge's battalion, were overrun, losing almost 300 men killed and many more wounded. Despite this and further crises during the day, the line held and a German breakthrough was prevented. The town of Ypres remained in allied hands and did so for the rest of the war.

A series of skirmishes followed over the coming days. On 5 November 1914 Loveridge received a serious injury to his left arm. He was apparently taking part in a charge when he observed an adjacent unit under heavy attack. He managed to make his way to some nearby British machine-gunners who, under his direction, turned their fire on the enemy and removed the danger. A little later in the day he was hit by shrapnel that wounded his arm in three places. By 18 November 1914 he was back in Britain being treated at the Western General Hospital, Manchester and at some point his arm became affected by gangrene. Several unsuccessful operations were performed to try to prevent the spread of the infection to his good flesh before a nurse spotted a scrap of his khaki uniform embedded in his wound. Once that was removed and the affected area cleaned, further infection ceased although he had already lost a good portion of his arm in the earlier surgery. He was clearly unfit for further active service and was discharged to pension on 22 January 1916. Contemporary press reports describe Loveridge as a 'sergeant' and a holder of the Distinguished Conduct Medal.

Thomas Loveridge.
(Christine Clarke)

His service record actually shows that he was returned to the rank of private in July 1915. The reason for this was that Loveridge had been proven to be a bigamist. He had married Isabella Fletcher in 1900 at Southam, Warwickshire but subsequently went through another marriage ceremony with Lilian Wellman in 1909. Although he had apparently separated from Isabella in 1907, he had never formally divorced her. When he enlisted, Lilian, naturally believing she was his wife, assumed she had become eligible for a separation allowance in respect of his being in the army. It seems likely that a family member tipped off Isabella (who was still living in Warwickshire) that Thomas had joined up and she (possibly believing that she was truly due the separation allowance) submitted the second claim that got him into trouble.

Loveridge attended court where he was unrepresented (the prosecuting lawyer

Recruitment form completed by Thomas Loveridge. *(Christine Clarke)*

took the unusual step of saying a few words on his behalf, probably due to his being seen as a war hero). He wore the ribbon of the Distinguished Conduct Medal and his left sleeve hung limply at his side. What remained of his arm was still very painful and required further hospital treatment but despite that he had recently provided valuable service by acting as a focus for the recruiting effort at Swansea. The court was clearly sympathetic to his predicament and bound him over in the sum of £5 for six months; the judge commenting that he had taken

Character reference for Thomas Loveridge. *(Christine Clarke)*

into account his good character (his 'extra' wife stated that she had spent 'the happiest time of her life' when with him) and his service to king and country.

Thomas Loveridge could not be said to have lived a healthy lifestyle in his post-army days. Family members recall him smoking small cigars and, so it is said, 'drinking like a fish'! Despite these habits which are, of course, much frowned upon today, Thomas lived to the ripe old age of 87 years.[10]

Glyn Lloyd was born in

Recruiting badge of Thomas Loveridge. *(Christine Clarke)*

Army Form B. 208.

Authority for Recruiting.

In Virtue of the Authority given to me by the SECRETARY of STATE for WAR, I hereby appoint you Thomas Loveridge of 9th Royal Warwick Regt. to recruit for the Regular Forces, and for the Special Reserve at Swansea District and adjacent thereto. Further, you are hereby directed to show this Authority, and report yourself to the Justices of the said County or place that you may receive the necessary assistance for Attesting and Billeting* any Recruits according to Law; and also to make yourself known to the Station Masters of the different Railways, that all Attested Recruits raised by you may travel at military rates.

Signed

Date

Station

* NOTE.—No unattested Recruit for the Regular Army and no Special Reserve Recruit, unless he is called up for drill, is entitled to be billeted.

Recruiting appointment form for Thomas Loveridge.
(Christine Clarke)

The *Rewa* was used as a troop transport before being converted to a hospital ship.
(Phillip Sillick)

Gorseinon, Swansea in 1897, the oldest of nine children born to Phillip and Selina Lloyd. As an adult he is believed to have worked in the steelworks at Gorseinon and attended the Seion Chapel for holy worship. With the coming of war he joined the 6th Welsh Battalion, which was the Swansea Territorial Force unit. These men were the so-called 'Saturday soldiers' in that they held down a job during the week and performed their soldiering in the evenings and at weekends. Indeed, when war was declared on 4 August 1914 the battalion was at its annual summer camp at Portmadoc where it formed part of the South Wales Infantry Brigade. In the changed circumstances of a declaration of war, it returned home to Swansea where it mounted guard on several nearby towns and industrial facilities. It is very likely that Glyn Lloyd was present at that time, although his detailed service record seems not to have survived.

Initially the 6th Welsh was earmarked for service in India, although those orders were soon changed to 'an unknown destination'. It left Swansea by train on 28 October 1914 after receiving a rousing speech from its commanding officer, Lieutenant Colonel Ninian Crichton-Stuart in which he proclaimed 'I am prepared – as I am sure you all are – to lay down my life for my country if it is required.'[11] He presented each man with a small piece of red, white and green ribbon to wear in battle as an aid to recognition of a friend. The battalion then left Swansea for Southampton where they embarked on the *Rewa*, a steamer of the British India Steam Navigation Company that had been requisitioned by the military for use as a troopship at the commencement of hostilities. (The *Rewa* was again linked to Swansea later in the war when some of its survivors were brought into the town in 1918 after the ship had been torpedoed in the Bristol Channel.) The *Rewa* soon set course for Le Havre where it disembarked the soldiers on 29 October 1914. Glyn Lloyd was among those who landed and was thus a member of only the third territorial unit to go overseas up to that time.

Glyn Lloyd (standing, extreme left) and some pals with gas helmets at the ready. *(Phillip Sillick)*

The battalion soon moved to St Omer where it was used mainly for line of communication duties for several months. During this time members of the battalion formed a guard of honour for the body of Lord Roberts, a hero of the Indian Mutiny, who had died while on a visit to France. The battalion then reassembled at Wizernes before going into the line on 5 July 1915. At the start of October 1915 it was moved to the area of Loos, where a major attack was to be made. When a portion of German trench was wrested from the control of the enemy it fell to the men of the 6th Welsh to dig a communication trench from the British front line to the captured trench. It was during this dangerous work that the battalion commander, Ninian Crichton-Stuart, who was a son of the Marquess of Bute as well as being the Member of Parliament for Cardiff, Cowbridge and Llantrisant, was killed in action.

Precise details of what Glyn Lloyd did at the front are regrettably unknown. It seems that at some point he was subjected to a gas attack near Ypres and his breathing was affected to such a degree that he was subsequently dismissed from the army on medical grounds. He died in 1926 from tuberculosis, the damage caused to his lungs by his wartime experiences obviously not helping matters.

Ninian Crichton-Stuart.
(Simon Peter Lee)

Glyn Lloyd (right) and a pal (possibly Timothy Jones). *(Phillip Sillick)*

Like Glyn Lloyd, a great many men returned from overseas service with injuries that had lasting effects on their health. In Glyn's case, as he died in 1926 he did not even qualify to be officially counted among the war dead, the cut-off point for that being set at 1921 to allow for those who survived the war but later died due to war-related wounds or injuries. Thus he does not appear in the list of those commemorated by the Commonwealth War Graves Commission and similarly his name does not appear on the cenotaph at Swansea. He died aged just 29, a single man. How long he might have lived had he not been injured during his military service is impossible to say.[12]

Hubert Anderson McKay was born in Beaufort, Monmouthshire in 1893. He enjoyed a peripatetic childhood as the family moved to Altoona in America on two occasions

Hubert McKay (left) and an unidentified chum. *(Pam McKay)*

before finally returning to Britain around the turn of the twentieth century. By the time of the 1911 census the family was living at St John's Road in the Manselton area of Swansea. Hubert's father worked as a sewing-machine agent, while his wife Mary ran the home. There were six children of the marriage living with them at that time, two of whom were employed in laundry work and two more were at school, while Donald was a 3-year-old toddler. Hubert was then aged 18 and worked at a local tin works. The household was completed by the presence of a lodger; the room rent no doubt being a useful supplement to the income required to support a large family.

At the outbreak of war Hubert was employed at the Mannesmann Tube Works in Swansea. He joined the army in September 1914 and served with the 12th Battalion Lancashire Fusiliers, seeing service at Salonika where he was wounded in 1916. After recovering from his wounds he was posted in June 1917 to the 2/6th Battalion of the Lancashire Fusiliers which was at that time on the Western Front. From July to early October 1917 the 2/6th Battalion was deployed at Nieuport, close to the Belgian coast. In early October 1917 planning was ongoing for a continuation of the allied offensive that had started on 31 July 1917. In a step-by-step manner the advance was edging slowly forward and a success had been achieved with the Battle of Broodseinde on 4 October 1917. The next target was to be Poelcapelle and it was intended that the 2/6th Lancashire Fusiliers would take part in the attack. An immediate problem was the advent of rain, which commenced on 4 October 1917 and worsened as the date of the planned attack grew closer. Once again the boggy soil of Flanders worked against the attackers as heavy guns sank up to their axles and on occasion even to their muzzles in the waterlogged ground while being hauled forward. Plank roads gave way under the loads put upon them or simply floated away, while the sodden infantry sheltered as best they

Moving an artillery piece in the mud.

could under hastily-provided corrugated iron shelters. Pack animals fought to gain a footing on duck-board tracks even as they were being assembled, any comparatively dry surface being preferable to them than the morass of mud and water in which they found themselves wallowing.[13]

On the early morning of 9 October 1917 the 2/6th Lancashire Fusiliers assembled with the other attacking units behind the villages of Frezenberg and Potijze. They were to move forward to the start line which lay just over 2 miles away, although this was easier said than done in the prevailing weather conditions. A combination of darkness, rain, mud (which sometimes was over a man's knees) and spasmodic German shellfire severely delayed the movement. Despite the best efforts of the sodden infantry, when the first units struggled up to the tapes which marked the start line for the attack, numerous gaps in the ranks were visible as a result of other units still being delayed by the mud.[14]

When the protective barrage began, its effect was much reduced by inaccurate fire from guns which clung precariously to unstable firing platforms and the deadening effect of deep mud on high-explosive shells, many of which simply buried themselves and refused to explode. It had also proved impossible to move some heavy guns forward in the time available, so their much-needed fire was unable to be added to the mix. Despite these problems Hubert McKay's battalion had the advantage of advancing over sandy soil which was much easier to negotiate than the mud that was prevalent elsewhere. Indeed, a small patrol actually entered the battered remains of Passchendaele village and found it deserted. However, events elsewhere on the battlefield decreed that, for the time being at least, the village could not be held and the patrol withdrew. Eventually a line was established and then defended against German counter-attack and shellfire. The advance had edged ever closer to Passchendaele village, even if it had proved impossible to hold for the moment. Once again the fog of war denies us the knowledge of precisely what happened to Hubert McKay but he fell somewhere on the battlefield, probably the victim of a bullet or shellfire. As the local newspaper put it: 'He died for the cause of all and the glory of the regiment.' Like so many of his fallen comrades, Hubert's body was not able to be given a proper burial and he is remembered on the Tyne Cot Memorial.[15]

Not all who served on the front lines in the war on land were soldiers, of course. Indeed, not all of them were men. At the time of the 1911 census Elizabeth Clement was living at the Cooper's Arms public house in Landore, Swansea with her family. Her father, William Clement, was the landlord. Also living at the property were his wife, Hannah, and the other children of the marriage: Mary Ann, Selina and Esther. William's widowed sister, Margaret Mayers, also shared the family home.

By the beginning of 1914 Elizabeth was the head nurse at the Llanelli Workhouse, a role she held until just after the outbreak of war in August 1914. Although the reasons are unclear – it might have been simple patriotism – it seems that Elizabeth was driven to offer her nursing skills in the service of her country at a time of war. By early September 1915 not only had she offered those services but she was actually on a ship in harbour at Malta and transferring to the SS *Mossoul* for the onward voyage to Salonika. She was a member of a French Red Cross team of doctors and nurses, sent to help the Serbian army wounded.

Memorial to the men of the Mannesmann Works at Swansea. *(Pam McKay)*

It was the Austro-Hungarian Empire that had identified what it saw as Serbian influence in the assassination of the Archduke Franz Ferdinand in Sarajevo on 28 June 1914. Despite the terms of a draconian and insulting ultimatum being largely accepted by the Serbs, the Austro-Hungarians had nevertheless decided that only military action could at least partly avenge the wrong they had suffered. Once that decision was taken, the interlocking alliances that tied the various countries of Europe into requirements of mutual support were activated. There seemed to be no-one with the statesmanlike qualities required to prevent the slide into war and, as Austro-Hungarian artillery shells fell on Serbian soil, one by one the other nations of Europe had duly taken their allotted places on the path to war.

Serbia was a poor country with an underdeveloped infrastructure and a shortage or even absence of the most basic services. Medical aid for the treating of wounded soldiers was an obvious area of need and the French Red Cross, among others, stepped in to try to fill the gap. The Austro-Hungarian armies had invaded Serbia on 12 August 1914 but surprisingly the Serbs had proved to be stronger than anticipated and by 24 August the only enemy troops still on Serbian soil were either dead or prisoners of war. Matters were not to end there, however. Both sides planned for further offensive action and it was the Serbs who struck first, attacking at Syrmia on 6 September 1914 before the Austro-Hungarians responded with their own attack on the following day. With these developments Nurse Clement and her comrades were soon to enter an active and therefore very dangerous war zone.

Leaving Malta at the end of September 1915, Nurse Clement had an early inkling of what was to come. Early in the voyage several bodies were sighted in the water, the victims of a submarine attack on a steamer a few days earlier. After a brief stop at the port of Piraeus, lifebelts were distributed to the passengers and the

Serbian army units on the retreat.

lifeboats were readied for any eventuality. The risk of attack was increasing daily. Salonika was soon reached, however, and disembarkation followed before a train was taken to the town of Nish.

At Nish there was an early indication of the risks that the medical team was running. An enemy aeroplane passed overhead and dropped several bombs on the medical building, a shed converted to hospital use in which Nurse Clement and her party were resting. Although the medical team escaped unscathed, nine Austrian prisoners were killed in the explosions. Nurse Clement was then moved to the village of Maladnavitz where another bomb attack took place. A move to Valyevo soon followed and at nearby Valion a camp hospital had been set up.

As it turned out, a great many of the early medical cases were suffering from typhus, although those numbers were swollen by the periodic arrival of wounded men from the front lines. By 10 October 1915 rumours that the fighting was not progressing in Serbia's

Elizabeth Clement, some nursing colleagues and a group of soldiers on Christmas morning, 1915. *(Alan Penhaligan)*

favour were commonplace and orders were issued that all medical staff should be ready to leave at short notice. A senior member of the medical team sternly told the doctors and nurses to remember that they were British and to behave as such in the current difficult and trying circumstances. It was noted that the sound of gunfire was getting ever closer. Conditions at the temporary hospital were primitive, as Nurse Clement recalled:

> The sights were horrible. Some of the poor fellows' faces were almost blown off, and some had no legs and arms, and were dying. The awful part of it was there was no provision for the poor fellows. There were no beds, and no food but bread, and that of poor quality.[16]

Between 11 and 17 October 1915 Nurse Clement still tended to the wounded while awaiting news of a possible evacuation to a safer place. On 18 October the move finally came and a train was boarded to transport the group further away from the fighting. Part of the move involved sleeping on railway station waiting-room floors and sharing a cattle truck with Austrian prisoners. Medical work for Nurse Clement resumed on 22 October when she was effectively commandeered to provide trained assistance to some French doctors. Hospital conditions were still inadequate, however; when a new batch of wounded arrived there were simply no spare beds to put them in. At this time she also extracted a bullet from a Serbian soldier and kept it as a souvenir.

Towards the end of October 1915 it proved necessary to once again change location in order to keep ahead of the advancing enemy. The nursing and medical party, which numbered about forty, again slept on the floor of a station waiting-room and later passed huge piles of war matériel, a sign of the growing efforts of the allied powers in the area. Prince Alexis Karageorgevitch, who had been excluded from the line of succession of the Serbian royal family, allowed the party to stay for a while at his villa. He was president of the Serbian Red Cross and had returned from exile to support the Serbian war effort.[17]

Close-up of Elizabeth Clement. *(Alan Penhaligan)*

By 30 October 1915 it seems to have been reluctantly accepted that the deteriorating military situation meant that getting home was becoming more important than providing unavoidably inadequate care to the wounded, with the risk of capture an ever-increasing threat. On the following day the nurses had to abandon all their belongings except what could be contained in their handbags. On 3 November the promise of a start on the long journey home proved to be illusory: there was no train and also no food or drink for a period of almost twenty-four hours. With the enemy guns growing louder by the hour Nurse Clement was, somewhat surprisingly, nevertheless placed on duty at a new hospital. She stated that this was at 'Athena', although this location has proved impossible to place on a modern-day map of the area.

When reporting for duty on 10 November, Nurse Clement heard with disbelief the news that she and her comrades were effectively prisoners of the Austrians. Her disbelief vanished when she observed some very tired-looking Austrian soldiers on

Prince Alexis Karageorgevitch.

duty outside her building with their bayonets fixed. The commanding officer of those men stated that the doctors and nurses were now to regard themselves as prisoners of war. The following days saw masses of enemy soldiers enter the town, some of whom simply passed through in pursuit of their enemy while others made themselves comfortable in the villa previously used by Nurse Clement and her colleagues. The nursing of wounded Austro-Hungarian soldiers, rather than Serbs, became common practice.

In the days that followed food became scarce, the weather deteriorated and it became very cold with snowstorms. The hospital was soon commandeered for the use of enemy troops and the nurses had to move yet again, by foot and by train, to Krushevatz. Here they were allowed to dine in the German officers' mess (though only on whatever food had been left by the officers), an unexpected kindness which was received with gratitude. The bare floor once again acted as a bed, with sleep being broken by the constant passage of soldiers through the room.

Orders were then received on 3 December to the effect that all prisoners were to be transported to Hungary. Moving by lorry and train, the only available food for a while was bread and cheese. If a transfer to cattle trucks seemed to be a move down the scale in terms of comfort, at least it was accompanied by some rice and water, served as a kind of slushy soup. An internment camp at Semendaria was then utilized as a waiting-place until a boat ferried the group across the River Danube and into Hungary. Wooden huts were then available for shelter but there was still little or no food. This was followed by a 3-mile walk on 6 December in very trying conditions before a house was used as a makeshift prison, with armed guards at the door. Soup, bread and coffee made up the irregular and inadequate menu at that time.

Life became a monotonous mix of confinement and poor food up until Christmas Day. At that point members of a holy order managed to provide the medical team with some biscuits but this was the only addition to the menu (of coffee and bread) on what should have been a special day. Divine service was attended by the nursing staff as well as a number of German officers, many of whom seemed to be inebriated and the officers' attempts to enter the ladies' quarters were repulsed. Some minor but enjoyable celebrations of Christmas Day took place in the privacy of the captives' quarters late at night and the national anthem was sung, albeit in hushed tones lest the enemy guards should take offence.

As 1916 dawned, the nursing group suffered several more weeks of waiting and wondering what would be their fate. Burns' Night (25 January) was celebrated before news finally came that they were to be moved once again and then formally handed over to the Hungarians. A journey to Keschemet followed where the transfer duly took place. The group was jeered by the local populace as it made its way to a hospital of a most obnoxious standard where they were detained for a night. A medical examination and interrogation at Pollitze followed, when

... Serbien muss sterbie

Austrian propaganda cartoon stating that 'Serbia Must Die!'

personal details regarding next of kin were also recorded. By 6 February 1916 Budapest was reached and it became clear that, as it seemed they were more of a problem than an asset to their captors, they would soon be released. This was accomplished by a route that took in Vienna before neutral Switzerland (where welcoming flowers were received instead of insults) was entered and then, as Nurse Clement put it, 'Now – England, home and beauty.'[18] After her return, Nurse Clement ventured abroad once more and lived for a while in Ceylon (modern-day Sri Lanka) before returning to Swansea.

A Swansea General Hospital doctor who was called up for medical service was Hamilton Ernest Quick. Quick had been born in Sydney, Australia in 1882 and was the son of Charles H. Quick, the works manager of the Anglo-French Nickel Company. At the age of only 18 months, Quick was brought to Britain where he spent the rest of his life. He was educated at the Swansea Grammar School and at the Royal College of Science, South Kensington where he graduated with a BSc in 1902. His medical training commenced at St Bartholomew's Hospital in London where he gained MB BS in 1906. He became a Fellow of the Royal College of Surgeons in 1909.

After holding positions in London and Southampton, Quick moved back to Swansea where he was appointed to the post of ophthalmic surgeon at the Swansea General and Eye Hospital. His work there was interrupted by the declaration of war in 1914. He had, in fact, applied for a commission as a lieutenant in the 3rd Welsh Field Ambulance in 1911 and would have played a part in what was the Territorial Force, the forerunner of the modern Territorial Army, which trained in peacetime and could be called upon in times of national emergency. When war was declared members of the Territorial Force could not be compelled to serve overseas although many men, including Hamilton Ernest Quick, did opt to do so.

The 3rd Welsh Field Ambulance formed part of the 53rd (Welsh) Division which was an amalgamation of numerous other Territorial Force units including twelve infantry battalions and contingents of engineers and signallers, to name but a few. The division initially remained in Britain, a possible deployment to India being cancelled in November 1914. In early July 1915 it was told to prepare for service in the Mediterranean and later in that month it sailed east via Alexandria and Lemnos. The 3rd Welsh Field Ambulance consisted of just over 200 men, with 10 horses and 24 vehicles. In early August the local press published a letter sent by Lieutenant Quick to his parents, written while he was still aboard ship:

> The weather is very hot from 9 a.m. to 4 p.m. and we are having a good time. You would laugh at our convict-like appearance just now, for we have nearly all had our hair cut short with the clippers all over the head, and the khaki rather heightens the effect but is much cooler and comfortable than the ordinary equipment.[19]

H.E. Quick at his wedding to Ruth Hellins. *(Heather Thomas)*

Quick added that schools of porpoises were often seen, the food was good and there was an onboard concert every night. All the men were 'in excellent spirits and delighted with the voyage'. Matters were about to change dramatically for the worse, however, as the convoy approached Suvla Bay, Gallipoli.

Gallipoli was a part of the Ottoman Empire. Shortly before the outbreak of war, the Ottoman Empire had signed a secret accord with Germany as a means of gaining support in the event of any problems with Russia that might affect Turkish interests. When, after war was declared on Germany, Britain commandeered two warships that were being built in British ports for the Ottoman navy, the Germans responded by despatching two similar ships to Turkey as replacements in an effort to improve their own standing with the Ottomans. With the British in pursuit of the German vessels, the Ottomans heightened tensions by granting the German warships passage through the neutral Dardanelles Strait to Constantinople, despite international law deeming such an act illegal. Command of the Ottoman navy was then given to a German naval officer and the strait was soon closed to shipping. The former German warships were renamed for use in the Turkish navy and, in a sortie into the Black Sea, they bombarded Odessa and sank several Russian ships. Russia declared war on Turkey in November 1914 and Britain, as an ally of Russia, did so soon afterwards, bombarding some Dardanelles forts for good measure and killing almost ninety Turkish soldiers.

The blockading and subsequent mining of the strait by the Ottomans made the shipping of supplies to Russia from Britain by that route impossible. Winston Churchill, as First Lord of the Admiralty, thought that a forcing and holding of the strait might not only help the Russian supply situation but also encourage Greece and Bulgaria to enter the war on the allied side. An appeal to Britain for assistance from Grand Duke Nicholas of Russia for a diversionary attack on the Turks, who were attacking Russia in the Caucasus, added weight to the idea. Churchill eventually persuaded the Cabinet to approve a plan for action in the Dardanelles.

When a primarily naval force with a small infantry contingent failed to force the strait due to Turkish gunfire and shipping losses due to mines, it was decided to commit larger ground forces to the endeavour. The force that stormed ashore at several locations on 25 April 1915 included French, Australian and New Zealand units as well as fusiliers from Lancashire, Dublin and Munster, among others. The troops found that the Turks, capably advised by their German officers, had placed their men in strong defensive positions and a withering fire was unleashed on the attacking troops. Of the first 200 men who came ashore from the troop-carrying SS *River Clyde*, only 21

In the trenches at Gallipoli.

reached the beach. Other units suffered similar rates of attrition and, although a foothold was established on each of the beaches attacked, the expected gains did not fully materialize. Months of stalemate followed, with neither side able to totally defeat the other, while the casualty lists grew ever longer.

In early August 1915 an attempt was made to force a decision by making landings at Suvla Bay. The 53rd (Welsh) Division began landing there on the night of 8/9 August 1915, a few days after the initial attack had gone in; an attack that had yet again been stalled by the tenacious actions of the Turkish defenders and the tough terrain. One battalion commander of the 53rd found that he had got his men ashore but had no idea of the exact location of the enemy or even the position of the friendly troops on his flanks with whom he was required to make contact. He decided to simply get his men inland and accordingly got them moving forward. They soon came under heavy rifle-fire; so much so that ground had to be made in a series of short rushes in order to minimize the risk of being shot. To make matters worse, the officer in question was then wounded by a shell-burst.[20]

It was into this maelstrom of activity, confusion and danger that Hamilton Ernest Quick found himself thrown. Although there seem to be no surviving records of his work ashore, there is no doubt that in such a bloody campaign he would have been

W Beach at Cape Helles, Gallipoli just before the final evacuation. A Turkish shell has exploded in the water in the background.

V Beach at Cape Helles, Gallipoli. Men, animals and matériel of all kinds crowd into the tenuous bridgehead.

extremely busy dealing with the numerous casualties, both of enemy action and disease, and with the front line never very far away, also under a not inconsiderable risk of injury himself. Matters were made worse by the rudimentary sanitary arrangements leading to frequent outbreaks of disease. As the months of 1915 dragged on with little progress, the climate, usually baking hot, began to change with the seasons so that gales, blizzards and driving rain added to the woes of the soldiers. A great many frostbite cases were recorded and had to be dealt with by the hard-pressed medical teams. By December 1915 London had had enough of the struggle and an evacuation commenced, ending in early January 1916. Ironically, it was the most successful part of a hard-fought but poorly-planned campaign. The British alone had lost over 21,000 killed and 52,000 wounded.[21]

Hamilton Ernest Quick had been promoted captain (Royal Army Medical Corps) and mentioned in despatches for his efforts at Suvla Bay. In 1916/17 the 53rd (Welsh) Division returned to the front in Palestine, although it seems that Quick was not with it, having been invalided home, possibly with typhoid. In 1917 he seems to have been working in North Wales, probably at a military hospital. Had he left any wartime memoirs they would have provided an enlightening but alarming read. Post-war, Quick returned to the Swansea General and Eye Hospital and perhaps somewhat oddly, being an eye surgeon, helped set up a venereal disease clinic. He continued to work at the hospital until his retirement in 1947. He had been secretary of the local branch of the British Medical Association and was a past president of the Royal Institution of South

Wales (based at Swansea Museum). Apart from his medical career, Quick had a great interest in conchology (the study of mollusc shells) and malacology (the study of molluscs as whole organisms). He developed a worldwide reputation in these fields and published numerous papers on the subjects.[22]

Wilfred John Victor Hancock had known Ceinwen Irene Jones since they were children, both living in the Plasmarl area of Swansea. In 1918 Wilfred was serving in the South Wales Borderers where he held the rank of corporal. Although the date of his arrival on the Western Front is not clear, he had returned home to Swansea in 1918 to recover from wounds received in action. Upon recovery he was destined to be sent back to the front for further active service with all the risks that that involved. It seems that this knowledge had cemented his feelings for Ceinwen, as on 3 October 1918 they were married at the Mount Pleasant Baptist Chapel, Swansea. Wilfred was 24 and his bride was 21. A short honeymoon in London followed before the happy couple returned to Swansea.

Hamilton Ernest Quick in later life.
(Heather Thomas)

Wilfred duly returned to the front in October 1918, while Ceinwen continued to live close to her family in Plasmarl and pursue her occupation of dressmaker and tailoress. She soon developed a heavy cold that promptly developed into a bout of influenza. This was at the time of the worldwide influenza epidemic of 1918, of course, and to contract such an illness could have life-threatening consequences. Wilfred, meanwhile, had reported sick to his unit medical officer in France on 16 October 1918, also suffering from what appeared to be influenza. On 21 October 1918 Wilfred was admitted to the 49th Casualty Clearing Station at Grevillers, France for urgent treatment.

Ceinwen was still confined to her sickbed when her sister Hilda brought her a communication from the military authorities informing her that Wilfred had, sadly, died while at the casualty clearing station. They had been married for just eighteen days. Shortly after this devastating news came a letter from Sister Dunn, the nurse who had attended Wilfred during his final hours. Sister Dunn wrote:

> I don't know how to begin this letter to you or what method I must use to break to you the news I must send you.
>
> Your husband, Corpl. Hancock, was received into this Hospital last night, or should I say early this morning, SICK. He appeared very ill indeed and had immediate attention, but grew rapidly worse and when I saw him at 8 o'clock, he was dying. He told me that he had only been ill since the 16th inst when he reported to his MO [Medical Officer] and was relieved duty. He complained of the usual symptoms of a heavy cold or influenza, and said that he was now almost allright [sic]. Of

Wilfred J.V. Hancock and Ceinwen Irene Jones at their wedding.
(Val and Ken Waite)

course I knew he was not; he was then sinking rapidly...

He was at this time lying on his side apparently not the least distressed, only by his appearance and pulse could one tell that he was passing away. He lingered on like this until half past ten when he just stopped breathing, absolutely without any effort.

I am sending you a lock of his hair, which is the only thing I can send you: his personal belongings will be sent home by the authorities.

Ceinwen Irene Jones.
(Val and Ken Waite)

Wilfred was buried in the Grevillers British Cemetery, France. Ceinwen never remarried, throwing herself into her work and travelling extensively by the standards of the time, even making one passage to America on a cargo boat.

Wilfred had become yet another victim of the 1918–19 influenza pandemic, sometimes referred to as 'Spanish flu', which is estimated to have killed well over 20,000,000 people, more than were killed during the four years of the Great War. Ironically, he had survived the dangers of the Western Front only to succumb to what was normally an everyday illness of no great consequence. It seems that Ceinwen, by contrast, had had a very lucky escape; displaying some of the symptoms of the disease but then making a full recovery.[23] Many others in Swansea were not so lucky, as described elsewhere in this work.

Notes

1. Bernard Lewis, *Swansea Pals.*
2. *London Gazette*, 27 July 1916.
3. *London Gazette*, 9 January 1918.
4. Ann Warin, *Dear Girl, I Escaped: Experiences of the Great War, 1914–1918.*
5. Information provided by Sue and Andy Thorndycraft.
6. Cuthbert Headlam, DSO, *History of the Guards Division in the Great War*, pp.31–2.
7. Information provided by Jean Morgan.
8. The Long, Long Trail.www.1914–1918.net
9. Basil Liddell Hart, *History of the First World War*, p.166.
10. Information provided by Christine Clarke.
11. *Cambrian*, 30 October 1914.
12. Information provided by Phillip Sillick.
13. Edmonds, *Official History*, pp.328–9.
14. Ibid., pp.330–31.
15. *South Wales Daily Post*, 18 October 1918; information provided by Pam McKay.
16. *Cambrian*, 18 February 1916.
17. Wikipedia entry for Prince Alexis Karageorgevitch.
18. *Cambrian*, 18 and 25 February 1916; information provided by Alan Penhaligan.
19. *Cambrian*, 6 August 1915.
20. C.H. Dudley-Ward, DSO, MC, *History of the 53rd (Welsh) Division, 1914–1918*, pp.33–4.
21. L.A. Carlyon, *Gallipoli,* p.645.
22. Information provided by Heather Thomas.
23. Information provided by Val and Ken Waite.

Chapter Nine (b)

The War at Sea

On 4 August 1914 at 11 pm the Admiralty in London sent a signal to all ships of the British navy, at that time the most powerful fleet in the world. The message was simple and stark. It read: 'Commence hostilities against Germany.'

If, over time, the main theatre of war developed into a stalemate on the Western Front, the war at sea still gave the Germans some hope of victory. While it was true that the German High Seas Fleet was well-armed and crewed, the plain fact was that the enormous size of the Royal Navy meant a German victory in the surface war was essentially out of the question. Ultimately, irrespective of skill and bravery, the British would win by simply having far more ships than their enemy and in a war of naval attrition there could only be one winner. Indeed, the German High Seas Fleet spent much of the war anchored safely in port, only occasionally sallying forth to try to tempt out, then isolate and destroy a small part of the British Grand Fleet. The German fleet hoped that several successful small-scale skirmishes might allow it to whittle away at the British force and eventually tilt the overall numerical superiority a little more their way.

However, by way of contrast, the undersea war waged by the German U-boat force offered up a real chance of success. The U-boats were a constant worry to the British naval and commercial fleets, regularly sinking shipping by torpedo or gun attack and laying deadly mines in busy waters. Germany hoped that by strangling Britain's trade routes, it could at least force its enemy to the negotiating table where it would have a strong hand to play based on the effectiveness of the U-boat fleet. Indeed, by 1917 allied shipping losses had reached critical proportions and it was only then that the principle of the convoy system was finally introduced by the allies with remarkable success.

In more traditional naval warfare it had been customary for naval craft to intercept

The U-boat threat was very real. German U-boat *U-14* is pictured in harbour. It was sunk by gunfire from an armed trawler in 1915.

**MEN OF BRITAIN!
WILL YOU STAND THIS?**

Nº 2 Wykeham Street, SCARBOROUGH after the German bombardment on Decr 16th. It was the Home of a Working Man. Four People were Killed in this House including the Wife aged 58, and Two Children, the youngest aged 5.

78 Women & Children were killed and 228 Women & Children were wounded by the German Raiders

ENLIST NOW

Poster issued after the German bombardment of Scarborough to encourage recruitment.

the unarmed merchantmen of its enemy and also those of neutral nations where it was suspected the cargo might be intended for enemy use. Ships would be stopped, cargoes examined and, in some cases, prize crews put aboard and the ship escorted back to the captor's port. Submarine warfare drastically changed that situation. It was very difficult for a submarine to stop a fast-moving vessel without opening fire and, even if a ship was stopped, it was then not usually possible to provide a prize crew from the small contingent of men aboard a submarine. In most cases the only option was to sink the vessel, ideally having first humanely evacuated the crew, which in itself posed problems of potential overcrowding if those captured were to be taken into the cramped confines of a submarine. The harsh answer was for the submarine commander to set aside the niceties of civilized behaviour (tempered by the fact that a brutal war was being fought) and simply sink the ship with or without warning. A warning at least gave crews the chance to take to the lifeboats and risk the perils of the open sea, while an unannounced attack greatly increased the danger of loss of life.[1] The Germans soon moved from 'restricted' submarine warfare (where a warning was given) to 'unrestricted' warfare (where it typically was not), although this practice was suspended in 1915 following American pressure after the sinking of the large ocean liner, the RMS *Lusitania*. On occasion it was very much down to the nature of individual U-boat captains as to which path they chose to follow. Unrestricted submarine warfare was, in any event, reintroduced by the Germans in 1917.

From an early stage of the war the former Swansea fishing trawlers, now under the control of the navy, attempted to clear the sea lanes of enemy mines; a difficult and dangerous task, especially when the slow-moving trawlers themselves became U-boat targets. An early loss was that of the *Harfat Castle*, a trawler of 274 tons that had been built at Middlesbrough in 1915 and then operated by Castle Steam Trawlers Ltd at Swansea. That boat was actually stopped by a U-boat 90 miles from Fastnet, the crew evacuated and the trawler scuttled. The *Benton Castle* hit a mine off Dartmouth and sank with the loss of ten lives, while the *Picton Castle* suffered a similar fate with twelve lives lost. The *Ruthin Castle* and *Carew Castle* also became victims of the very mines they were deployed to deal with. In the latter two cases the loss of life was nine and three respectively.

Other Swansea-based ships were lost in addition to those from the trawler fleet. Several ships went to the bottom bearing names that harked back to the town of Swansea. Among these were the *Ilston* (sunk 1915), the *Caswell* (scuttled 1916) and the

Bishopston (sunk 1917). The *Batoum* was a 4,000-ton oil tanker that was worked out of Swansea by Associated Oil Carriers Ltd (J.I. Jacobs and Company). In July 1915 it was damaged by a U-boat but her captain managed to beach her prior to her eventual refloating and repair. The incident cost six lives, however. The *Batoum* was an unlucky ship as she had a second encounter with a U-boat almost two years later. On that occasion she was sunk off Fastnet, although only one life was lost.

The protection of the port of Swansea and its maritime traffic in the nearby shipping lanes was another concern; this was initially addressed by the stationing at Swansea of a mish-mash of ships that formed an auxiliary force protecting shipping at Swansea for the duration of the war. The auxiliary force consisted, at varying times, of a number of 'drifters, trawlers, motor-launches, paddle-steamers, and other vessels'.

The Swansea Auxiliary Patrol Depot started off by using the armed yacht *Ombra* as its 'nominal vessel'. A nominal vessel was essentially used as the base at a particular port from which naval officers and ratings could operate. In many cases they would actually serve their time on other vessels, using the nominal vessel and its crew as a depot for pay and administrative purposes. The *Ombra* was soon needed elsewhere and was replaced at Swansea by the armed trawler *Longset*. This vessel did not last too long at Swansea either, being lost to enemy action in February 1917. One of its crew members was Edmund

The merchant seamen memorial at Swansea.
(Author)

William Bullock, an engineman and Royal Naval Reservist who was 39 years of age and lived at Kilvey Terrace, Swansea. The *Longset* had struck a German mine off Nell's Point, Barry Island; the mine probably laid sometime earlier by an enemy submarine. Bullock and seven of his shipmates did not survive the sinking. The *Longset* was duly replaced at Swansea by another trawler named *Shikari* that was later renamed the *Shikari II* after the navy, rather thoughtlessly, decided to name a new destroyer *Shikari*. This forced the name change, as a destroyer was regarded as senior to a trawler and thus had first call on the name.

The patrol vessels were on almost constant duty, patrolling the Bristol Channel and the approaches to Swansea in an attempt to detect and deter the activities of enemy submarines. The spotting and destruction of mines was another of the hazardous tasks undertaken in all sorts of weather. Reports concerning possible enemy activity had to be investigated and ships provided with escorts, at least for the start or end of their journey to or from Swansea. Other work included the rescue of crews from vessels that had been lost due to enemy action or accident, as well as the picking up of air-crews that had ditched in the sea. The remnants of the Swansea trawler fleet were also afforded some protection from the U-boat menace by the patrol as they went about their business, although several of them were lost due to mines or submarine activity. In a single week over 171 tons of fish were safely brought ashore by slow-moving Belgian trawlers that had made Swansea their temporary home; ample testimony to the general effectiveness of the patrol arrangements.

In the early part of the war about twenty-five large vessels were entering the harbour at Swansea every week and as well as offering some protection to those visitors, it

An armed motor-launch of a type that may have patrolled out of Swansea. *(David Davies)*

was also the task of the patrol to examine incoming vessels to detect any contraband cargo of possible use to an enemy that might be stored on neutral ships. It was estimated that only about 1 per cent of the ships departing Swansea were lost to enemy action but given the volume of ships using the port, this still added up to a considerable number. It also did not prove possible to prevent the enemy callously sinking the hospital ships *Rewa* and *Glenart Castle* in the Bristol Channel in February 1918. On the plus side, when the *William Middleton*, a military transport ship, came under attack the patrol was able to drive the enemy away without any losses. Other duties were of a less dramatic nature. When a large gorse fire broke out on Lundy Island, members of the Auxiliary Patrol landed and put it out, lest its fierce light illuminated the surrounding waters to the benefit of the enemy.

The patrol learned as it went along and was not set into a rigid pattern of patrol and other duties. Indeed, a seemingly erratic approach to the timing and direction of patrols made it more difficult for the enemy to anticipate things. When in 1917 the British submarine *C6* was in the area, the opportunity was taken to perform practical submarine detection and harassment without the risk of being hit by a torpedo, always assuming an enemy submarine did not take the chance to join in the fun. This certainly helped the patrol to fine-tune its techniques in light of real experience. Changes were also made to the manner in which sweeping was carried out in June 1918, after six American navy submarine-chasers were temporarily allocated to the area. Gunnery practice was performed time after time to ensure accuracy, while the use of the new hydrophone in submarine detection was also practised.[2]

The patrol members appear to have made a very good impression on the people of Swansea, with one Corporation official recalling:

> The Naval Officers responsible successively for all the varied activities...will always be remembered in Swansea and it is due as much to their vigilance as to the fine loyalty of the officers and men under them that the enemy's efforts were in so large a measure robbed of success.

No doubt that sentiment was echoed by a large element of the Swansea population who plied their trade or had family members who did so in the potentially dangerous waters around wartime Swansea.

At the start of the war the manpower of the British navy had been rapidly augmented by the calling-up of reservists. One of those reservists was Daniel James Taylor, a Swansea man who had previously seen action while serving aboard HMS *Goliath* during the Boxer Rebellion of 1900 in China. Taylor had been born in 1883 and was the son of

James and Mary Taylor of Well Cottage, Llangennith. He was a modest 5 feet 5 inches in height with brown hair and blue eyes, had a scar on his forehead and a fresh complexion. His naval career had commenced in 1898 with HMS *Impregnable*, a training establishment, with further training being undertaken aboard HMS *Lion* and HMS *Black Prince*. He also served on HMS *Cambridge* which was a gunnery-training ship based at Plymouth, as well as HMS *Vernon*, a torpedo-training ship, and several other vessels. It seems the only 'real' action that he had seen in a war situation was that aboard HMS *Goliath* off China during the period 18 June to mid-August 1900. He left the navy in April 1905 at the age of 22 and became a member of the Royal Fleet Reserve, which meant that he would undergo an annual week of training at sea and be liable to recall in an emergency until he reached 55 years of age.

In 1914 he was living in Reynoldston on the Gower Peninsula and was employed as a postman. He was indeed recalled to the navy upon the outbreak of war and posted to HMS *Good Hope*, a *Drake*-class armoured cruiser that had been built at Glasgow in 1902. By 1914 her design was already showing its age and had, in fact, been surpassed in speed and strength by more recent additions to the fleets of several nations.

It was, nevertheless, still an imposing ship. HMS *Good Hope* displaced just over 14,000 tons and was over 500 feet long with a crew of around 800 men. She was lacking in firepower, however, having only two 9.2-inch guns as her main armament, as well as sixteen 6-inch guns, half of which were deployed behind casement doors that were so close to the waterline that, in a heavy sea, the guns risked being swamped and the gunners drenched. These guns were essentially unusable in such conditions. If the basic design of the *Good Hope* left much to be desired, matters were not helped by the fact that about 90 per cent of her hastily-mustered crew consisted of naval reservists such as Dan Taylor with much of the remaining 10 per cent being new recruits. Hard-nosed and relevant naval experience was, therefore, in very short supply on board the *Good Hope*;

HMS *Good Hope*.

a potentially disastrous failing in time of war.

In September 1914 HMS *Good Hope* became the flagship of Admiral Sir Christopher Cradock's newly-formed South American squadron. The role of this squadron was to patrol down the coast of South America and prevent German ships from attacking allied shipping on the trade routes of the South Atlantic. As well as HMS *Good Hope* (which had the recalled Dan Taylor aboard from 13 July 1914), Cradock could call on the services of HMS *Monmouth*, a County-class armoured cruiser that was fitted with fourteen 6-inch guns, many of which were close to the waterline and thus prone to similar problems that beset some of the guns on HMS *Good Hope*. Even worse, HMS *Monmouth* had been on the point of being scrapped, with her best days behind her, when the commencement of hostilities earned her a hasty reprieve. It was said that she was crewed by a mix of 'naval reservists, coast guardsmen, boy seamen and naval cadets'; a willing group, no doubt, but not one that would be the equal of a well-trained German crew on a modern ship in a wartime action at sea.[3] The state of *Monmouth*'s engines was also a cause for great concern, although notwithstanding these problems, she duly took up her post and awaited events in the harsh waters of the South Atlantic.

Cradock also had available the armed merchantman *Otranto*, a converted former cruise liner of the Orient Lines Company, now armed with six 4.7-inch guns. Given its inherent weaknesses, having been designed for comfort rather than naval warfare, this ship was intended only for dealing with similarly-armed merchantmen of the German forces. In any unforeseen action with a German warship there could only be one outcome and that would not be favourable to the *Otranto*. The final component of Cradock's command was the light cruiser *Glasgow*, a ship of almost 5,000 tons with an armament of two 6-inch guns, ten 4-inch guns and a well-trained crew of regular sailors under a good captain.

Cradock knew that his main task was to find and sink the German light cruiser *Dresden*. This was a ship of just over 3,000 tons and ten 4.1-inch guns. It also sported two torpedo tubes. When war commenced the *Dresden* was in the western Atlantic and waiting to be relieved from her duties by the larger and better-armed *Karlsruhe*. This simple and routine relief operation was swiftly forgotten on the coming of war and both ships were ordered by the German naval command to remain on station and attack British shipping as the opportunity arose.

Even allowing for the *Karlsruhe* now joining forces with the *Dresden*, Cradock's task was about to become much harder. This was because the German Vice Admiral Maximilian Reichsgraf von Spee was travelling across the Pacific Ocean with the armoured cruiser *Scharnhorst* as his flagship and the *Gneisenau*, another armoured cruiser, in support. Although he was desirous of getting his ships safely back to Germany, von Spee realized that the chances of doing so successfully were slim, given the distance involved and the likely British opposition he might meet along the way. He decided to attack allied trade routes along the western coast of South America and in the South Atlantic. In

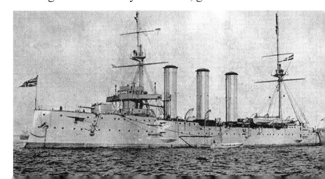

HMS *Monmouth*.

order to concentrate his forces, von Spee arranged a rendezvous at Easter Island with two additional ships, the *Nurnberg* and the *Leipzig*, while the *Dresden* rounded Cape Horn in order to keep the appointment. He now had five ships with which to attack the shipping lanes or confront any British forces in the area.

When Admiral Cradock heard that as well as the *Dresden*, he might need to deal with ships of the calibre of the *Scharnhorst* and *Gneisenau*, he wired the Admiralty in London for reinforcements. A confusing and occasionally ill-informed exchange of messages ensued, although in the final analysis only an elderly and mechanically-troublesome battleship in the form of HMS *Canopus* was sent to join him. He was advised to use the *Canopus* as a 'citadel' and gather his other ships around her. Admittedly, *Canopus* did possess large-calibre guns but their design was outdated and they were slightly outranged by the more modern guns of the German ships. This was a major drawback as it allowed an enemy to bombard an opponent while remaining safely out of range. A further complication was that, due to ongoing engine problems, *Canopus* was currently restricted to a sailing speed well below that of the rest of Cradock's force. In a pursuit or retreat situation, such a handicap might have drastic consequences. A vulnerable enemy might escape if the pursuers were limited to the best speed that *Canopus* could manage, while should Cradock need to speedily retire from an action he would either have to abandon the slower ship to her fate or remain with her and risk the consequences of attack by a superior force. Ultimately, Cradock resignedly shuffled *Canopus* off to calmer duty in protecting the coaling vessels that every 1914 fleet needed to supply its boilers at sea and she played no part in the subsequent fighting around the port of Coronel, on the coast of Chile.

Rear Admiral Sir Christopher Cradock, KCVO, CB, SGM. Killed in action at the Battle of Coronel.

SMS *Scharnhorst.*

By 27 October 1914 Admiral Cradock had arrived off the west coast of Chile. He then sent HMS *Glasgow* to the port of Coronel to collect any mail and signals that might have arrived from London. After pondering the advisability of entering and possibly becoming trapped in a neutral port, the *Glasgow* finally entered the harbour at Coronel on 31 October. The German squadron was soon alerted to the presence of a British warship in the harbour and von Spee devised a plan that would see the *Nurnberg* steam past the Coronel harbour entrance simply to confirm that the *Glasgow* was actually there, while the other German ships formed an arc in the surrounding waters that would ensnare the British ship once she left port. This plan was thwarted, however, when Captain Luce of the *Glasgow* became so suspicious of the increased enemy radio signal traffic that he hastily left the port before the trap was set.

Cradock was still uneasy about the adequacy of his force in meeting the German threat. He had, however, been assured by the Admiralty in far-off London that his force was quite sufficient to deal with any eventuality. This Admiralty view was predicated on Cradock using HMS *Canopus* in an effective manner but his doubts about the usefulness of that vessel had led him to assign it to essentially non-combatant duties; a course of action that had received no adverse comment from London. In Cradock's mind it must have seemed that he simply had to carry out the task with whatever he had to hand if his obligations of honour and duty as a naval officer were to be met. With *Glasgow* having rejoined his squadron, Cradock ordered his ships to spread out and look for the enemy. He actually only expected to find *Leipzig*, the latest location of the other German ships being unknown to him. He found the enemy three hours later in the shape of four menacing German warships: *Leipzig* with, to Cradock, her most unwelcome comrades, the *Scharnhorst, Gneisenau* and *Dresden* close at hand. Cradock sent a wireless signal to HMS *Canopus* which was now some 300 miles away, still escorting the colliers. It said simply: 'I am going to attack the enemy now.' It proved to be the last that *Canopus* ever heard from him.

On sighting the enemy both sides began to jostle for position. With the Germans steaming south the British, who had been heading north, changed course so that the opposing forces soon formed parallel lines, some 15,000 yards apart and both moving south. The Germans were confident that they had the measure of their enemy and began to narrow the distance between the two lines. At about 11,500 yards and just after 7 pm on 1 November 1914 von Spee opened fire, each German ship concentrating its fire on a particular opponent to ensure that no enemy vessel was left untroubled.

The guns of the *Scharnhorst* were trained on HMS *Good Hope*. The first salvo fell 500 yards short; the second salvo flew 500 yards too far. The officers and men on the *Good Hope* who had a view of the action so far must have mentally braced themselves as they anticipated where the *Scharnhorst*'s third broadside would fall. It duly crashed into the forward gun turret and foredeck of the *Good Hope*, resulting in a maelstrom of smoke and flame. Thus even before the British flagship had got off a single shot, it had been deprived of one of its main weapons in the shape of its forward gun. HMS *Monmouth* suffered similar punishment at the hands of the *Gneisenau*. Despite this setback, Cradock still attempted to close the range so as to get his smaller guns within range of the enemy. As the sun went down, an added disadvantage came into play. The

SMS *Gneisenau.*

British ships were now highlighted against the glowing backdrop of the slowly-disappearing sun, while the German ships had the benefit of being in semi-darkness.

When darkness finally came it made little difference to the fighting. By then the *Good Hope* and *Monmouth* were both so well ablaze that the Germans did not have to use their powerful searchlights to locate the enemy. They merely aimed at the flames, which were regularly enlivened as further German shells slammed home. Despite the pounding, Cradock remained defiant and *Good Hope* returned the occasional shot against its tormentors while still narrowing the range. At 5,000 yards German gunfire effectively stopped her dead in the water and she simply heaved with the swell for a short time, little more than a blazing wreck. A little after 7.50 pm a huge explosion occurred on the forward part of the *Good Hope* and it quickly broke away and sank, leaving only the after-part afloat. This drifted out of sight and must have sunk shortly afterwards.

In the meantime HMS *Monmouth* had also been sunk by her adversaries. The ship had been listing so much that the guns on her port side could no longer be used but despite the extent of the damage the White Ensign still flew, indicating that she had not surrendered and there were signs of movement on her twisted deck. The Germans were reluctant to fire again on a foe that was obviously crippled but as the White Ensign had not been struck and there were indications that the ship was capable of at least some controlled movement, the *Nurnberg* eventually fired several shells into the *Monmouth* with the result that she rolled onto her side before totally capsizing and sinking.

HMS *Glasgow* had managed to avoid any serious damage, despite more than 600 shells being hurled in her direction. Only five of those had struck home but even then damage was minimal while casualties amounted to only four men with slight wounds. *Otranto*, meanwhile, had played no real part in the confrontation. German shells had started to straddle her while her own guns remained silent as the range was well beyond their capabilities. Realizing that there was little he could usefully do, her captain exercised some sensible discretion and withdrew her from the action.

About 800 men were lost on the *Good Hope* (there were no survivors) including Admiral Cradock. Dan Taylor was also lost. He was well-known among the Gower villages of Swansea, his postal round bringing him into daily contact with a great many people. He had also been active in the local community, being scout

Some of the guns of the *Scharnhorst.*

master of the troop in Reynoldston. He left behind his wife and three children at the family home of Glen View, Upper Reynoldston. It had been his misfortune to be posted to sea in what was essentially a scratch force made up of mainly part-time sailors and largely decrepit old ships. That combination was bound to founder once it encountered a force of professional seamen deployed in more modern ships. Dan Taylor was 33 years old and is commemorated on the Portsmouth Naval Memorial. It would have been scant consolation to his family that within five weeks all of the German ships from the Coronel encounter would be hunted down and sunk by a vengeful British squadron near the Falkland Islands. Admiral von Spee and two of his sons were among those lost.[4]

The threat to allied shipping posed by German submarines was a matter of great concern throughout the war. By 1917 the situation was achieving critical status as the U-boats seemed to be going from success to success in terms of allied shipping sunk. Germany actually hoped that the mounting losses in hard-to-replace ships, coupled with the resultant reduced imports of food and other material to Britain, would have the effect of forcing its enemy to the negotiating table. The loss of material imports that were vital for the war industries together with the similar loss of foodstuffs meant that the very means of waging war were under threat, while the prospect of enforced food rationing would soon become a fact of daily life in Britain.[5]

Not all the ships heading to or from Britain were carrying food or war material, however, and one Swansea man sailed on a ship charged with a special mission. Frederick John Woollard had been born in Swansea in 1877, the son of Frederick Smith Woollard and his wife Ann. Frederick senior worked in the butchery trade while his son, after a spell as a boilermaker, seems to have opted for a working life close to or on the sea and by 1911 he was a labourer at the Swansea docks. In 1898 he had enlisted in the Royal Naval Volunteer Reserve and had undergone training on the *Colossus*, the *Crescent* and the *Australia*. Frederick was described as being 5 feet 4 inches tall, with blue eyes and a fair complexion. He had a tattoo of a cross on his left arm. On 2 February 1914 he was presented with the Royal Naval Reserve Medal for Long Service and Good Conduct, having spent a month at the end of 1913 in training on HMS *Russell*. By around this time he seems to have found employment at the Mannesmann Tube Works at Swansea, in its timber section.

As a naval reservist Frederick John Woollard was called up on 3 August 1914, as the military authorities watched the developing political crisis with increasing concern. He was eventually posted to HMS *Laurentic*, a former cruise liner which had been commissioned into the navy to serve as a transport ship before being converted to an armed merchant cruiser by the fitting of a number of 6-inch deck guns. The *Laurentic* was owned by the famous White Star Line and was an impressive ship, being 565 feet long and weighing almost 15,000 tons. In her civilian life she was able to carry 230 passengers in first class, 430 in second and 1,000 in third. It had been planned to use the *Laurentic* and her sister ship the *Megantic* on the Canadian passenger trade routes. The war swiftly put paid to those long-term plans but not before she had come to the attention of the public in a cause célèbre of the time.

In July 1910 Inspector Walter Dew of Scotland Yard travelled aboard the speedy *Laurentic* in order to overtake a slower-moving vessel that was headed for Canada, upon which travelled a person of great interest to the British police. As the SS *Montrose* neared Quebec harbour, Inspector Dew, with the co-operation of the local authorities, boarded the vessel in the guise of a harbour pilot. He duly introduced himself to Doctor Hawley Harvey Crippen and arrested him on suspicion of the murder of his wife in London. Crippen was brought back to Britain, tried, found guilty and hanged at Pentonville Prison in November 1911.

In January 1917 the *Laurentic*, with Frederick Woollard aboard, sailed from Liverpool for Halifax, Nova Scotia. Also aboard were 43 tons of gold bullion with a value of about £5,000,000 in 1917, equal to about £215,000,000 at 2007 prices. The gold was intended to be used to pay for vital war material and it was stored in the second-class baggage room. On the night of 25 January 1917 the *Laurentic* was passing Fanad Head, off the north coast of County Donegal, when it struck a mine that had been laid earlier by the German submarine *U-80*. A second mine was soon struck and the ship began to settle in the water. A number of men had been killed in the explosions which had also destroyed the engine room, cutting off the power so that neither the radio nor the pumping systems could be operated. The lifeboats were launched, not without difficulty on a stormy night, and those who were able to do so quickly departed the ship which soon sank in 125 feet of water. Rescue efforts were hampered by the bad weather and, when boats did finally reach the scene, they found that many of the men in the lifeboats had perished; some from wounds sustained and others from exposure to the freezing winds. About 350 fatalities were recorded.

Of Frederick Woollard there was no sign and he is remembered on the Plymouth Naval Memorial. It was more than seven years before his will was proven and his effects, amounting to just under £290, were settled on his widow Catherine at her Brynmelyn Street home in Swansea. The family had a very hard war. In 1918, the year after Frederick was lost, his brother Sam was killed in action in France while serving with the King's Scottish Light Infantry. Ironically, the German submarine *U-80* was surrendered at the end of the war as part of the Armistice terms. It was later broken up ... at Swansea.

The wreck of the *Laurentic* was certainly not forgotten, given the value of its cargo, and between 1917 and 1924 99 per cent of the gold ingots were recovered by Royal Navy divers, although it seems that perhaps twenty-two ingots proved impossible to find and so still await a salvage team's attentions.[6]

In February 1917 the U-boats sank 520,000 tons of allied shipping. In March this rose to 564,000 tons, while April yielded a spectacular total of 860,000 tons. The navy's new and all-powerful dreadnoughts, as well as its cruisers and destroyers, were driven by fuel oil rather than the traditional coal and bringing heavily-laden oil tankers to Britain from America presented the German submarines with an abundance of tempting, slow-moving targets. The Royal Navy destroyer fleet was expected to be of great help

HMS *Laurentic*.

in hunting down the undersea threat but it was already thinly stretched in its defence of the Grand Fleet and ensuring the safe passage of men and matériel to France, as well as attending to the myriad other duties that fell to its overworked ships.

The introduction of the convoy system in 1917 certainly eased the problem posed by submarines, as did technological advances such as the hydrophone underwater listening device and the depth-charge. One of the simpler but certainly innovative measures introduced to combat the U-boat threat was the deployment of 'Special Service' ships, more commonly known as 'Q-ships'. These were essentially slow-moving merchantmen and as such were ideal targets for the German submarine fleet but Q-ships came with an unpleasant surprise for the enemy. Hidden on deck was an assortment of concealed guns manned by a volunteer crew of naval personnel. The idea was simple: present a U-boat captain with an easy kill and the chances were that, rather than 'waste' an expensive torpedo, he would be quite likely to surface so that a few well-placed (and cheaper) shells fired from the deck-gun of the submarine could quickly despatch what he saw as an easy target. In reality, once the submarine had surfaced and was visible, the covers would be taken off the Q-ship guns, the White Ensign hauled aloft to indicate that the Q-ship was a military vessel and, if all went according to plan, the hunter would become the hunted.

The Q-ship modus operandi was quite simple. At the first sight of a submarine periscope a portion of the crew would adopt a false posture simulating panic and the lifeboats would be quickly filled and lowered, leaving the ship an apparently helpless, drifting target. The reality was somewhat different and the rest of the crew would remain on board in concealed positions, ready to uncover and man the guns once the U-boat commander had been tempted to the surface. This clearly required Q-ship crews who could display a resolute and calm disposition as those left on the ship would, initially at least, be unsure whether a torpedo might soon strike home with possibly catastrophic results. There was usually a lifeboat or two left on board for use in that unwelcome eventuality and the lifeboats that had set off earlier would always be fairly close by to try to pick up survivors should the plan not work as expected and the Q-ship, rather than the submarine, be sunk.

On 19 March 1917 Q-ship designation HMS *Q36* (sometimes known as the SS *Peveril* or *Polyanthus*) was commissioned into active service. By 30 March *Q36*, under the command of Commander Guy R. Dolphin, Royal Naval Reserve, was sailing off Cape Barfleur in the English Channel. The condition of the ship's crew could at best be described as 'raw', with some members being unfamiliar with the ship as well as their shipmates. Dolphin had been instructed in what was required of a Q-ship and its commander and crew. Indeed, he had been encouraged to discuss relevant issues with other Q-ship commanders who had already encountered enemy submarines. The ship's crew had also been rehearsed in the basic requirements of their roles, though it could hardly be said that the training was in any way comprehensive. Few of them had any previous Q-ship experience. It is an old

A Q-ship, in this case HMS *Tamarisk*, *Q11.* **No image of** *Q36* **appears to have survived.**

military axiom that 'no plan survives its first contact with the enemy' and this was amply demonstrated with tragic consequences in the case of HMS *Q36*.

HMS *Q36* included a Swansea man among her crew. Thomas Charles Croft was born in 1898 (his service record states it was 1897, indicating that he may have misrepresented his age to the military authorities) and was 19 years old when he set sail in March 1917. He lived at Major Street, Manselton and was described as being of a dark complexion with dark hair and brown eyes. He was 5 feet 5 inches tall and had been a pre-war tin worker in one of the multitude of metal-processing works that hugged the banks of the River Tawe at Swansea. Croft had begun his wartime service in the summer of 1915 before completing a signalling course later that year. He was able to swim, a skill not possessed by a surprising number of sailors, many believing that in the event they should end up in the dark, deep sea, swimming would only prolong their ordeal before death overcame them. Croft's role, in the event of contact with an enemy submarine, was as part of the 'abandon crew', the element of the crew that faked panic and promptly evacuated the ship in the hope that the U-boat could be tempted to the surface and thus expose itself to fire from the hidden Q-ship guns.

The 'standard' plan for Q-ships went wrong from the start for HMS *Q36*. Rather than spotting a submarine periscope and thus being allowed a little time for the sham evacuation to take place and the hidden gunners to move to action stations, Commander Dolphin was startled to find his ship suddenly under fire from a submarine that had already surfaced, with its low profile remaining unseen by the ship's look-outs in a choppy sea. Even after three shots had missed the ship, the location of the submarine remained a mystery to Dolphin and his crew. A strong breeze and a rough sea probably didn't help the German gunner's aim and, as the firing continued, Dolphin saw almost all the shells fall harmlessly into the sea.

Engagement with an enemy submarine should, of course, have been the fundamental desire of every Q-ship commander and crew. In this case the enemy had already surfaced, so there was really no reason to complete the fake 'abandon ship' routine. Indeed, it might be safer for the 'abandon crew' to remain on board a substantial and well-armed ship rather than set off into a choppy sea in a much smaller lifeboat.

Dolphin, however, still ordered the sham abandonment to take place with the requisite amount of 'fake' panic being displayed, despite this not being required by the current situation. It was then that things started to go awry. Deciding that the lifeboats on the port side were the most appropriate to be lowered given the location of the enemy and the condition of the sea, disaster soon struck. One man was detailed to lower each of the two lifeboats using the necessary apparatus. Unfortunately the boats, once partly lowered, were no longer visible to the men that were lowering them. The after-lifeboat, when fully laden with crew members, was lowered unevenly so that the bow became partly submerged. When this became all too apparent, an urgent order was given to release the after fall apparatus and when this was done the rear of the aft-boat was unceremoniously dropped into the sea.

The momentum of this sudden action meant that the bow of the aft-boat came up suddenly and under the stern of the forward-boat which was still being lowered; thus that boat was capsized towards the side of the ship, pitching its occupants into the sea. Although efforts were made by the aft-boat to pick up those who had been capsized, five men were sadly drowned. One of them was Thomas Croft, whose swimming skills proved inadequate in the harsh waters of the ocean. He was seen swimming at one point but then disappeared from view, never to be seen again.

To make matters worse the submarine then dived, depriving the hidden gunners of an opportunity to sink it and increasing the risk of HMS *Q36* being torpedoed. The port-side gun crew also proved to be missing from the ship. It transpired (according to a subsequent Court of Enquiry finding) that these men, demoralized by a couple of German shells that hit the ship near their location, had simply jumped into the sea hoping to be picked up by the lowered lifeboats, one of which was now floating upside-down. The surviving men from the gun crew claimed to have been blown overboard by an exploding shell, although the lack of any significant physical injuries counted against their testimony in that respect. Three of their number had been drowned in the incident. A German shell that exploded near the starboard gun crew was responsible for the death of Able Seaman Mason, while Ordinary Seaman Sadgrove was wounded in the leg. The assistant paymaster, acting without authority, had thrown the Q-ship's secret books overboard before sending an SOS signal and then a further message (an incorrect one at that), claiming that the ship was sinking. The Court of Enquiry believed that this sort of behaviour was symptomatic of a crew that had been poorly led and, in parts, been found wanting and prone to largely unnecessary panic.

The court noted that the thrust of Commander Dolphin's written orders for 'action stations' seemed to be predicated on the fact that the ship would, in fact, be sunk; ignoring the fact that the prime aim of Q-ships was to remain afloat in order to sink the enemy submarine. This might well have had a demoralizing effect on his crew, even before an action commenced. He had envisaged getting so many men off the ship and into the supposed safety of the lifeboats that when the evacuation was actually completed he found that a shortage of men left on board had led to communication problems, hindering the combat-effectiveness of his ship.

Captain Otto Steinbrinck of *U-65*, which tussled with *Q36*. Steinbrinck, pictured here in 1947, was convicted of being a Nazi and a member of the SS after the Second World War.

Nine men had been killed in this sad affair, among them Thomas Croft who had left his home in Swansea to voluntarily help his country in its hour of need. His reward had been a tragic and unnecessary death, largely caused by the incompetence of those on whom he depended. The Court of Enquiry subsequently decreed that Commander Dolphin was to be removed from his command of HMS *Q36*.

Even after this sad incident matters did not improve much for the ill-fated HMS *Q36*: she was sunk on 6 November 1917 while acting as a decoy west of Gibraltar, with the loss of one hand. Perhaps Captain Dolphin's worries had not been entirely ill-founded after all.[7]

Notes
1. John Terraine, *Business in Great Waters*, p.7.
2. WGAS, TC/53 and information provided by David Davies.
3. Robert K. Massie, *Castles of Steel*, p.203.
4. TNA, ADM/188/349; information provided by Huw Jones.
5. Massie, op. cit., p.715.
6. TNA, BT/377/7; information provided by Charles Wilson-Watkins.
7. TNA, ADM/339/1 and ADM/339/1/8603.

Chapter Nine (c)

The War in the Air

The baby of the armed forces during the Great War was, of course, the air force. Early attempts at putting a man into the air had relied on such things as kites, airships, balloons or gliders. The Wright brothers in America had worked towards a powered and controllable fixed-wing aircraft and, after a number of false starts, finally took to the air in December 1903. Military minds soon saw the potential for using the new technology for their purposes, although there were conflicting views on how such a novel service should be organized. In 1908 the British prime minister took the time-honoured path and asked a committee to consider the issues and report back.

The report of the committee recommended the creation of a single military aeronautical service to be named the Royal Flying Corps (RFC). The competing demands of the army and navy would be met by creating a flying wing for each, while there would also be established a central flying school for the instruction of those intrepid types who wished to risk life and limb in the newfangled inventions. A factory capable of producing suitable flying machines for the armed services was also to be provided. After the customary pause for mulling things over, a Royal Warrant was duly issued allowing for the creation of the Royal Flying Corps on 13 May 1912.[1]

Recruitment poster for the Royal Flying Corps.

One such 'intrepid type' who sought employment in this new arm of the services was Lewis Laugharne Morgan, who had been born in Swansea in 1897. He was the son of William Laugharne Morgan, a Swansea businessman who also became a councillor on the Swansea Corporation. Before the war Morgan junior had worked as a bank clerk with the Capital and Counties Bank at Shoreditch in London. With war declared he initially joined the 6th Welsh Battalion, which was essentially the Swansea Territorial Battalion, made up of men who worked by day and trained for the military by evening and in annual camps. In 1916 it seems that Morgan applied for a transfer to the flying service and he reported for duty with the 2nd Reserve Squadron at Reading on 16 October 1916. In February 1917 he was sent to the Central Flying School at Upavon in Wiltshire and by March 1917 he had been assigned to the D Squadron there, with the rank of flying officer. In the same month he was posted to 40 Squadron on the Western Front.

The size of the new aerial force had grown quickly. By July 1916 there were twenty-seven squadrons of aircraft on the Western Front alone. The aircraft were used for reconnaissance, photographing the enemy trench systems and acting as observers for the artillery so that range corrections could be signalled where the fall of shot was proving to be inaccurate. Another role was that of preventing the enemy from using their own aircraft to further their military aims by engaging them in aerial combat whenever the chance arose.[2] Bombing by aeroplane was in its infancy at that time and projectiles were simply dropped by hand in the hope that they would hit or at least land close to their intended target. Early flying machines were also unable to fire a machine gun through the propeller blade of the aircraft without damaging it, so frequently a hopelessly inadequate handgun was used to take optimistic shots at enemy aircraft. Technological innovation soon stepped in to remove these problems and in short order bomb racks were fitted, allowing a crewman to release the bomb-load by pulling on a cable in the cockpit, and an interrupter mechanism was devised that allowed a machine gun to fire directly ahead and through the arc of the propeller blade, greatly increasing the accuracy of its fire.

In 40 Squadron Morgan found himself rubbing shoulders with Mick Mannock, who would subsequently become one of the Great War's most celebrated flying aces. In fact, Morgan actually started destroying enemy observation balloons and aircraft before Mannock had claimed his first kill. On 2 May 1917 Lewis Laugharne Morgan brought down a German observation balloon during a special mission designed to reduce the observational activities of the enemy. On that day four such balloons were brought down by 40 Squadron. Mannock only managed to bring down his first enemy balloon on 7 May 1917 but went on to score a staggering total of sixty-one kills or possible kills (some being unconfirmed). During these dangerous escapades Mannock also earned himself a Military Cross and bar (meaning he won the award twice), a Distinguished Service Order and two bars, and a Victoria Cross. He was killed on 26 July 1918 after flying low to inspect the wreckage of an enemy aeroplane that he had downed. As he did so, he was met by a hail of small-arms fire from the enemy trenches and was subsequently killed when his aircraft crashed to the ground in flames.

Morgan brought down his first enemy aircraft on 6 May 1917 at about 3.00 pm near the south-east corner of the town of Lens. He was on 'offensive patrol' duty at a height of 10,000 feet when he saw an enemy aircraft, which he believed to be an Albatross single-seat aeroplane, flying below him. He dived down onto the unsuspecting enemy, emptying three-quarters of a drum of ammunition into the aircraft. The effect was instantaneous and deadly; the Albatross falling vertically towards the ground while engulfed in flames and narrowly missing another British aeroplane during its fatal descent. It was seen to crash into the ground with the pilot, if still alive, being unable to control it.[3] On 7 May 1917 Morgan succeeded in bringing down another enemy observation

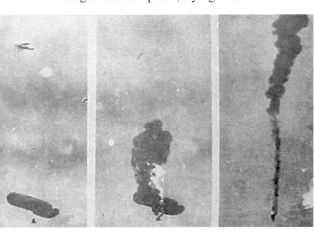

A bombed balloon plummeting to the ground.

An Albatross DIII aeroplane.

balloon and was subsequently awarded the Military Cross. His citation read:

> For conspicuous gallantry and devotion to duty. He crossed the lines at a height of under 100 feet, and destroyed a hostile kite balloon. Previously he attacked a hostile scout at close range and brought it down in flames. He has shown great gallantry in many combats.[4]

Morgan was clearly beginning to acquire the skills that could make him an excellent pilot in the dangerous skies over the Western Front. His luck changed, however, on 26 May 1917 when his aircraft was hit by enemy fire, probably from a ground battery rather than an enemy aircraft. The engine was damaged but Morgan managed to ease the aircraft back over friendly territory before landing. His right leg had been broken and his right foot injured in the incident, although he was fully conscious and able to explain what had happened to the stretcher-bearers who came to meet him. Regrettably, it later proved necessary to amputate his right leg.[5]

This was obviously a major setback for Morgan's flying career, yet he was not prepared to accept that he could no longer play a part in the work of the Royal Flying Corps. A number of medical boards were held to consider his case, each one postponing a final decision as Morgan's recuperation continued. By March 1918 he was judged, despite the permanent nature of his injuries, to be fit for home service if not deployment to the front. He was also passed as fit to fly (despite having an artificial limb) and given the rank of lieutenant. He was sent to join 50 Squadron, a unit which was devoted to home defence in trying to intercept German aircraft as they attempted to attack targets in Britain. His role there was that of aerial combat instructor, for which his previous combat experience would stand him in good stead.[6]

On 28 April 1918 Lewis Laugharne Morgan took off in an SE5 (Scout Experimental) aircraft from Bekesbourne in Kent. After flying a short distance it became apparent to

those on the ground that the aircraft was in trouble. Morgan quickly turned the craft back towards the airfield, clearly intent on making an emergency landing, but instead hit a railway embankment that ran alongside the airfield. He was killed in the crash and was subsequently buried in a Canterbury cemetery with full military honours.

[Postscript: the author attended his nephew's birthday party the day after writing about Lewis Laugharne Morgan in December 2013. He was surprised to see that one birthday present, a Hornby train set, included a model carriage emblazoned with the words 'William Laugharne Morgan, Swansea...best house coals...' It was the business of Lewis's father at Swansea. The company has not been active in Swansea for around half a century.]

Lewis Laugharne Morgan. *(Cambrian)*

Another airman from Swansea was Allan Harold Bates. He had been born in 1896 and was the son of Archibald Bates, an ironmonger who had premises (the Utility Stores) on St Helen's Road, Swansea. Bates junior had attended the Technical College at Swansea as an engineering student and had worked for a time in an aeroplane factory before enlisting. He was sent to an officer cadet training battalion at Lincoln College, Oxford before joining the Royal Flying Corps. His first role was to simply ferry aeroplanes over the Channel to St Omer. He was then posted to 25 Squadron of the RFC on 6 April 1917.

On 13 April 1917 he took off with Sergeant William Barnes and flew over the Noyelle-Godault area of the Pas de Calais. The plan was to bomb a railway junction near Lens in combination with five other aircraft. As the mission progressed, a flight of five other aeroplanes was seen to be approaching the bombing group and the new arrivals were initially taken to be friendly. They were actually German and they

Allan Harold Bates. *(Cambrian)*

promptly attacked the British aircraft, hitting two of them including that of Bates and Barnes. Both stricken aircraft were seen to lose altitude, although they seemed to be under a measure of control and it was hoped that safe landings could be achieved. However, in the case of Bates and Barnes the aeroplane descended rapidly and crashed into a house, killing both men.

The crew of the other aircraft did manage to land behind enemy lines and were taken prisoner. Bates and Barnes had had the great misfortune to meet in aerial combat none

An SE5A aeroplane, the unit marking having been obscured to suit the censor.

other than Manfred von Richthofen, the famed Red Baron flying ace of the German Air Force. It was an uneven fight: the Red Baron had already claimed forty-two aerial victories while Bates and Barnes had only arrived at the front in the previous two weeks and had minimal combat experience. The result of that level of experience versus inexperience was entirely predictable and the British aeroplane was soon shot from the skies. Richthofen went on to chalk up a total of eighty 'kills' before being himself killed in action on 21 April 1918. Ironically, although there is some debate, it seems probable that the Red Baron was killed by fire from the ground (probably a machine-gun bullet) rather than by fire from an enemy aircraft.[7]

German fighter ace Baron Manfred von Richthofen.

Thomas Llewelyn Davies was the son of William and Margaret Davies of Dillwyn House, Brynhyfryd, Swansea. Davies junior had been born in 1893. His father, who hailed from Carmarthenshire, ran a grocery store in Swansea. By 1911 Thomas was training to be a teacher but, with the advent of war, he joined the Royal Field Artillery. Although his military service record seems not to have survived, he was obviously well-suited to the task, winning a Military Cross and advancing to the rank of major at only 25 years of age. His Military Cross citation reads:

> For conspicuous gallantry and devotion to duty in reorganising a battery which had lost all its officers, N.C.Os., and gunners. Two days afterwards he not only commanded the battery in an attack, but personally laid the guns, and it was due to his splendid example that the battery was able to change its position and come into action again with the rest of the brigade. He displayed throughout the operation a complete disregard of hostile fire.[8]

At some point he was transferred to the Royal Air Force [formed in April 1918 from the RFC and the RNAS (Royal Naval Air Service)] and it is likely that he was stationed at the Artillery and Infantry Co-operation School near Winchester. His role was probably that of observer, while a qualified pilot flew the aircraft. The co-ordination between artillery and infantry was of prime importance when making attacks to try to ensure that barrages fell where they were most needed and in a manner that did not harm the allied infantry. Given the confusion of battle that prevailed on the ground, it was also natural that advantage should be taken of the view from the air which was less likely to be hampered by terrain of varying heights and the dust and smoke of battle. Davies' artillery expertise would have been a valuable addition to this arm of the aerial service. However, aircraft technology was still in its infancy and accidents were a regular occurrence as engines failed or inexperienced flyers made critical errors. On 16 September 1918 Davies was taken up in an RE8-type aeroplane which subsequently crashed, resulting in his death. His father undertook the administration of his estate, which amounted to just over £300.

Another Swansea man to lose his life in an air accident was Noel Parry Davies. He had been born in 1899 and both his parents were deceased by 1918, although there were family links to Queen's Road, Mumbles. He had been educated at the Swansea Grammar School where he played rugby for the school team and had subsequently found employment with a banking firm in London. On reaching the age of 18 in 1917, he had joined the Royal Naval Air Service and commenced his training at the Crystal Palace in London, which was being used for this purpose. Following training, he had performed airborne reconnaissance for naval units although, after two months spent at Vendôme in France, he appears to have returned for further training in postings in Britain; first at Cranwell, near Sleaford, Lincolnshire and latterly at Calshot, near Southampton. On 8 April 1918 he was flying over Edinburgh when the machine developed engine problems and Davies was killed in the resultant crash. He was buried at the Bethel Chapel, Sketty.[9]

John Lawrence Hughes had been born in Swansea in 1892. His father was a commercial traveller for a brewery company and the family lived at Eaton Grove in Swansea. Hughes had been educated at Swansea Grammar School before going up to Cambridge and was regarded as extremely promising. He had planned a profession in dentistry but, on the declaration of war, abandoned his studies and enlisted as a private in the Royal West Kent Regiment. His promise did not escape the attention of the military authorities, however, and in August 1915 he was commissioned into the 17th Welsh Battalion with the rank of second lieutenant. The 17th Welsh was one of the so-called 'bantam' battalions, consisting of men who could not meet the usual minimum height requirement for service in the army. In July 1915 the battalion moved to Prees Heath Camp in Shropshire, proceeding in September 1915 to Aldershot for further training. It was then inspected by the king in late May 1916 before embarking for France at the end of the month.

In June 1917 Hughes returned to Britain with a view to being trained as an observer with the RFC, a role he quickly mastered and put into practical use. He flew on observation missions in the summer and autumn of 1917 as the battle raged around Passchendaele and Ypres. On 1 October 1917, while returning from a flight mission his aircraft was brought down, resulting in his death as well as that of his pilot, Lieutenant Charles Oliver Rayner, whose parents lived in Vancouver, British Columbia. The loss of their son must have hit the Hughes family very hard, especially as another son was already a prisoner of the Germans, having recently been captured.[10]

Losses among air force personnel were understandably lower than those of the army and navy. The number of personnel involved in the aerial arm of the military, while very important, came nowhere near the number of men serving in the army and navy. That said, given that the technology of powered flight was very new, being a pilot or navigator was a very dangerous role. Even if a man was lucky enough to avoid being shot down, there was still a major risk of technical failure and resultant death, with use of the parachute also being in its infancy at that time.

Notes

1. Peter Hart and Nigel Steel, *Tumult in the Clouds*, pp.14–15.
2. Ibid., op. cit., pp.101–02.
3. TNA, TNA/AIR/1/1222/204/5/2634.
4. *London Gazette*, 18 July 1917.
5. *Cambrian*, 1 June 1917.
6. *Mumbles Press*, 2 May 1918.
7. Information provided by Gareth Morgan and Gwyn Prescott.
8. *London Gazette*, 9 January 1918.
9. *Cambrian*, 12 April 1918.
10. *South Wales Daily Post*, 8 and 18 October 1917.

Chapter Ten

Swansea's Foreign Legion

The Great War broke out at a time when Britain still had a worldwide empire and it did not take long for many of the countries that made up that empire to come to the aid of the old country. In Australia, for example, the prime minister immediately pledged the full support of his country in aiding Britain. Indeed, an Australian force was sent to German New Guinea to seize German possessions as early as September 1914. Recruiting for an Australian expeditionary force began at once and by the end of 1914 over 50,000 men in Australia had volunteered for active service in what became the Australian Imperial Force, with the intention of supplementing the British forces.

The Canadian government declared war on Germany on 5 August 1914, despite having a very small standing army of just over 3,000 men and hardly any navy at all. Once again the need to defend the mother country seems to have stirred the hearts of many Canadian men with the result that within two months more than 32,000 had volunteered. New Zealand also declared war on Germany as soon as the conflict commenced. Similarly, despite some internal opposition (a likely hangover from the earlier British wars with the Boers), South Africa also entered the fray on the side of Britain. Ironically, the South African Prime Minister Louis Botha and his Defence Minister Jan Smuts had both previously been thorns in the side of the British during the Second Boer War of 1899–1902. Many Indian units were also deployed in aid of the war effort including some to the unfamiliar, for Indian soldiers, environment of the Western Front. Many other outposts of empire helped the British cause in whatever way they could.

Britain had expanded her empire enormously in the previous 200 years, of course. That had opened up possibilities for men from Swansea to set up in business or ply a trade in various parts of the empire and many had taken due advantage of the prospects for commercial advancement and, in some cases, simply better living conditions. With the coming of war a great many men whose birth roots lay in Swansea opted to come back and help their former homeland by enlisting in the armed forces of the country in which they were currently living, then return to Europe to assist in the fight against Germany and her allies. As might be expected, the fates they suffered at the front differed in a number of ways.

Donald Herbert Odo Hopkins had been born in Swansea around 1894. His father was George Herbert Hopkins, a doctor who was for a time the resident medical officer at the Swansea General Hospital as well as being in practice with Doctor Arthur Davies at 5 Picton Place, Swansea. At the age of 2 Donald had emigrated with his parents to Australia and later attended the Brisbane Grammar School where he joined the school cadet force before finding work as a 'jackeroo'.[1] This involved working on a sheep or

Recruiting at Melbourne.

cattle station with a view to gaining the necessary skills and experience to eventually be able to manage such an undertaking on his own account. Donald was 22 years of age in April 1916 and had previously attempted to enlist in the Australian forces, only to be rejected on the grounds that his chest measurement did not meet the required standard of 34 inches. However, as losses mounted among the first volunteers, it became expedient to relax the requirements with the result that Donald was eventually allowed to enlist in the Australian army.

He was medically examined at Brisbane in April 1916 when his expanded chest measurement was recorded as just under 34 inches, which was by then good enough for the army. He stood at just over 5 feet 7 inches tall and weighed a little under 9 stone. The second toe on his right foot was noted as missing. He was clearly not the 'strapping digger' of popular imagination but nevertheless had the grit and determination to overcome his physical shortcomings and gain entry into what was later recognized as one of the hardest-fighting forces in the allied army.

Donald Herbert Odo Hopkins. *(Cambrian)*

A period of intense training followed before, on 7 October 1916, he embarked on the SS *Ceramic* for the voyage from Sydney to Plymouth, arriving in England in late November. He left Britain on 12 December 1916 and duly arrived at the training camp at Étaples, France; known as 'the bullring' to all who endured its forced marches, regular drill and fierce bayonet practice. Towards the end of December 1916 Donald was assigned to the 49th Infantry Battalion of the Australian Imperial Force. This battalion had been formed by a mix of equal numbers of Gallipoli veterans who had served there with the 9th Battalion and new recruits of mainly Queensland men. His early days with the battalion were unhappy, however, as he promptly came down with a case of mumps that necessitated his admission to the 39th Casualty Clearing Station before the seriousness of his condition saw him admitted to the 25th Stationary Hospital at Rouen. He was then transferred to a convalescent depot before finally rejoining his battalion on 28 January 1917.

SS *Ceramic.*

In March 1917 he attended a school of instruction and remained there for almost a month. In the summer months he was promoted to the rank of lance corporal before being promoted once again, this time to corporal, upon the death from wounds received in action of Lance Sergeant Thomas Foster, a former Birmingham man who was serving in the same battalion. By this time it is very likely that Donald would have played a part in the Battle of Messines which ran from 7 to 14 June 1917 and was marked by the detonation of nineteen large mines placed in tunnels that had been carefully, and silently, dug under the German front line. The result was about 10,000 German casualties and the capture of all key objectives by the allied forces, which included the 49th Battalion in their number. It was probably during this battle that Thomas Foster, the man from whom Hopkins inherited his promotion, received the wounds to which he would later succumb. Sadly, it seems that Donald's promotion in place of Foster was

Attestation form for Donald Hopkins.
(National Archives of Australia, B2455, Hopkins, DHO, 2678)

Australian soldiers near the front line.

quite literally a case of walking into a pair of 'dead man's shoes'.

Donald's battalion was next involved in the Battle of Polygon Wood, so-called after a young plantation forest that lay along the planned line of advance of the allied troops. The advance began at 5.30 am on 26 September 1917 under a massive artillery barrage that was described as sounding like a 'roaring bushfire' by men who were well-acquainted with such things back in Australia. Once again, all objectives were secured before a series of German counter-attacks was beaten off. There was, of course, an inevitable cost to pay for such gains and the Australian casualties amounted to about 6,000 men killed or wounded. The 49th Battalion had lost 24 men killed, with 77 men and 6 officers wounded.

Donald Hopkins was among those killed. His lieutenant wrote to Donald's parents, telling them that he 'was one of my most trusted NCOs. His unassuming, gentle manly behaviour compelled admiration and respect from all who knew him, and if spared he would certainly have advanced in the profession.' The officer explained that Donald and his comrades had reached an objective and were pausing until the allied artillery barrage had lifted and the next stage of the advance could begin. While waiting, the troops were

Report of the death in action of Donald H.O. Hopkins.
(National Archives of Australia, B2455, Hopkins, DHO, 2678)

FIELD SERVICE.   Army Form B. 2090A.

REPORT of Death of a Soldier to be forwarded to the War Office with the least possible delay after receipt of notification of death on Army Form B. 213 or Army Form A. 36, or from other official documentary sources.

REGIMENT OR CORPS   **49th Battalion A.I.F.**   Squadron, Troop, Battery or Company

Regimental No. **2678**   Rank **CORPORAL**

Surname **HOPKINS**   Christian Names **Donald Herbert Odo**

Died — Date **26th September 1917**   Place **BELGIUM**

Cause of Death* **KILLED IN ACTION**

Nature and Date of Report   **Field Return (A.F.B.213) dated 6th October 1917.**

By whom made   **Commanding Officer 49th Battalion A.I.F., B.E.F.**

* Specially state if killed in action, or died from wounds received in action, or from illness due to field operations or to fatigue, privation or exposure while on military duty, or from injury while on military duty.

State whether he leaves a Will or not   (a) in Pay Book (Army Book 64)   (b) in Small Book (if at Base)

(c) as a separate document

All private documents and effects received from the front or hospital, as well as the Pay Book, should be examined, and if any will is found it should be at once forwarded to the War Office.

Any information received as to verbal expressions by a deceased soldier of his wishes as to the disposal of his estate should be reported to the War Office as soon as possible.

A duplicate of this Report is to be sent to the Fixed Centre Paymaster at Home, or to the D.F.A.G., Indian, Expeditionary Force, or Field Disbursing Officer, as the case may require, together with the Deceased's Pay Book (after withdrawal of any will from the latter). If the deceased's Small Book is at the Base, it should be forwarded to the War Office with this Report.

Station and Date   **Australian Section**   Signature of Officer in charge of Section   **Captain**
3rd Echelon GHQ. BEF   Adjutant-General's Office at the Base   Officer i/c Records.

W2088/M1768—500,000—H. & Sr5—Forms/B2090A/2.

subjected to German shellfire of a heavy calibre and one of these had landed close by and killed Donald by its concussion. His body was apparently unmarked and his death was said to be instantaneous. As the officer put it: 'He died a painless and glorious death, as a soldier fighting for his beloved King and country – bravely facing the foe.'[2]

His family subsequently inserted a death notice in the columns of the *Queenslander* newspaper of Brisbane. It ended with the verse:

Memorial stone at the Blackboy Hill Camp in Australia. *(Satsuro)*

On fame's eternal camping ground
Their silent tents are spread,
And glory guards in honour round
The bivouac of the dead.[3]

Donald Herbert Odo Hopkins was single and 23 years of age when he met his death. His belongings were sent to his mother, who was also the beneficiary of his will, and consisted of his pyjamas, a shirt, a masonic apron in a case, a 'housewife' (a small case for needles and thread), postcards, books and a few other odds and ends.

Another Swansea man who had emigrated to Australia was James Southwood Thomas. He was a labourer aged 37 years in 1916 and at about that time his mother still lived in Richard Street, in the Manselton area of Swansea. Once again he was a comparatively small man but obviously intent on 'doing his bit' for king and country by

serving with the Australian forces. In fact, he stood at just 5 feet 4 inches and weighed a little under 9 stone. His chest when expanded only reached just over 34 inches and he was already showing signs of a receding hairline. He clearly was a man who liked a tattoo; displaying a pair of clasped hands, a heart, two flags and a star on one crowded forearm, while the other was graced with an illustration of a fully-rigged ship.

When first applying to join the armed forces Thomas stated that he had served five years in the naval reserves, presumably in Swansea, although the form does not clarify that point. He was posted to the Blackboy Camp near Perth, a training camp for new recruits.

A formidable enemy: a German infantryman on the Western Front.
(Bundesarchiv Bild /183/RO5148)

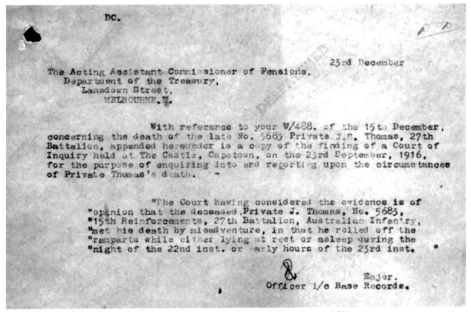

Result of a Court of Enquiry into the death of James Southwood Thomas.
(National Archives of Australia, B2455, Thomas JS, 5683)

It seems that Thomas was not cut out to be a perfect soldier. Having enlisted in June 1915, he promptly came to the attention of his superior officers by first going absent without leave, for which he was fined 5 shillings and docked a day's pay, and then being found drunk and disorderly in Hay Street, Perth. For that offence he was fined two days' pay and discharged from the service. He completed a second application some thirteen months later, in July 1916. By that time he was a labourer rather than a fireman, as he had previously stated, and his age had not increased despite the passage of thirteen months! The army, it seems, was prepared to let bygones be bygones and duly re-enlisted him. Private Thomas was first assigned to a pioneer unit after reporting for duty on 19 July 1916, before being placed in the 15th reinforcements for the 27th Infantry Battalion.

On 28 August 1916 Thomas was embarked at Adelaide for the long sea journey to the Western Front. One of the stops on the voyage was at Cape Town, South Africa and here the Australian infantry disembarked for a short stay in the old castle which was still used for military purposes. It is possible that Thomas had enjoyed some free time in Cape Town since, when Private McKearney saw him at about 10.30 pm on 22 September, he formed the opinion that Thomas was recovering from the effects of a drinking session. Indeed, if Thomas had been drinking it seems that he had not fully slaked his thirst since he told McKearney that he 'knew a way to get out of the castle and was going to try'. Private Summers also saw him and also came to the conclusion that he was under the influence of alcohol. Thomas gathered up his army blankets and told Summers that he was going to sleep outside. Exactly what happened after that is unclear. It is possible that Private Thomas did indeed try to get out of the castle, or he might have simply settled down on the castle ramparts to sleep off the effects of the alcohol. The sad fact is that he was not seen again until his lifeless body was found in the dry moat of the castle on the following morning. He had fallen about 50 feet and his death was judged to have been instantaneous.

A Court of Enquiry was convened to hear the available evidence and a judgement of death by misadventure was arrived at. The court felt that the chances were that Thomas had simply rolled off the rampart while resting or asleep and had fallen to his death in the dry moat. Thomas's mother, who had previously been widowed, lodged a claim with the Australian authorities for payment of a war pension in respect of her deceased son. This was still under consideration in December 1919 (more than three years after his death), with the main issue being whether 'the soldier's death was the result of his employment in connection with warlike operations'. Whether a pension was eventually awarded is not clear but bearing in mind that allied troopships were often exposed to the risk of deadly attack by enemy submarines, it does seem a little harsh to treat the mother of a man thus, whatever his personal failings had been, when he had voluntarily enlisted and was prepared to place himself in mortal danger for what he saw as a just cause. Mrs Thomas died around 1922. Twenty-five years later Walter Thomas, a surviving brother of James Southwood Thomas, was gratified to be told by the Australian military authorities that James's sacrifice had been remembered during an ANZAC (Australia and New Zealand Army Corps) Day service at Cape Town.[4]

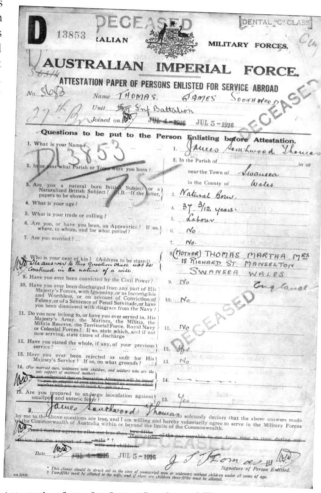

Another Swansea man who returned from overseas was James Simpson. Up until 1911 he had lived with his widowed mother, two brothers and a sister at 10 Odo Street, Hafod. He had been born in Swansea in 1890 and now, as a grown man, worked at the Cwmfelin Tin Works in Swansea. He was single and during or shortly after 1911 he seems to have decided to uproot himself to Canada where he gained employment as

Attestation form for James Southwood Thomas.
(National Archives of Australia, B2455, Thomas JS, 5683)

James Simpson.
(Cambrian)

a sampler, although in precisely what line of business is unclear. Once again it seems that his patriotic emotions were aroused when he saw his country of birth engaged in a life-or-death struggle with a European neighbour and in June 1915 he attested his willingness to serve overseas in the Canadian army. He had no previous military experience, which was not uncommon for recruits at that time. He was called up for service in February 1916 and his medical examination revealed him to be 5 feet 8 inches tall with a 34-inch chest, 38 inches when expanded. He had blue eyes and brown hair and was of a medium complexion. There were two small scars on the fingers of his left hand; possibly the result of his former work in the tinplate industry in Swansea. He was passed as fit and soon began his training for service in the Canadian Expeditionary Force.

Simpson eventually joined the 27th Battalion of the Canadian Expeditionary Force, unofficially known as the Winnipeg Battalion. In 1917 the battalion was attempting to advance in the final stages of the Third Battle of Ypres, an offensive that had been launched as far back as 31 July 1917. On 6 November the battalion, and with it James Simpson who had by then been promoted corporal, formed up close to the objective of their advance, the village of Passchendaele. Since the first day of the battle on 31 July the weather had worsened considerably, often leaving both attackers and defenders wallowing in waterlogged trenches and shell-holes. Despite this, over several months the allies, at heavy cost, had advanced slowly forward, one painful step at a time. With the advent of winter, ground conditions were deteriorating even further but the British high command nevertheless decided that another attack was necessary.

It seems there were probably several factors in that decision. The French army had been badly shaken by its costly reverse at Arras in April 1917 and required both the direct and indirect support of its allies to maintain some semblance of morale among its soldiers. It was also thought that another 'show' by the British and Empire forces would lend indirect support to a planned French attack in the Champagne region. The British were also planning an attack at Cambrai and action on another part of the front would help to keep prying German eyes focused elsewhere, while at the same time wearing

A morass of mud: the shell-torn battlefield.

down the enemy. Finally, it would be helpful if the Germans could be forced off the ridge that ran near Passchendaele so that the allied soldiers could winter on the higher and thus better-drained ground in slightly better conditions than they would experience on the soggy plain below.[5]

As usual, the start of the attack was heralded by a powerful barrage that commenced at 6 am. The weather was favourable compared to that experienced in the late summer and autumn months, with a clear sky that later clouded over but thankfully produced no rain. In any event, some of the attackers were still reported to be 'knee deep, and in places waist deep in mud and water' as they struggled forward. However, still they went on, despite the unwelcome attentions of enemy aircraft strafing the infantry. One battalion had placed a line of rolled-up army greatcoats on the ground to clearly mark the start line for the attack, much as young boys would place pullovers to mark the goal-posts for a game of football. A keen (if not exactly hawk-eyed) German pilot observed these empty greatcoats, concluded that they were enemy infantry and promptly machine-gunned them.[6]

James Simpson's battalion was the first to fight its way into Passchendaele village, capturing it at 7.40 am and taking prisoner more than seventy Germans and nine machine guns. The rest of the day was spent in consolidating what had been captured. One man of the 27th Battalion, Private J.P. Robertson, was awarded a Victoria Cross for his bravery in wiping out an enemy post. Part of his citation gives a vivid account of the fighting as he closed with an enemy machine-gun post and reads:

> Private Robertson rushed the gun, killed four of the crew and then turned the gun on the remainder. After inflicting more casualties and carrying the captured gun, he led his platoon to the final position and got the gun into action, firing on the retreating enemy. During the consolidation his use of the machine-gun kept down the enemy sniper fire. Later when two of the snipers on his own side were wounded, he went out and carried one of them in under heavy fire but he was killed by a shell just as he returned with the second man.[7]

His Victoria Cross award was, of course, posthumous. Sometime during the attack James Simpson also fell. His body was never found, probably due to the effects of constant shelling of the ground or if it was found, it proved not possible to identify it and he would later have been buried beneath a headstone simply as 'A Soldier of the Great War. Known unto God', to quote the words devised by Rudyard Kipling for use in such cases. Kipling himself lost a son during the conflict.

Another former Swansea lad who made the long journey back from Canada to Britain and the Western Front was Thomas Emlyn Davies. In 1916 he was living in the small hamlet of Zelandia, Saskatchewan. He had left the family home, which may have been in Glantawe Street, Morriston around 1911 and gained employment in Canada as a bank clerk with the Union Bank of Canada.

Davies had indicated his willingness to return to Europe and fight in May 1916. At that time he stated that he had previously served for four years with a unit of the yeomanry, a volunteer mounted force. He was 5 feet 10 inches tall with

Thomas Emlyn Davies.
(Cambrian)

brown eyes, light-coloured hair and a fair complexion. He was eventually assigned to the 28th Battalion of the Canadian Expeditionary Force. The battalion had been on the Western Front since mid-September 1915 and had spent the early months of 1917 in or near the front lines. Although the battalion played a full part in the capture of Passchendaele village, Thomas Emlyn Davies did not take part in that affair. In fact he had been wounded sometime earlier, suffering a compound fracture of the right thigh. Despite treatment being administered, the wound finally proved to be fatal and he died on 3 November 1917. As he had died while out of the forward areas there was time to properly arrange his burial and he lies in a marked grave in the Potijze Château Grounds Cemetery, Belgium.[8]

Bertram Donne Trethewey was the son of Richard Trethewey of Walter Road, Swansea. Bertram had been born in 1889 at Brentford, though the family later moved to Swansea where his father was a representative of the Great Western Railway Company.[9] They lived for a while at King Edward Road before moving to Walter Road. It seems that Bertram's father had probably been able to secure a position on the railway for Bertram, as by 1907 he was also employed by the Great Western Railway Company at Swansea. He worked in a clerical capacity in the 'DSO' department which was probably concerned with the transportation of iron ore for use in the metal-processing works that were a mainstay of the town's economy. This did not last for long, however, and just over a year later Bertram tendered his resignation.[10]

He subsequently left Britain for South Africa where he took up a post at the Witwatersrand Gold Mining Company in the Transvaal. At the beginning of the war he joined up with the South African armed forces and was deployed to German-controlled South-West Africa where he fought against the Germans until they surrendered in July 1915. He was then sent to the Western Front and contemporary press reports state that he was wounded in July 1916 at a time when his unit, the 4th Regiment, South African Infantry, was engaged in the attacks on Trones and Delville Woods. The South African 4th Regiment was called the South African Scottish and had been raised from members

Delville Wood: the scene of heavy fighting in 1916. It earned itself the nickname of 'Devil's Wood'.

of the Transvaal Scottish and the Cape Town Highlanders. The fighting for Delville Wood was particularly fierce, with only about 750 of the 3,100 men of the South African Brigade who took part in the attack being able to muster for a roll-call when they were relieved on 20 July 1916.[11]

It was April 1917 before Bertram was able to rejoin his unit. After the usual tours of duty in and out of the line, the South African Infantry Brigade was deployed in the Battle of the Menin Road which commenced on 20 September 1917. The brigade was to advance towards Poelcapelle, passing close to

Men of the 4th South African Regiment.
(Delville Wood Museum)

Hanebeek Wood as well as Borry Farm, a German position that had previously caused great trouble to allied troops. However, an innovative use of a creeping barrage consisting of high-explosive and smoke-shell shielded the attackers from the worst of the enemy machine-gun fire and enabled the wood to be essentially surrounded. Once the barrage lifted, Borry Farm was attacked from front and rear and quickly overrun by Bertram's 4th Regiment. Four strongly-held German pillboxes were also stormed by men of the 12th Royal Scots and a contingent of Springbok soldiers.[12] The next stage of the advance was swept by machine-gun fire from a nearby hill, resulting in the 2nd South African Regiment losing half its strength as it struggled forward. When the brigade was finally relieved during the night of 21/22 September 1917 it had lost 16 officers and 237 other ranks killed. The wounded amounted to about 1,000 men out of a total attacking force of 2,500.[13]

Bertram Donne Trethewey was among the officers killed. He had previously been promoted second lieutenant while in the field. His commanding officer, Lieutenant Colonel D.M. Macleod, wrote to Bertram's father very much in the fashion of the time:

> Please accept our deepest sympathy in the loss of your son. He was a gallant soldier and true gentleman, adored by his men, and a comrade to be trusted and proud of at all times. He met his death on the morning of the 20th inst., leading his men. He did not suffer, as his end was very sudden. I hope that it will console you somewhat in your sorrow to know that he died nobly playing the game.[14]

Bertram Donne Trethewey. *(Cambrian)*

It was indeed a deadly game that he had played. The administration of his will was left to his father, his estate being valued at just over £129, a sum equal to about £5,500 in 2005.[15] He lies buried in the White House Cemetery, St Jean-les-Ypres, which is north-

Symbol of the 1st South African Infantry Brigade.

east of modern-day Ieper (Ypres during the war).

Many men with Swansea links returned to Britain to help the allied cause. One man had made the journey in the opposite direction, from Australia to Swansea, before the war had arrived. Born in Kangaroo Mount, New South Wales in 1887, Japhet Lazarus Kelly (commonly known as Dan or Daniel) was one of nine children born to John and Mary Ann Kelly. John Kelly was a farmer of Irish descent. It appears that Dan Kelly travelled alone to Britain, though exactly when is not known. In 1915 he gave his next of kin as his sister, who still lived in Australia. It is likely that he found employment in or close to Swansea and his name appears on a contemporary list of the first men who left for the Western Front in 1915 as part of the Swansea Battalion (the 14th Welsh). He would have served on the Somme and in the Ypres Salient, both extremely dangerous places during 1914–18. He probably took part in the attack on Mametz Wood where the Swansea Battalion suffered almost 400 casualties out of the 676 men it committed to the attack; about 100 of them being killed or dying later of wounds received.

By July 1917 the ravages of war and a shortage of recruits saw the Swansea Battalion strength severely reduced from the 1,300 men it could call on in 1915. Indeed, when the battalion took part in the Third Battle of Ypres on 31 July 1917 it committed only 470 other ranks to the attack plus about 20 officers. While the attack, one of the biggest of the war, achieved its early objectives, it cost the Swansea Battalion about eighty men and four officers killed, although Daniel Kelly managed to come through that traumatic experience.

The early days of August 1917 saw the battalion holding the ground captured in the attack of 31 July 1917. There was rifle and shellfire from the enemy to contend with, as well as having to remain in the uncomfortable and waterlogged shell-holes and portions of damaged trench that formed the new front line. After spending time near a location known as Iron Cross as well as at Stray Farm, the battalion was moved to an abandoned works for a day to rest and re-fit before it was ordered to move back up and hold the front line to the west of the Steenbeek stream. It seems that it was during this move, made on 5 August 1917, that Dan was killed in action. The surviving records are silent on exactly how he met his fate but it was likely to be from shellfire which was the single biggest killer on the Western Front. He was still single and 34 years of age at the time of his death. His body was not properly recovered and he has no known grave, being

A shattered road and knocked-out tank. Although early tanks helped in attacks they were very prone to mechanical failure and were not, on their own, a war-winning weapon in 1917/18.

commemorated on the Menin Gate memorial at the city of Ypres.[16] Sadly his younger brother, Herbert Norman Kelly, also did not survive the war, being accidentally drowned while in training with the Australian Light Horse at Liverpool, New South Wales in November 1917.[17]

Patriotism seems today to be regarded as an old-fashioned and outmoded mindset. It is often surprising to note how the men of Australia, Canada, South Africa, New Zealand and a number of other parts of the Empire willingly volunteered for active service in support of Britain in the Great War (and indeed, in the Second World War as well). They came of their own accord and included a large number of former Swansea lads in their midst. As in the case of Daniel Kelly, many who were already in Britain did not hesitate to voluntarily join the allied cause with all the risks that entailed. As has been demonstrated above, many of them met their deaths in the defence of the old country and its ideals. The modern-day reader may well regard patriotism as a largely outdated concept but must nevertheless surely admire the selflessness of those who have preceded us and fought and died for what they saw as a just cause.

Notes
1. Australian Roll of Honour and National Archives of Australia B245, Hopkins, DHO, 2678.
2. *Brisbane Courier*, 23 November 1917.
3. *Queenslander*, 3 November 1917.
4. National Archives of Australia, B2455, Thomas, JS, 5683.
5. G.W.L. Nicholson, *Canadian Expeditionary Force, 1914–1919*, p.312.
6. Ibid., p.324.
7. *London Gazette*, 11 January 1918.
8. Library and Archives Canada, RG150, accession 1992–93/166, Box 2357 – 33.
9. *South Wales Daily Post*, 1 October 1917.
10. Register of Lad Clerks in the GWR Company (via Ancestry).
11. The Long, Long Trail.www.1914–1918.net
12. Miles, *Official History*, pp.263–5.
13. Ibid., p.267.
14. *South Wales Daily Post*, 1 October 1917.
15. National Probate Calendar (via Ancestry).
16. Commonwealth War Graves Commission.
17. National Archives of Australia, B2455, Kelly, H.N. N82234; information provided by Lesley Taylor.

Chapter Eleven

The War According to Captain Blackadder

To many modern readers the Great War can be summed up in a small number of well-known phrases or images: 'Lions led by donkeys', 'Generals swigging brandy in posh châteaux far from the Front', 'futility', and so on. The media sometimes reinforce this view with, for example, Captain Blackadder spending much of his time on television in *Blackadder Goes Forth* trying to avoid taking part in attacks that are designed to simply move his commanding officer's drinks cabinet several inches closer to Berlin, while Sir Douglas Haig is seen airily sweeping toy soldiers off a map and into a dustpan as yet another attack fails.

This view of the Great War had been previously inculcated into the general

Confederate dead behind a low wall at Marye's Heights, Virginia. It was natural to seek whatever cover was available or could be quickly fashioned. So it was with the trenches of 1914–18.

consciousness of the nation by its constant repetition in a swathe of 1930s' memoirs that were mainly written by a particular class of person that had seen active service during the war. Thus the well-known memoirs and war poetry of Siegfried Sassoon and Robert Graves, among others, are thought by many to be typical of the experiences of all who served when, in reality, they often represent only the views of a particular section of the officer class rather than the common soldier. In a similar vein, while it is undoubtedly entertaining, one could hardly call the stage and film musical *Oh, What a Lovely War!* an accurate portrayal of history.

'War is hell' was the remark made by a general of another era to whom the trenches of the Great War would not have been totally unfamiliar.[1] It is obviously impossible to win a war without risking the lives of a nation's young men and, in accepting that sad but inevitable fact, it is then unavoidable that an army general or naval admiral will, at some point, commit his men to an enterprise that might not succeed, almost certainly resulting in deaths. This fact cannot be avoided, even in today's world of guided missiles and precision drone strikes. If a country wishes to prevail over an enemy by capturing its territory, then 'putting boots on the ground', to use the modern phrase, still runs the risk of failure and deaths.

A book of this nature is not the place to discuss in detail the question of whether Britain was right or wrong in going to war in 1914, essentially to aid 'poor little Belgium' against the German invader. Suffice to say that, at the highest levels, Britain feared that a Europe dominated by a militaristic Germany that had its soldiers and ships stationed in both France and Belgium was a real threat to British interests which simply could not be ignored. There was a major risk that Britain's all-important trade routes to her Empire and the rest of the world could be interrupted at a time of crisis in the future by the presence of enemy troops and guns just across the English Channel. Although not strictly bound by its treaty obligations to assist Belgium, it was obvious to those in power in Britain that the expansionist Germany of 1914 had to be confronted, if not immediately then surely very soon, if Britain's place in the world was to be protected. Many in the general population had similar worries.

Once that commitment had been accepted, it is difficult to see how the war could have ended other than by victory or defeat. Diplomatic moves seemed unable to break the impasse and it was clear that Germany had no intention of giving up the territory it had gained, other than to force of arms. The German army bestrode large chunks of France and Belgium and that was where it fully intended to stay. The human cost of forcibly evicting the invader from 1914 onwards was clearly going to be high but it was one at which

Kaiser Wilhelm II, the leader of an increasingly militaristic Germany in 1914.

the allies did not baulk. If we look forward to 1940 it is impossible to imagine Winston Churchill deciding to sit back and do nothing further had Britain been invaded by Nazi Germany, resulting in a portion of the country, for example running from Bristol to Norwich, being under the German jackboot. Churchill, and I am sure the mass of the British people, would have strained every sinew, regardless of loss, to push the invader out. Indeed, it was only the intervention of the king in 1944 that prevented Churchill himself from accompanying the D-Day invasion force to Normandy!

Upon declaration of war in August 1914 the rapid expansion of the British army, which was quickly swelled by Lord Kitchener's keen but totally untrained volunteers, placed a great strain on the apparatus of command. It must be remembered that, at the outbreak of war, Britain had available an expeditionary force of about 129,000 fully-trained infantrymen in six divisions, plus about 6,000 cavalrymen and 31,000 artillerymen. However, in the early days of the war the threat of a German invasion seemed very real and two infantry divisions were held back in Britain to defend the island against that possibility. Men of the regular army were also brought back from overseas postings for service at the front; their places abroad often being taken by some of those who

Winston Churchill: who could imagine him accepting the permanent presence of an invader on a large chunk of British soil?

had previously served as part-time territorial soldiers.[2] Kitchener's appeal of August 1914 had looked for 100,000 men to come forward. By the end of the month he had 300,000 volunteers; by the end of December 1914 the figure had risen to over 800,000.[3]

The men who were to command this vast new army could not simply be pulled out of a military storage depot that was handily stocked to the brim with fully-trained officers, as no such convenient place existed. Initially, many of those required for command purposes were simply 'dug out' of retirement and placed in command of units, many of which were New Army recruits, i.e. Kitchener's volunteers, who knew little about military matters and were still undergoing training. The 'dug-outs' understandably proved to be a mixture of good and bad: some deftly adapted to the requirements of twentieth-century warfare, while others remained firmly rooted in the former days of small-scale colonial actions and thus proved to be unsuitable for command in the present war. As time went on, other commanders were promoted as their merits became apparent, whether they had been noticed while in lower command roles or even while serving in the ranks. However, all this naturally took time and battles had to be fought in the interim using the leadership that was actually available, whether it was good, bad or indifferent. There can be no doubt that several battles suffered from poor-quality staff work with inadequate planning and unsatisfactory co-ordination between units. When men who had perhaps previously commanded no more than a battalion of about 1,300

German soldiers entrain for the front.

men were suddenly put in charge of a brigade of around 5,000 men, it is unsurprising that they struggled with unfamiliar problems and made mistakes along the way. On the cruel field of battle, such mistakes often brought with them a heavy cost.

The typical Great War general is often portrayed as being both unthinking and uncaring, prodding his men into pointless attacks with little chance of victory but almost certain death. The reality was somewhat different. The British Expeditionary Force on the Western Front was fighting in coalition with its French and Belgian allies and this meant it was occasionally required to make certain attacks, the main object of which was simply to assist an ally. That was certainly the case on the Somme in 1916, when a British-led attack was required by the French to help divert German forces from their ferocious attack on Verdun. Similarly, the British attack at Arras in 1917 was delivered largely to assist the main assault on the Germans, which was to be made by French forces under the direction of French General Philippe Nivelle.

It is absurd to suggest that any general would commit his men to battle, totally indifferent as to whether they would live or die. The unavoidable fact, as already stated, is that in any military action involving contact with an enemy, men will die. Every death is, of course, a tragedy but death is regrettably what happens in war and the early volunteers knew that that was the stark reality of their situation. That was the choice they made voluntarily; they were prepared to put their lives at risk for the sake of their country and its allies. Some were led by men who, for whatever reason, eventually proved to be not good enough; quite different from being led by someone who did not care what fate befell his men.

The attack of 1 July 1916, the infamous 'First Day on the Somme', was essentially a disaster. The effects of a massive British pre-attack bombardment had been overestimated, with the result that the Germans were waiting as the British infantry left their trenches and advanced into a hail of machine-gun fire. It was indeed a tragedy but, thankfully, one that was never repeated on that scale for the remainder of the war. Lessons, very hard lessons at that, were learned from that terrible experience and the knowledge gleaned was put to good use in later attacks. That knowledge was also circulated to all levels of the army, indicating what did and, just as importantly, what did not work when attacking the enemy. Training was changed to reflect the new reality of war and, over time, new tactics and weapons were developed to counter the strength of the enemy as he awaited the next attack in his trench or bunker. A clear learning process was undertaken and poor commanders were removed (including, over time, two commanders of the Welsh Division).

In the Second World War Winston Churchill spent an anxious night before the D-Day invasion worrying that a failed landing would produce no favourable outcome but possibly result in the deaths of 20,000 men.[4] It is also worth remembering that General Eisenhower, overall commander of the Allied invasion force, famously prepared two messages to be broadcast in the immediate aftermath of the D-Day landings in Normandy. The one he actually used announced the successful landing of Allied troops on Hitler's *Festung Europa* ('Fortress Europe'). The second, which thankfully he did not need to use, paid tribute to the courage of the Allied forces but stated that the landing had failed and the troops had been withdrawn. In the unsent message, he went on to accept full responsibility for the failure on his own shoulders. At a time of war, such is the very thin line between success and failure.

In November 1918 when the defeated German army marched out of France and Belgium, it did so under the gaze of a British high command including many of the generals who had taken part in the early battles of the war. They were different men in 1918, however; their strategy, tactics and weaponry having evolved to meet the new demands placed upon them in four years of brutal fighting. Evolution of that kind is not a trait that is usually associated with donkeys and thus, in my view, largely undermines the 'lions led by donkeys' notion.

Additionally, most Great War British generals did not opt to sit in a safe château far behind the line, swigging brandy while their men died at the front, as sometimes suggested. Indeed, no fewer than 78 generals of British or Empire origin were killed in action or died of wounds during 1914–18, while almost another 150 were wounded.[5] In 1815, almost 100 years before the battles of the Great War, it was certainly the custom for commanders like Wellington and Napoleon to be present on the field of battle, galloping from point to point in order to control and direct their men. At Waterloo the allied forces amounted to about 118,000 men, of whom some 25,000 were British, led by the Duke of Wellington. In 1918 Sir Douglas Haig had slightly over 2,000,000 men under his

Dwight D. Eisenhower. A great weight rested on his shoulders as he awaited early reports from the D-Day beaches. He knew the landings could have been a disaster.
(www.eisenhower.archives.gov.)

Wellington at Waterloo. With the small armies of his day he was able to exert personal leadership on the battlefield. *(Robert Alexander Hillingford, image in public domain)*

command on the Western Front. To cover the field of battle of an army that size would clearly require quite a lot of galloping. It was, of course, an impossible and undesirable task. In 1914 at a key moment in one battle Sir John French, then the British commander-in-chief, had set off, largely unaccompanied, to view the forward positions of his army, with the result that as the battle developed he could not be contacted. When the chance came to strike back at the enemy it passed by, the command headquarters being paralysed by the absence of the one man with the authority to give the order to attack.

Communication, in the pre-radio and cell phone days, was a constant problem for both men and commanders in the field. During the chaos resulting from an attack it was often left to 'runners' to be sent back over a war-torn battlefield to report progress (or the lack of it) to those in command, so that suitable further action could be contemplated. These runners frequently became victims of shot or shell even before their messages could be delivered, leaving the commander devoid of vital information. The field telephone was a very useful device but it worked via a wire that, in an attack, was rolled along the ground as the infantry advanced and was thus subject to damage from shellfire or even the hasty transit of men and transport moving about the battlefield. Such problems naturally limited the knowledge of a commanding officer regarding just how well an attack was going. Was it time to call a 'retire' as an attack was possibly stalled, or should reinforcements be sent forward as victory might be within reach? This was frequently a key question, the answer to which was often just a best guess in the absence of any reliable information coming back from the front.

A Great War general was actually best placed at some distance behind the front lines so that he was, hopefully, able to receive updates on the progress of an attack and formulate the necessary actions to improve the chances of success or exploit a favourable situation. That position is little different from that of General Dwight D. Eisenhower, the Allied commander in the invasion of Normandy in the Second World War. He certainly did not storm ashore with the invading troops but remained at his headquarters in Britain so that he could take whatever action was necessary, based on reports that actually managed to reach him from the chaos of the beaches. His influence on events, had he instead been lying down under fire on an enemy-held beach, would have been minimal. Warfare had clearly changed in scope and scale since the far-off days of the personal leadership displayed by Wellington and Napoleon. We cannot blame the Great War generals for that.

Another word regularly trotted out by the press when covering Great War issues is 'futile'. The dictionary definition of 'futile' is 'incapable of producing any useful results; pointless'. The action that brought Britain into a war against Germany was the invasion of Belgium, a British ally. The ultimate aim of any British Expeditionary Force sent to help the Belgians had to be the removal of the invader from Belgian soil. This could not be achieved without a regrettable loss of life, as stated earlier. The Germans were never going to voluntarily withdraw and planned to hold what they had gained by force. Therefore, according to the dictionary definition of futile, it would be logical to assume that at the end of the war Belgium was still under the German yoke, despite all the attacks made and battles waged on the Western Front. This was clearly not the case. Admittedly at enormous cost in both lives and matériel, the invader had been removed from both Belgium and France, indicating that the action taken had eventually achieved the required result and therefore cannot be regarded as futile.

It is sobering to recall that in 1939 Britain went to war to assist Poland and after almost six hard years of fighting, the invader was removed from Polish soil only to be replaced by another (Russian) regime that suppressed the Polish people for almost fifty years. If Poland was not truly free between 1945 and 1989, then were the 1939–45 attacks of the Western Allies, made to eventually free it from German control, also to be regarded as futile? As Britain had declared war against Germany in 1939 in defence of Poland, was the aim of a free Poland actually achieved by the Allied victory in 1945? The Western Allied forces had certainly done their best, had suffered accordingly and cannot be blamed for the military and political considerations that resulted in Poland becoming a mere vassal of the Soviet Union at the end of the war. In my view the outcome for the Belgian people in 1918, i.e. being free again, was far better than the outcome for the Polish people in 1945, yet it is the Great War battles that are repeatedly

Haig and his generals. They learned from their sometimes bitter experiences and in the last three months of the war they had the Germans in constant retreat.

referred to as futile. This cannot be correct and the achievements of the Great War generals and their men in freeing Belgium and France surely deserve greater recognition. The sacrifices made, heavy as they were, were not made in vain.

It is not an easy thing to reduce the terrible losses of the First or Second World Wars to a basic analysis of the stark numbers relating to those killed. It is this awful arithmetic of war that has, in my view, largely contributed to the poor opinion of the Great War generals among the general public in Britain. Every war-related death was, of course, a tragedy and when looking at almost any war memorial in Britain, it is striking to note that the list of those lost in 1914–18 is far longer than the corresponding losses for 1939–45. However, the bare figures do not tell the full story. It is common for the press to attribute the higher Great War losses to the generals' profligate use of their men in so-called futile battles but what must be remembered is that in the Great War the bulk of the British army confronted the main body of the German army on the Western Front for the entire duration of the conflict. Casualties were sustained on a daily basis during all of that time, even in sectors of the front where no major attacks were currently being made. Shellfire and sniping from the enemy, often less than a football pitch away, resulted in a continual rate of attrition that added on a daily basis to the total losses sustained.

By contrast, certainly in terms of the main British area of military effort in the Second World War, it should be noted that, apart from a six-week period in the summer of 1940 (leading up to the Dunkirk evacuation), the British army did not fight on the Western Front in any real strength again until the Normandy invasion in 1944, some four years later. There were, of course, campaigns in other parts of the world – especially Italy, Burma and the Western Desert – but the forces deployed there were far fewer than had been deployed on the Western Front in 1914–18 and the rates of loss were correspondingly lower (although, of course, still potentially deadly to the individual soldier). Also in 1914–18, as in 1939–45, the British army was fighting on other fronts such as the Dardanelles, Italy, Egypt and Palestine, Mesopotamia and Macedonia among others, suffering losses in every campaign.

The seemingly higher losses of the Great War compared to the 1939–45 conflict must, at least in part in my opinion, be put down simply to the greater length of time that the British army spent in close proximity to its greatest and most dangerous enemy in the Great War, namely Germany. The losses cannot solely be ascribed to inferior generalship. Indeed, if there were undoubted catastrophes in the Great War, we have only to look at the Second World War to give us similar examples of poor leadership. The failed defence of France in 1940, the fall of Crete in 1941, the fall of the 'impregnable fortress' of Singapore in 1942, the raid on Dieppe in 1942 and the brave but ultimately unsuccessful airborne attack at Arnhem in 1944 all reinforce the fact that the Great War generals were not the only ones to find that, as the old military axiom goes, 'no plan survives its first contact with the enemy', often with tragic results.

Notes
1. Quote from William Tecumseh Sherman.
2. Martin Middlebrook, *Your Country Needs You*, p.26.
3. Charles Messenger, *Call to Arms*, p.96.
4. http://www.bbc.co.uk/history
5. Frank Davies and Graham Maddocks, *Bloody Red Tabs*, p.22.

Chapter Twelve

Remembrance

The Great War produced casualties on an unprecedented scale and posed immediate problems for the military authorities in relation to what to do with the bodies of the fallen. At the time it was very rare for the body of a serviceman to be returned to Britain for burial. This was unsurprising as most died in distant parts of the Empire and the transportation of a body was impractical in almost all cases. Indeed, even in cases where a return did occur, the cost of transportation fell on the family of the deceased and, given the expense involved, it was very likely that the family would need to be financially well-off to meet the cost. This risked a 'double standard' within the armed forces, with the bodies of the well-to-do being returned home while those of the less well-off remained in 'some corner of a foreign field'. In fact, in the period up to mid-1915 there were less than thirty repatriations of bodies from the field of battle to Britain.[1] In mid-1915 a ban was introduced on the repatriation of any more bodies. This was not invoked on the grounds of cost as the man's family would, in any event, be expected to meet the expense. It was more to do with the sheer logistical effort entailed in bringing a body back to Britain from the front lines in an appropriate manner that satisfied requirements in relation to both the dignity of the deceased and the health of those involved in the transport.

This edict did not meet with universal approval. The better-off resented the fact that their money could no longer secure the passage home of the body of a much-loved father or son so that the important rites of mourning could be carried out in the presence of the deceased. Many of the less well-off were unhappy that, their husband or son having laid down his life for his country, that country now seemed to think that its obligation had ended and no further thought was given to the emotions of those left behind at home to quietly mourn in the absence of a body. There would be no nearby grave to visit, so a vital aspect of the mourning process would be also absent. Despite these misgivings, the scale of the fighting and the long casualty lists coupled with the enormous logistical efforts of keeping a vast army in the field meant that the issue of dealing with the dead essentially stood in abeyance for the remainder of the war. It was simply not a priority and they were necessarily buried where they fell.

Despite this, even during the war there was a need for those who had suffered the loss of a loved one to have the opportunity to honour them. Annual drumhead services were held in Swansea during the war; the one staged in Victoria Park in April 1917 being attended by about 5,000 people. The annual drumhead services had actually been organized since the early 1900s by the Swansea branch of the United Services Brigade to remember the dead of the Boer Wars. So it was natural that, in due course, the far greater losses of the Great War should also be commemorated alongside those of earlier conflicts. Those taking part in the 1917 ceremony included the Swansea police band,

Victoria Park and the Boer War memorial at Swansea.
(Dave Westron)

representatives of the army, Royal Navy and Royal Flying Corps, the tramways, the Salvation Army bands, the Red Cross, boy scouts and girl guides and a host of other organizations as well as the usual coterie of local dignitaries.[2]

Similarly, in July 1917 a 'huge congregation' was present in the Albert Hall at Swansea to honour the fallen. This event was organized by the Swansea branch of the Naval and Military War Pensions and Welfare League. The keynote address was delivered by the Reverend Captain H.C. Mander who, as well as paying homage to the dead, bemoaned the fact that at home many men were taking their pleasures as usual – were following their ordinary habits; multitudes of the people seemed to fail to realise what this war meant...the man who lived his normal life today was nothing short of a traitor, and not acting honourably to those to whose memory they were at that moment paying tribute.[3]

Similar events were staged at Mumbles and Sketty in November 1917.[4] The Mumbles War Shrine to the fallen was unveiled before the end of the war in September 1918, although within three weeks or so the park in which it was located had to be locked from dusk to dawn to prevent the shrine being damaged and the flowers trampled, or even stolen, by the unruly children who frequented it in the evenings. Some things, it seems, never change.[5]

The signing of the Treaty of Versailles in June 1919 resulted in the staging of a Victory Parade (also referred to as the Peace Day Parade) in London on 19 July 1919. Almost as an afterthought, a cenotaph of wood and plaster was erected along the route of the parade. The word 'cenotaph' derives from Greek and means 'empty tomb', a structure erected to the memory of someone who is buried elsewhere and as such it was a fitting design to the memory of those Britons who lay in France and Flanders and in a host of other countries where the Great War had been fought. Designed by Edwin Lutyens, it became the focal point for the laying of wreaths by members of the public in memory of a loved one whose body was buried overseas or had not been found. Such was its popularity that it was decided to retain the structure but to rebuild it in Portland stone and this was done during 1919–20. It then became the focal point of the national service of remembrance; a role it continues to perform up to the present day.

Swansea followed suit in erecting a cenotaph to a design by the borough architect, Ernest Morgan (who had himself seen active service) and which design seemed to have been heavily influenced by the London monument.

The town had, of course, played a full part in the war, sending perhaps 15,000 of its sons to serve in the military according to contemporary reports. Almost 3,000 never came home and it is likely that perhaps another 6,000 or so came home after being wounded. Many would bear the scars of their service for the rest of their life in the form of physical or mental injury. It was only natural that the sacrifice made by those who did not return should be permanently marked in some way.

The Swansea Corporation had established a War Memorial Committee and this had been instrumental in raising £9,000 in public subscriptions which eventually allowed the erection of the cenotaph to

The Menin Gate at Ieper (Ypres). The inscription on the outer face reads: 'To the armies of the British Empire who stood here from 1914 to 1918 and to those of their dead who have no known grave.' The 'Last Post' is still sounded at the gate every night.

proceed, as well as providing a sum of money for the benefit of the children of local men who had given their lives in the cause of freedom. Early discussions regarding a memorial had included the suggestion, championed by Sir John T.D. Llewelyn, that the memorial should be of practical use to the town and a new hospital ward or an institution to help disabled soldiers were among the initial proposals.[6] The cenotaph that was finally decided upon took the form of a pylon some 30 feet high, set on a base of white steps. It was surrounded by a sunken court of memory in the form of an irregular octagon of about 60 feet by 40 feet. The inside of the walls of the court of memory were 6 feet high and affixed to them were the bronze plates proudly bearing the names of the fallen of Swansea. Both Portland and pennant stone had been used in the construction.

For a name to appear on the

THE LAND ON WHICH
THIS CEMETERY STANDS
IS THE FREE GIFT
OF THE BELGIAN PEOPLE
FOR THE PERPETUAL RESTING PLACE
OF THOSE OF THE ALLIED ARMIES
WHO FELL IN THE WAR OF 1914-1918
AND ARE HONOURED HERE

Inscription at Tyne Cot Cemetery. The cemetery contains almost 12,000 burials of Commonwealth soldiers together with the names of another 35,000 whose burial place is unknown. *(Author)*

A large crowd gathered to see the unveiling of the cenotaph at Swansea. Sir Douglas Haig had laid the foundation stone a year earlier. He had been enthusiastically welcomed by large crowds and had also been made a Freeman of the Borough. *(Cambrian)*

cenotaph at Swansea it was necessary for a family to make application to the Corporation and provide the necessary details. Given that many 'Swansea' men might have been living elsewhere at the outbreak of war or had died while serving in units with no obvious link to Swansea, this was a very necessary process. It did mean, however, that the names that actually appeared on the cenotaph did not represent in any way a 'definitive' list of Swansea men who had made the ultimate sacrifice as, for all sorts of reasons, the relatives of the deceased might choose not to apply or might not even know that they had to apply for the inclusion of a particular name on the memorial.

Allowing for that caveat, there were still almost 2,300 names on the cenotaph at Swansea when it was unveiled on 21 July 1923. As in the case of London, the cenotaph at Swansea, prominently positioned on the seafront, was able to be easily visited by those who had lost a father, husband, son or brother during the war. As such, it probably met a latent requirement for the bereaved to at least partially satisfy their emotional needs in the absence of

The cenotaph at Swansea. *(Author)*

a nearby grave to visit.[7]

The cenotaph at Swansea mirrored the national monument and became the fulcrum for the annual local service of remembrance. In Swansea, however, there was another day that was marked by thoughts of remembrance. From the war's end in 1918 until well into the 1930s, 10 July was marked in Swansea as Mametz Memorial Day. This was the anniversary of the attack by the Welsh Division on Mametz Wood on the Somme in 1916. Although the attack was successful in clearing the wood of Germans, success came at a cost with over 4,000 men of the Welsh Division being killed or wounded in several days of hard fighting. The Swansea Battalion (14th Welsh) took part in the attack and suffered about 400 casualties with around 100 of them being killed or subsequently dying of their wounds. The effect on the town of Swansea was searing and 10 July became an important date in the town until more pressing concerns about Nazi Germany diverted attention elsewhere in the late 1930s.

If the Swansea cenotaph provided a central mark of remembrance, local communities also felt the need to record the losses that they, too, had suffered and this manifested itself in a variety of local memorials; in plaques in churches and in printed rolls of honour, to name but a few of the numerous expressions of collective mourning and grief. Churches were, of course, the obvious focal point for prayer and remembrance during the war.

A token that was presented to a man who served and survived the war by the Hafod Isha Works at Swansea. *(Noel and Alan Cox)*

Although the war posed difficulties for churches of all religious persuasions it is probably true to say that most were able to endorse the war as being a 'just' one while still being uneasy about man killing his fellow man. As well as the usual prayers for victory and the safety of those in danger, the churches often acted as collection points for a range of war-related charities. In April 1915 St Jude's Church, for example, raised modest sums for the Prince of Wales Relief Fund, British Red Cross, Indian Soldiers, the Belgian Relief Fund and the Serbian Relief Fund.

However, it was as sites for memorials that churches came to the fore, particularly after the war's end. Once again the total accuracy of what is recorded on these memorials is not always entirely correct but it is very likely that, allowing for the odd error or omission, they were clearly well-intentioned and reasonably accurate and certainly remain among the best records we have of how the war affected particular local communities or groups. Bearing in mind the potential shortcomings of these largely contemporary memorials, it is worth examining a few of the records. The parish of St Joseph's at Swansea recorded 122 men of the parish as having died during the war. For the Brunswick Methodist Church the losses were 12 men, although happily 150 were recorded as having served and returned home. For the Trinity Calvinist Methodist Church the figures were four killed and forty-five returned. The Carmarthen Road Congregational Church (now the United Reform Church) listed 160 men and 2 women as serving, with 27 deaths. The Swansea Hebrew Congregation recorded nine fatalities. Swansea businesses and public services also remembered their dead. For men who had worked on the docks the figure was 35 killed; the postal service lost 26 men; the Hafod Isha Works lost 11; and the borough police force recorded 10 men killed. The Swansea Grammar School recorded almost eighty old boys killed,

A 'Dead Man's Penny' to a man who served and did not survive the war: David Howell Evans of the Swansea Battalion, killed in action 10 May 1918. These plaques were presented to the next of kin of all British war dead. *(Jason Muxworthy)*

while for Dynevor School the figure was forty-nine. The memorial to the fallen of Fforestfach and district recorded forty men killed.[8]

As mentioned earlier, these memorials and annual ceremonies of remembrance were the public form of a great outpouring of grief for those who had been lost in a conflict of unprecedented scale. However, there can be no doubt that a far greater outpouring of grief took place in private, behind the drawn curtains of countless households in Swansea and its districts, and this on every day of the year rather than merely on an annual occasion. In those homes the dead were mourned in oft-darkened rooms and bitter tears

Memorial plaque in a Swansea church.
(Jason Muxworthy)

must have frequently coursed down pallid cheeks. In some homes small areas of a room were set aside for the display of memorabilia of a much-loved relative who would never return to the place he called home: a faded photograph, a medal or two, a 'Dead Man's Penny' and perhaps a poignant last letter home, written in the squalid and dangerous confines of a trench, at a windswept airfield or aboard a rolling ship on a storm-lashed sea. These were the cherished treasures that were lovingly displayed and were often all that was left to show that such a man had once breathed and lived and loved. For many families this was all they had to cling to in the anguish of despair; fond memories of a happy past which stood in stark contrast to an uncertain and often lonely future. No matter what they perceived as the rights and wrongs of fighting for a just cause, the plain fact was that for a great many of those left behind, the beating heart had been ripped out of their family. Even today, 100 years after the start of the Great War, many families can still turn with reverence to the faded but still treasured mementos of a man that most of them never knew but one they did know had nobly 'done his bit for king and country' according to the spirit of the time and had finally paid the ultimate price. Such men are truly not, and never should be, forgotten.

Yet what exactly did they die for? When looking back at the two world wars that scarred the twentieth century it is easy to think that the Second World War was the 'just' war, with its battles being fought and losses accepted as the price of defeating the evil of the Nazi and Japanese regimes. The First World War, by contrast, seems to be not so clear-cut to many. The losses were far heavier, yet the Kaiser was clearly not a Hitler and the world was spared the horror of the death camps that later flourished under the Nazis. It needs to be remembered, however, that Britain did not go to war

Tyne Cot Cemetery. A very small portion of the 12,000 graves with a Great War German bunker (pillbox) between the trees. *(Author)*

in 1939 in protest at the death camps but rather in defence of Poland, much as the Britain of 1914 had gone to war in defence of Belgium and France. Both Hitler and the Kaiser intended to hold sway over Western Europe by way of military might and it is hard to imagine anyone arguing that Poland in 1939 or Belgium and France in 1914 deserved to become mere vassals of a greater German empire. It is an old but very true saying that all that is needed for evil to succeed is for good men to do nothing. In both wars Britain decided to do something (although little that was of immediate and practical help to Poland) and subsequently paid a heavy cost in what was a just cause in both cases.

In my view the thorny question of why we fought in the Great War is neatly and simply answered in the poetry written by two veterans of the Great War; two men who had come through the horrors of the Western Front and as such had a perspective on it that is beyond the understanding of both the author of this work and the modern-day reader. Bernard Newman and Harold Arpthorp had no link to Swansea but I suspect they were speaking for many Great War veterans when they penned *The Road to La Bassée* in 1934. Twenty years after the battles they had fought during 1914, they travelled back to the Somme on what was essentially a pilgrimage to the battlefields. The poem they later wrote outlined their astonishment at the fact that the war-torn ground they remembered had been so quickly reclaimed by nature, with the old trench lines being hard to pick out in a now verdant green landscape. They were also

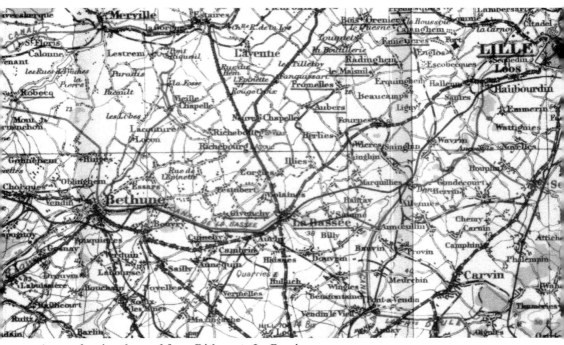

A map showing the road from Béthune to La Bassée. *(Author's collection)*

surprised to see 'kiddies playing marbles on the road to La Bassée', an area that had seen heavy fighting in 1914. Even more disconcerting to them was the sight of an ice-cream van parked at a once much fought-over crossroads. The final shock was the sudden appearance of a bus, serenely wending its way across the idyllic countryside on its now regular route from the village of Béthune to La Bassée, something that was unimaginable during the bitterly-contested war years. They concluded the poem:

> And I wondered what they'd think of it – those mates of mine who died –
> They never got to La Bassée, though God knows how they tried.
> I thought back to the moments when their number came around,
> And now those buses rattling over sacred, holy ground,
> Yes, I wondered what they'd think of it, those mates of mine who died.
> Of those buses rattling over the old pave close beside.
> 'Carry on! That's why we died!' I could almost hear them say,
> To keep those buses always running from Béthune to La Bassée!

They and millions like them believed in 1914 that when evil men attempted evil deeds, the freedom of a nation was surely worth fighting for. Thus they fought and a great many died but a Belgium and France painfully prised free from the oppressor's grip in November 1918 belies the old myth that their sacrifice, tragically high though it was, was in any way 'futile'.

Fred Gammon returned to Swansea in 1995 to lay flowers at the cenotaph in memory of his father, Samuel Gammon of the Swansea Battalion, killed in action at Mametz Wood, 10 July 1916. Samuel had not been forgotten almost eighty years after his death.
(John Powell)

Notes

1. Information from members of the Great War Forum (1914–1918.invisionzone.com).
2. *Cambrian*, 6 April 1917.
3. *Cambrian*, 20 July 1917.
4. *Cambrian,* 9 November 1917.
5. *Mumbles Press*, 12 September and 10 October 1918.
6. *Cambrian*, 7 February 1919.
7. *South Wales Daily Post*, 20 and 23 July 1923; *Swansea Herald of Wales*, 28 July 1923.
8. National Inventory of War Memorials.

Select Bibliography

Manuscript sources:
Admiralty records, TNA, London.
Air Ministry records, TNA, London.
Board of Trade records, TNA, London.
Service Records, Library and Archives, Canada.
Service Records, National Archives of Australia.
War Office records, TNA, London.
West Glamorgan Archive Service Records, series D/D; H/E; TC.
Other manuscript material as indicated in the footnotes.

Periodicals:
Cambrian.
South Wales Daily Post.
Swansea Herald of Wales.
Other periodicals as indicated in the footnotes.

Secondary sources:
Alban, J.R., 'The Activities of the Swansea Belgian Refugees Committee, 1914–16', *Gower* magazine, Volume 26, 1975

Beckett, Ian, *Home Front 1914–18* (TNA, 2006)

Carlyon, L.A., *Gallipoli* (Bantam Books, 2003)

Cesarani, David (ed.), *The Internment of Aliens in Twentieth-Century Britain* (F. Cass, 1993)

Edmonds, J.E., *Official History of the War: France and Belgium 1917* vol. II (reprinted by IWM and the Battery Press, undated)

Gilbert, Martin, *First World War* (HarperCollins, 1995)

Griffiths, Ralph A. (ed.), *The City of Swansea: Challenges & Change* (Alan Sutton, 1990)

Headlam, Cuthbert, DSO, *History of the Guards Division in the Great War* (reprinted by the Naval & Military Press, undated)

Lewis, Bernard, *Swansea Pals: A History of the 14th (Service) Battalion, the Welsh Regiment, in the Great War* (Pen & Sword Books, 2004)

Liddell Hart, B.H., *History of the First World War* (Book Club Associates, 1993)

Mainwaring Hughes, W.T., *Swansea's Mayors and Civic Events* (published by the author, undated)

Marden, T.O., *History of the Welch Regiment*, Part II (Western Mail & Echo Ltd, 1932)

Marwick, Arthur, *The Deluge: British Society and the First World War* (Norton Library, 1970)

Massie, Robert K., *Castles of Steel: Britain, Germany and the Winning of the Great War at Sea* (Pimlico, 2005)

Messenger, Charles, *Call to Arms: The British Army, 1914–18* (Weidenfeld & Nicolson, 2005)

Middlebrook, Martin, *Your Country Needs You* (Pen & Sword Books, 2000)

Miles, Wilfred, *Official History of the War: France and Belgium 1916* (reprinted by IWM and the Battery Press, undated)

Nicholson, Col. G.W.L., *Official History of the Canadian Army in the First World War: Canadian Expeditionary Force 1914–1919* (Queen's Printer, 1962)

Peace Pledge Union, *Refusing to Kill: Conscientious Objection and Human Rights in the First World War* (Peace Pledge Union, 2006)

Purnell Partworks, *History of the First World War* (BPC Publishing, 1971)

Steel, Nigel & Hart, Peter, *Tumult in the Clouds: The British Experience of the War in the Air 1914–18* (Coronet Books, 1998)

Storey, Neil R. & Housego, Molly, *Women in the First World War* (Shire Publications, 2013)

Terraine, John, *Business in Great Waters* (Leo Cooper, 1989)

Index

(NB: The name of Swansea appears *passim* and has therefore not been indexed unless it forms part of another entry; e.g. Swansea Market, Swansea Metal Exchange, etc.)